BY PAUL SOLMAN
AND THOMAS FRIEDMAN

LIFE AND DEATH
ON THE
CORPORATE
BATTLEFIELD
How Companies Win, Lose, Survive

SIMON AND SCHUSTER
· NEW YORK ·

SIMON AND SCHUSTER and colophon are trademarks
of Simon & Schuster
Designed by Irving Perkins Associates
Manufactured in the United States of America

10 9 8 7 6 5 4 3 2 1

Library of Congress Cataloging in Publication Data

Solman, Paul.
    Life and Death on the Corporate Battlefield

    Includes index.
    1. Corporations—United States.   2. United States—Commerce.
I. Friedman, Thomas.   II. Title.
HD2785.S58   1982   338.7′4′0973   82-10413
ISBN 0-671-25564-9

TO RACHEL, JOANNA, AND JAN;
TO COREY AND CHRISTY

Contents

Preface

Long before this book was written, when we first became interested in business, we discovered to our dismay that many of our assumptions about it were false. We also discovered that we were by no means alone in our ignorance—that our friends and colleagues were as uninformed as we were. So we set about, in a very modest way, to educate ourselves, and eventually, as these things often happen, wound up educating others.

In our attempts to make some simple sense out of what is often thought of as a hopelessly confusing subject, we have arrived at a rather unconventional view of American business. It's not an academic view, although we have spent time at Harvard and elsewhere learning that perspective. It's not a corporate view, although we have watched business work from the inside. And it's not an ideological view, although we have been exposed to ideology from all sides. Instead, it is the view of two journalists trying to depict, as vividly as possible, what has come to fascinate them: how business really works.

Naturally, we are deeply in debt to many people and institutions that helped us shape our thoughts. First, the Nieman Foundation for Journalism; its curator, Jim Thomson; and Dean Lawrence Fouraker provided the opportunity for study at the Harvard Business School. Then WGBH-TV afforded us the opportunity to explain business (among other things) on television, and thus made possible *Enterprise,* the PBS documentary series, to which we owe so much. Special thanks must go to the series'

9

Beth Satter, Ben Loeterman, and Zvi Dor-Ner, as well as Bob Diamond and John Kiser.

Harvard professors who graciously gave of their time in discussing business issues with us during our formative work on *Enterprise* include Joseph Bower, Colyer Crum, Ray Goldberg, Steven Greyser, James Heskett, Warren Law, Theodore Levitt, Quinn Mills, Michael Porter, Tom Raymond, Richard Rosenbloom, Wickham Skinner, Robert Stobaugh, and Hugo Uyterhoeven. Jim Michaels of *Forbes* also was an early influence.

When it came to writing our book, the guidance of Professors Robert Glauber, John Meyer, and Steven Star was invaluable. Louis Banks, of *Fortune* and the Sloan School, and John Rosenblum and James McKinney of Harvard, were encouraging from the very beginning. Thanks also go to Walter Kiechel III and John Clarkeson, Richard Rosen, Mickey Friedman, Charles Matthews, Laura Shapiro, Jeffrey Klein, Joe Klein, Alan Jehlen, Marie Behan, Martha Cochrane, Deirdre Rosenberg, and especially, Jan Freeman and Christy Newman who were extremely helpful in their comments, advice, and support.

We are also grateful to the people who shared their business experiences with us: chief among them Bruce Henderson of the Boston Consulting Group, Charlie Waite of Greylock, Henry Kloss of Kloss Video, Howard Anderson of the Yankee Group, Wesley Cohen of Carnegie-Mellon, Dean LeBaron of Batterymarch, Professors Elon Kohlberg, Steven Star, Robert Glauber, and Jay Light of Harvard, Bob Moore of Babson College, and our friends Ed, Ron, Maury, and Tim.

Finally, we would like to extend our deepest thanks to Daphne Abeel, Susan Bolotin, Jonathan Coleman, and John Sterling for their great encouragement and help; to Amanda Urban, our much-prized agent; to Fred Hills, our much-prized editor; and of course, to our parents and families, prized above all.

Introduction

There's an enormous amount of talk these days about the "bottom line"—so much that the phrase has crept into conversation about religion, politics, sports, and even sex. Not that Americans really measure everything in terms of profit and loss—or their social equivalents—of course, but we certainly do like to think of ourselves as a tough, pragmatic people interested primarily in results.

But in our near obsession with results, we seem to have overlooked the critical importance of something else: *process*. This oversight is especially limiting to our understanding of business—and especially disturbing· in these uncertain economic times. How, after all, did we get to the bottom line in the first place?

The bottom line is only one set of numbers; *behind* it is a complex world in which many forces combine to determine which products get made, how they are made, when they are made, for whom, and by whom. The bottom line will tell you if a company made or lost money, but you have to journey behind it to learn how and why it happened.

Why should we care? Simply because in many ways our country *is* its businesses—a fact which, in good times at least, is as easily overlooked as it is obvious. No matter that economists are usually no better than palm readers at predicting the future; business can and must be understood. There are clear reasons why workers are laid off in industry A and scarce in industry B;

why one company goes bankrupt and its rival prospers; why competition is fierce in one sector of the economy and not in another. But most of us are as confused about business as we are dependent upon it. This is true even of most businesspeople.

In California, General Electric closes one of its old factories and is seen by the public and local business as a prime example of a hardhearted corporation leaving its dedicated workers out in the cold. In North Carolina, however, GE opens its new, more efficient factory and is hailed as a beneficent company creating new jobs and infusing capital into a chronically depressed area. Same company, same business process, but you would never know it from the public reaction or media coverage.

Our thoughts about business are all too often muddled. Many of us fear the size of huge American corporations—yet we hope they are large enough and strong enough to vanquish foreign competition and provide more jobs.

As workers and managers, we presumably want the company we work for to be as profitable as possible so that we can get a raise; but as consumers we complain when faced with what we think are exorbitant charges for products or services.

We're happy we can choose among fifty different kinds of breakfast cereal if we happen to like breakfast cereal. Those of us who don't, think it's another instance of corporate wastefulness—although we sure are glad we can get so many different types of soup.

Why this double vision? Perhaps it's just a result of our difficulty in seeing the business process as a whole. It's an understandable problem, given that—in this country, at least—many businesses do not "Business" make: which is to say, companies do not act as one, do not always have common interests or shared goals.

The truth is that companies fight each other constantly. They wage war across an enormous corporate battlefield, as it were, and it is out of this struggle that we wind up with fifty different kinds of breakfast cereal, dozens of types of soup, plant openings and closings, and a great deal more.

It's a struggle that can be extremely subtle. Victory on the corporate battlefield does not necessarily depend on sheer firepower. Some businesses will succeed precisely because of their large size, but others will fail because of it. Here a small business's size can make it "agile" one week and "weak and vulnerable" the next.

It's also a struggle that can seem quite confusing. Much that goes on in business stems from competitive conflict, and conflict, by its very nature, tends to obscure the issues that bring it about. This battlefield, like most others, is cursed with a terrible din and thick, nearly impenetrable smoke. Both are disorienting, not only to the public, but to the corporate combatants themselves. Companies can have the hardest time keeping their bearings. Is that a foxhole up ahead, a place of refuge where a business can protect its position? Or is it a death trap, easily overrun by competing firms? Should Exxon have bought that electrical-equipment company to outflank its sister oil companies and grab a piece of a new, burgeoning industry? Or was it walking blindly into a multimillion-dollar disaster?

When to fight, how to fight—even whom to fight—are questions not easily answered on the corporate battlefield.

Not that businesses *always* fight—or really want to. They're just like most soldiers on a real battleground: they would much rather be out of danger—and would do almost anything to keep out of harm's way and minimize the risk to themselves. But as every soldier knows, sometimes the only way to protect yourself is to go on the offensive.

It can be a hell of a choice. In combat of any kind, your need to be safe today may expose you to danger tomorrow, while your struggle for long-term security can get you killed. The result can be great indecision. After all, it's not hard to be indecisive when you know your basic urge for self-preservation may turn out to be self-destructive.

But what are we to make of such ambiguity? Since there's little, if any, romance in the image of the reluctant soldier, it cannot hope to satisfy our seemingly insatiable need for heroes and villains. So we mythologize it. We mythologize the business process almost as much as we do war. Some of us believe that corporations *love* competition, while others think that companies hate competition so much they always conspire to stamp it out.

Some believe that firms thrive on risk; others, that companies never take risks.

If only business weren't held back by government regulation, the free market could work exactly as it's supposed to, you may say to yourself. Or do you say instead: if only business were regulated much, much more, the system could work as it should?

There is the myth of the coldly calculating big businessman who is in complete control. And there is the myth of the dashing, freewheeling entrepreneur who could revitalize the nation if only given the chance.

The number of myths and misconceptions about business is so large that many businesspeople despair of ever being understood. Not liked, mind you (although they wouldn't mind that either), but merely understood. Many businesspeople complain that even their counterparts in other industries have little idea of what goes on in other corners of the corporate battlefield.

This book, then, is an effort to explain, without reverence or rancor, the *how* of business. It is a guide to life on the ever-changing corporate battlefield. We began the 1970s amidst cries of "Gulf—Out of Angola Now!" when that African country was still a colony of Portugal, and Gulf Oil was considered an exploiter of its people, but we ended the decade with a vice-president of the world's fifth-largest bank explaining in a hushed, plushly carpeted corridor that he considered a loan to Angola for the construction of a refinery "safe" because "the Communists there will make sure the oil keeps flowing."

This book is not an argument for or against our economic system or a vision of what it should be, but an exposition of American business as it is actually taught and practiced. It will attempt to explain, for instance, why so many executives put their self-interest ahead of their companies'; why IBM failed to vanquish all its rivals in the computer industry; why a tobacco company went into the beer business; why Mobil and U.S. Steel got into a pitched battle for Marathon Oil, offering 1½ times its stock price; why entrepreneurs are often fired by the companies they build; and why a brilliant, highly successful inventor couldn't find a banker or venture capitalist to back him.

Our subject is the all-too-human ways in which professional

managers guide their companies through the corporate battle-field—the ways in which they make decisions. In the following chapters, we will show that some of the results of this process are economically productive, while others are distinctly counterproductive.

There is a national debate going on now about the training and goals of modern managers, about the high-powered, know-it-all, number-toting MBA's who supposedly run American business. We have tried to trace the steps of those managers from business school to the confusing world of the corporate battlefield. Our premise is that no matter how you feel about the practices and practitioners of business, it is hard to argue for or against them without first fully understanding them. But begin to realize how companies and their managers fight, and why they win or lose, and your attitude toward the breakfast-cereal aisle of your supermarket—or the next major corporate takeover—will be irrevocably altered.

LIFE AND DEATH
ON THE
CORPORATE
BATTLEFIELD

CHAPTER ONE # The Hawk/ Dove Factor

Competition. For corporate executives, it is the dominant theme in their working lives. They compete in the service of their companies against other firms, and they compete for their jobs against the people who work beside them.

But if there is a myth about business more deeply held than any other, it is that corporate competition is really a sham. Or, put another way, *the corporations are in cahoots.*

This myth gets an awful lot of mileage. After all, how else can one explain all those top executives sitting on each other's boards of directors—and in each other's golf carts? Surely they must be planning as a group, synchronizing their business strategies, and fixing prices.

But in truth, competition is the rule, not the exception, in business. Just consider the following:

- An Englishman named Wilson Harrell comes to America in the 1960s, buys a small company that makes a spray cleaning liquid, and turns it into a small money machine. No sooner has he done so than the Goliath of groceries, Procter & Gamble, brings out a rival product to chase him from the market. He retaliates with guerrilla warfare, and wins.

19

- Giant Gillette has had the lion's share of the world shaving products business since the turn of the century. King C. Gillette invented the disposable razor blade in 1895 after a fellow inventor suggested that Gillette come up with something which, "once used, is thrown away, and the customer keeps coming back for more." On this invention a multinational corporation was built; patents and perspicacity won it as secure a position atop its industry as that of any company in the world. Yet Bic, a European pen manufacturer with no experience in the shaving business, threatens the entire Gillette franchise with the ultimate Gillette-ian concept: a disposable *razor*.

- In 1970, the Savin Corporation acquires the rights to sell a copying machine that uses a liquid chemical, rather than a powder, which Xerox uses. The machine, manufactured in Japan by the Ricoh Company, is touted by Savin as cheaper and more reliable. In 1975, with $60 million a year in company sales, Savin launches an ad campaign against $4-billion-a-year Xerox. Radio comedians Bob and Ray banter about copiers, Bob consoling Ray for his purchase of a Xerox instead of a Savin. The ad ends as Bob says, "Here's a set of plastic seat covers for your Edsel."

> RAY: "How'd you know I drive an Edsel?"
> BOB: "Oh, it just seemed inevitable."

Savin's sales more than triple in three years. But then Ricoh decides to sell its copiers itself in the U.S., and becomes a competitor of Savin.

- In early 1980, $5-billion-a-year Johnson & Johnson, the nation's seventy-fourth-largest industrial corporation, announces that it is pulling out of the disposable-diaper market in the United States. Its share of the $1-billion-a-year market has dropped from 12 percent to 8 percent in the previous six months; annual sales are down from $120 million to $80 million.

The company had been selling a conventional disposable diaper at a premium price. When its primary competitors, Procter & Gamble and Kimberly-Clark, then introduced fitted diapers with elasticized legs (Luvs and Huggies, respectively), the parents who were willing to pay a premium price for disposable diapers "traded up" to the elastic-leg ones. Johnson & Johnson's strategy to nail down the premium part of the market didn't and couldn't work because it didn't have an elastic-leg product. The company had spent millions testing the market and perfecting its conventional disposable diapers. Its withdrawal from the market resulted in an estimated $15-million loss.

Some companies do conspire to eliminate competition, of course—fixing profits, driving competitors out by blackmailing suppliers, bribing officials—and the results can be as criminal as the practices are. But even in those industries where it is attempted, conspiracy does not guarantee success.

Examples of corporate competition run into the millions, even in this day of conglomerates and markets dominated by a handful of companies. There's Coke versus Pepsi, the television networks against one another, supermarkets against convenience stores, plastic against wood—fierce battles, all waged on the corporate battlefield.

Yet with all the evidence of competition around us, we still cling to the notion that true competition is dead, or at least dying. It appears to be a question of logic: how can competition exist to such an extent—how can it be said to pervade our economic system—when our major corporations are so huge and our industries so concentrated? If business is combat, how can anyone survive against—let alone defeat—Procter & Gamble or Xerox or IBM?

A common answer is government regulation, which restrains such giants from certain predatory practices, but it is by no means the whole answer. There is something inherent in the very nature of the corporate battlefield that keeps competition alive. It explains much of what goes on behind the bottom line: the strategies and tactics that businesses employ in their winning—and losing—efforts. It even explains success and failure, and the nature of corporate combat itself.

Bruce Henderson is an expert on how and why businesses compete. As King Gillette introduced modern shaving, so Bruce Henderson introduced modern strategic corporate consulting— in 1982, a $350-million industry which pays graduates of the top five business schools upwards of $60,000 a year to join one of the most glamorous professions in America.

For years, corporations have been hiring people to give them advice—about legal problems, public relations, advertising, marketing, and so on. Bruce Henderson's innovation was to formalize the consulting profession by concentrating on just one type of analysis: corporate strategy. Henderson believed that the most important challenge to any company was its competition in the marketplace. To succeed, a company has to compete. To compete, it must have an analysis of its market and a strategy— often, a whole host of strategies.

After a Tennessee boyhood, a Vanderbilt University education in engineering, a 20-year career in the electrical industry, and a degree from the Harvard Business School, Henderson set up the now-legendary Boston Consulting Group in 1963. The Boston Consulting Group is the world's foremost practitioner of "corporate strategy" thinking, and Bruce Henderson is the theoretician behind the thinking.

Henderson is a large man in his sixties. He dresses conservatively and speaks in a soft Southern accent. He talks as if you had been listening to him for years—as, indeed, his clients have been. He will stop suddenly and ask a tough question to see if you're following him, and he is not above deriding you if you aren't. He has the blunt, sometimes abrasive manner of a high-ranking officer who has spent his life in the trenches of corporate warfare.

His career began in 1938 at a small manufacturer of electric motors named Leland Electric. Henderson was put in charge of pricing incoming orders. Pricing policy came from above; he merely applied it. After work, he would question the sales manager of the company about the whys and wherefores of that policy. He was told there was only one hard-and-fast rule: If the competition cuts price on an item, so will Leland.

"And I began to find myself wondering," Henderson explained: "If every competitor matches every price, how does any company ever gain or lose customers?"

The manager provided the answer. He would make a special deal. He would take the president and the purchasing agent of one of Leland's customers out for a clambake on the beach where there was no telephone, get them slightly drunk, and then start kidding them about Leland's own prices' being too high. Eventually, the customer would say, "Well, then, why don't you give us a lower price?"

And the Leland manager would say, "Well, if we did, you'd only go off and get someone to match it someplace else."

"Oh, I wouldn't do a thing like that," the customer would answer.

So, in the spirit of camaraderie, the Leland man would say, "Hell, I'd give you a twenty-percent cut in price if I knew I had a firm commitment from you that you'd really give me your business for the next year."

Then they would strike the deal—not putting anything on paper—and Leland would start selling them at the lower price to shut off the other supplier.

In this case, the other supplier was huge Westinghouse, and when one of its sales managers got wind of the Leland deal, he bawled out the Leland manager at the next trade convention. "You Leland people said you were going to try to keep to book prices and you all went up there and you cut the price on *our* customer!"

An agreement to keep to book prices was illegal. It amounted to price-fixing. In other words, here was a cartel—and Leland Electric was breaking it.

Henderson considers this a perfect illustration of how even cartels can fall prey to competitive forces. "Unless it's to the advantage of *all* the parties to stick to it, a cartel won't work," he says. "While small companies have the most to gain by being part of a cartel—because their costs are usually higher and so they like the artificially high prices—they also have the most to gain by breaking the cartel, because it's very hard for a larger competitor to retaliate. Why? Because if you're a large company like Westinghouse, and you have to cut your prices to match a small competitor like Leland, you've got to take more loss of profit than even his total *sales*."

So for all Westinghouse's frustration, it just wasn't worth its while to have a price war with Leland Electric, since Westinghouse had so many more similar products and so much more volume on which it would have to lower prices. Or so Henderson concluded.

Henderson's first question about pricing thus led to a much larger insight about competition in general: *The bigger the elephant* (in this case, Westinghouse), *the better the monkey's* (Leland's) *odds.*

Those less enamored of the "free market" than Bruce Henderson point out that until the government began to referee such fights, many an elephant crushed many a monkey. (The continuation of antitrust litigation, even by the free-market Reagan Administration, bears witness to the need of policing our competitive system in order to preserve it.) But in today's regulated jungle, Henderson's monkey-elephant rule does often hold. To see why, let's go back to the story of Wilson Harrell versus Procter & Gamble.

Harrell's greatest triumph was his purchase in the early 1960s of an obscure wholesale cleaning spray liquid called Formula 409 and his subsequent nationwide retailing effort. By 1967, Formula 409 had a 5-percent share of all U.S. cleaning products and fully half of the spray-cleaning segment. It was a comfortable franchise, a comfortable living. Harrell didn't have to worry about stockholders (his company was closely held) or big competitors (the spray-cleaner market just wasn't very large).

And then along came Procter & Gamble—the Goliath of home products, the company all its competitors fear—fresh from a recent victory over a new liquid cleaner called Lestoil ("Less Toil with Lestoil"). Wilson Harrell's business had run into a problem: it had become successful enough to attract attention.

Procter & Gamble was just the sort of company to pay close

attention to its market. The firm was established in Cincinnati in 1837 when William Procter, a candlemaker from England, and his brother-in-law James Gamble, a soapmaker from Northern Ireland, realized that there wasn't much difference between their trades and set up an office and backyard "factory": one wooden kettle with cast-iron bottom for boiling fat into tallow.

Even in those days, the company was casting its product net as widely as possible. In 1850, its letterhead read:

PROCTER & GAMBLE
Manufacturers and Wholesale Dealers in
Star, Adamantine & Tallow Candles,
Rosin, Palm, Oleine, Toilet & Shaving Soaps
Pearl Starch, Lard Oil, &c, &c.

In 1879, P&G's most famous product, Ivory Soap ("the only Laundry Soap that successfully answers for Toilet Use") was introduced. The product seemed to have so much potential that the company put the enormous sum of $11,000 into an advertising budget, and Procter's son wrote the first ad: "Ivory . . . is $99^{44}/_{100}$ percent pure." Moreover, "It will float."

By the time Wilson Harrell had built his Formula 409 business, Procter & Gamble had been following its Ivory Soap formula for nearly a century: come up with a new household product and find a catchy way of selling it to the public. The company's methods had been greatly refined, of course, with questionnaires, individual and group interviews, and all sorts of mathematical and psychological analyses accompanying and monitoring every phase of a product's introduction, from its physical quality to the color of its package.

But the basic theme at P&G was the same: establish a new product, sell it to the retailers who already handle your other products, and advertise heavily enough to ensure capturing a strong percentage of the market (a large "market share").

It was natural, therefore, that a new type of cleaning agent would catch P&G's eye as soon as it became successful. To protect its own advantage, P&G would have to snare as much of the new business as possible by coming up with a competing product. In 1967, it began test-marketing a spray liquid cleaner called Cinch.

Just as P&G had used its vast resources to create, name, package, and promote Cinch with very costly market research, it would now "test-market" it, distributing Cinch only in Denver, Colorado, and chronicling its sales with scribelike devotion. (A national launch of the product, given P&G's heavy emphasis on costly advertising and promotion, would have been too risky without first making sure Cinch was worth the investment.)

In this competition, Procter & Gamble had the clear advantages of the much larger company. It could pour millions into the effort without requiring an immediate return. One would think that the money would be able to buy enough knowledge about consumers and how to please them to crush the likes of Wilson Harrell.

There is, however, another side to size. The little company can move more quickly, can hit and run. It doesn't get mired in the mud of large-scale management and bureaucracy. While Procter & Gamble was proceeding deliberately, step by step, Wilson Harrell got wind of its plans and discovered that Denver was to be the first test market.

Harrell's tactic was perfectly suited to his company's diminutive size. He subtly withdrew Formula 409 from the Denver market. He couldn't just pull it from supermarket shelves, of course, because Procter & Gamble would notice. But he could stop advertising and promoting the product. When a store ran out of Formula 409, he would discourage the salespeople from refilling the shelves. It was guerrilla warfare: moving quickly and quietly to foil the enemy. And it worked. Cinch did extraordinarily well in the test market. The Procter & Gamble team in charge of Denver could now proudly return to world headquarters in Cincinnati and proclaim their project a success. A combination of their own vanity and an abiding faith in Procter & Gamble's ability to conquer all blinded them to Harrell's machinations.

When Procter & Gamble began its national launch of Cinch (in what's called a "rollout" because it usually proceeds region by region), Harrell retaliated. His strategy was to make the Procter & Gamble executives discouraged about their new product. He had pumped up Procter & Gamble's expectations as much as possible with his manipulation of the Denver market, and now had to make the ensuing reality as bleak as possible. So he strapped together his 16-ounce size of Formula 409 with his half-gallon size and sold them for $1.48 retail—a huge cut in the normal retail price of the two. The idea was not simply to cut price, however—Harrell did not have enough money to survive a lengthy price war with Procter & Gamble—but to load up the typical spray-cleaner consumer with what Harrell figured would be about six months' worth of product. He advertised and promoted the bargain heavily.

Thus while Procter & Gamble was pursuing traditional new-product strategy—putting much of its huge Cinch investment up front in a concerted national advertising campaign—Formula 409 users were, in business jargon, "out of the market." They didn't need any more spray cleaner. The only customers left were new users, and there weren't nearly enough of them to justify Procter & Gamble's expenditures on Cinch. Within a year, the impossible happened. Procter & Gamble withdrew its new spray cleaning product from the shelves, despite its remarkably successful test market.

It was a close shave for Wilson Harrell. For those with small companies, it usually is, and all the more so when a giant company like Procter & Gamble points itself in your direction. But Harrell knew the psychology of big companies. He knew their self-confidence. He knew they were inclined to believe positive results from a test market when they had already invested heavily in a new product. He was betting that Procter & Gamble was simply too big to watch him closely. It was an elephant grown so large that the monkey could usually hear it coming and dart out of the way.

Bruce Henderson has spent a lifetime observing, analyzing, and formulating the competitive strategies of companies.

"This little company I worked for in the Thirties, Leland Electric, made motors for gasoline pumps," he explains. "It made more gasoline-pump motors than any other company in the United States. Now, I didn't see any real question about that then, and only began to realize long, long afterward that it was a very interesting and peculiar fact, with tremendous implications, if you started to think about it."

Why was a little company with only a few hundred employees able to make and sell gasoline-pump motors at a much lower price than big companies such as General Electric and Westinghouse, and make a profit besides?

Because they were selling *different* motors, says Henderson. To most of us, the difference might not seem significant. Gasoline-pump motors, after all, have one function—to pump the gas when the handle is squeezed—and to consumers they all seem much alike.

But to the gasoline-pump manufacturer who buys and installs these motors, the differences are immense. Gasoline-pump motors have to be explosionproof. Most of the manufacturers had special designs for their particular motor: a slightly different shaft, or a slightly different way of mounting it, or slightly different specifications for the ventilation. Since Leland Electric's main business was making these relatively expensive motors, it started from scratch with a basic design tailored to the special purpose of the product.

Westinghouse also made a gasoline-pump motor. But since Westinghouse's main business was a standard, lightweight, general-purpose motor, the company took it and turned it into an explosionproof gasoline-pump motor by housing it in a cast-iron frame that cost much more to produce.

Westinghouse had the cost of the standard motor to begin with, the cost of the frame, and the cost of getting it all certified. Then the company had to run the motor down a production line, which interrupted the flow of what would otherwise be a high-production item.

Leland's costs on gasoline-pump motors were therefore half Westinghouse's costs.

Since cost and price are major components of a product's essential nature, Henderson concluded that Leland Electric was really selling a different product from Westinghouse's, even though they seemed the same. Leland's motor was not only cheaper, but also better suited to its particular purpose. Since the small company had much more riding on the motor's reputation, and the customers knew it, they seemed to *trust* the Leland motor more.

That's how little Leland could survive against mighty Westinghouse: by finding its own "product niche." As Henderson points out, there often are enormous variations in cost for essentially the same product—perhaps because of the overhead generated by having more than one product, or by the differences in marketing costs, or by the fact that a particular product design is focused instead of general.

There are an unbelievable number of these cost variations, which each successful company tends to attribute to its greater wisdom: "Our costs are good," they say, "because we're better managed; therefore we make a profit." But the truth is that their costs are inherently lower than the competition's because there is a fundamental difference in the way they do business, which gets reflected in cost.

These differences are a key to competition. They will help determine the niche a company can find, and can then defend against all enemies.

Henderson puts it this way: "For each competitor, its niche is that combination of customers and services with respect to which it *alone* has a competitive advantage over any and all competitors."

Henderson then goes one crucial step further. He says there is the potential for an *infinite* number of niches.

These niches are potentially limitless because they are forever changing. As competitors adapt to each other and make adjustments to increase the value of their mutual differences in the marketplace—which itself is always changing—then the boundaries of the niches change too. That's why you find a supermarket across the street from a twenty-four-hour-a-day, seven-day-a-week convenience store, with both selling many of the same items, and both making money. At the supermarket you get variety. You can get three different brands of peas in five different-size cans. At the convenience store, you can get only one kind of peas—one brand, one size—but you can get it at any hour of the day or night.

"Many times I've come home from the airport after a long trip," says Henderson. "I know the milk in the refrigerator is going to be sour. I stop by the corner store out near my home in the suburbs at nine at night—I don't even know its name—and I get a quart of milk. All right, so the supermarket sells it cheaper, but I couldn't care less. I want that milk for breakfast next morning. Both the small store and the supermarket are selling the identical product in the same market, but what the customer wants in one case and what he wants in the other are different enough that you can separate your customers into what I choose to call the *competitive segments*. In other words, every competitor who survives has a segment of the market."

Although the convenience store is charging him more for a container of milk, as long as he and the other customers don't mind (or don't notice, which amounts to the same thing), the store will hold its niche.

Not that the higher prices can't sometimes rub the public—or the government—the wrong way. Some niches are highly controversial. At the foot of Boston's fashionable Beacon Hill several years ago, an independent Gulf gasoline station began charging 50 percent and more above the going rate for gasoline. It had five competitors within several blocks, but it was the only one to stay open all night and Sundays. Its high rates received a great deal of bad publicity, yet the station apparently took in enough money to cover its high rent and twenty-four-hour-a-day operating costs. (It even charged customers 50 cents to use its air pump for tire inflation.)

Then the government stepped in. The owner was taken to court for illegally high rates—"price gouging"—and was vilified publicly for taking advantage of skyrocketing gasoline prices and insecurity over supplies. But he was also offering a "unique" product for which some people, for whatever reasons, were willing to pay a premium.

Sometimes, when a business's product niche is unacceptable by law, both the business and the government may find that the cure can be worse than the disease.

In the spring of 1980, Bruce Henderson quietly invited seven chief executive officers of U.S. corporations and an equal num-

ber of regulatory people from the Carter Administration to establish a bridge of communication between the two sides. The
group included several bureau heads of the Federal Trade Commission, a senior member of the Anti-Trust Division of the Justice Department, and the general counsel of a Senate anti-trust
committee.

About halfway through the day, the chief executive of a very
successful corporation got up and said, "I don't know if I'm
doing the right thing and I want your opinion. We have a product in which we're steadily gaining market share. It's up to fifty
percent of the world market now. And it's growing. Are we doing
something bad? Is our domination *wrong?*"

No one had an answer. "Our profit margin has been steadily
improving," the executive continued. "It's now up to a fifty-per-
cent return on assets, pretax [the national average in 1980 was 11
percent]. Is that bad? Is there something wrong with us? Is this
illegal?"

Finally, somebody asked, "Well, what's so special about the
product?"

"Nothing," the executive answered. "It's been in existence for
a hundred years. It's nothing more than an ordinary rod of a
standard-specification steel with threads on each end."

Henderson asked the next question: "Who are your competitors?"

"The world's largest steel companies," the executive replied.

The regulators, needless to say, were daunted by the problem.
The purpose of anti-trust legislation is to prevent huge competitors from controlling a market. But how do you prevent a *small*
company from cornering a market by competing against huge
competitors?

One of the regulators then spoke. "You're not selling steel
rods," he said; "you must be selling a service of some kind. Just
exactly what is this thing you're selling?"

"It's a sucker rod used in oil well pumps," the chief executive
replied. "And of course, if a rod breaks and you don't have a replacement for it, you've got thousands of dollars in losses because of a piece of steel that's worth hardly anything—as a piece
of steel, that is. But to you, it's priceless.

"So we carry stocks on site, have helicopters on call, keep tabs on what consumption is, all kinds of things, so that our customers will never be out of sucker rods, no matter what happens. And that kind of security is hard to put a price on."

"Well, what about the steel companies?" asked the regulator. "Can't they do the same thing?"

"No. Their problem is moving millions of tons of steel. They look at tonnage. They don't really look at the fact that you can get a very high profit margin on a very specialized function which has nothing to do with the basic skills, culture, and focus of a large steel company."

The executive's quandary was no small challenge to the assembled regulators. It suggests that a company can dominate a market by quality of product and that the only alternative to its dominance may be to handicap the company, and thus, by extension, handicap its customers.

When a regulator looks down the road a piece, he or she sees that if a company becomes large enough—no matter how efficiently it grew—it poses a problem to society by reason of its very size. But Bruce Henderson thinks the market can often take care of the "dinosaurs," just as he thinks the sucker-rod manufacturer eventually will face competition in his highly remunerative niche.

Sometimes government regulation can wind up working against the competitive nature of the corporate battlefield because of the differences between short-term and long-term conditions. Take the history of the steel industry. In 1903, United States Steel had more than 70 percent of domestic steel production. It led a cartel-like amalgamation of companies which held prices artificially high. Lowering steel prices was unlikely to increase demand or use, so why bother?

What happened to U.S. Steel? It set what amounted to "umbrella" prices for the group and was guaranteed a steady rate of return by the subsequent lack of any stiff price competition. There was little incentive to modernize its facilities and keep pace with modern technology, and that led to timidity and stagnation. The net result was that U.S. Steel has lost about two-thirds of a percentage point of the entire U.S. market *per year,* on average, for almost eighty years. It's down to less than 20 percent now. With obsolete assets and intense foreign competition, it will find it difficult to recover.

So the amalgamation spelled defeat for the steel giant. But suppose that U.S. Steel had dramatically *lowered* prices instead of joining the group—lowering prices to the cost of production. A price cut of this magnitude would have forced much of the competition out of business and left the market to U.S. Steel. In that event, it would have been the Anti-Trust Division's mandate to step in and preserve competition by moving against U.S. Steel for what's called "predatory pricing."

It's an extremely complex problem. Consider the steel industry's navigation of regulatory waters during the early Sixties, when it found itself between Scylla and Charybdis. Scylla was predatory pricing. Charybdis was then-Attorney General Robert Kennedy.

"Remember what Bobby Kennedy did when the steel companies raised prices in 1961?" asks Henderson. "He got the steel executives out of bed at four o'clock in the morning and said, 'If you don't lower the price, we're going to audit your personal tax returns.'"

Down the prices went, and to millions of Americans Bobby's brother Jack became a very popular President. But why had the prices gone up at all? Because there was no cutthroat competition in the steel industry. If there had been such competition, the prices would have gone down. And then the company with the lowest costs—the biggest steel company, which had been under an anti-trust threat all that time—would have been guilty of trying to put all the small competitors out of business by predatory pricing.

"Ah," sighs Henderson, "a criminal offense. The government was going to come down on them if they cut prices or if they raised prices. So they had an implicit agreement among themselves: We're not going to start a war. As a consequence, in an effort to hold the prices up, U.S. Steel's market now shrank and companies like Armco and Allegheny Ludlum moved into specialties, prospered, and grew. The competition moved from price into product and customer specialization. So the market gets cleared one way or the other, but not necessarily by price alone. It gets segmented in other ways. What we're talking about is a very complex set of competitive relationships."

Indeed, on January 12, 1981, *The Wall Street Journal* ran the following front-page story: "LITTLE GIANTS: MINI-MILL STEEL-MAKERS, NO LONGER VERY SMALL, OUTPERFORM BIG ONES." The market has punished the cartel behemoths, who were clamoring for so-called "trigger prices" to protect them from cheaper foreign competition.

To Bruce Henderson, each business on the corporate battle-field has its own territory, or niche, and each niche has its own *raison d'être.* He acknowledges that the resulting proliferation of products has been strongly criticized for conditioning us to make choices on the basis of artificial, meaningless differences among name brands. Breakfast cereals are often cited as a prime example: Bran Buds, Bran Chex, All-Bran, 40 Percent Bran Flakes, and Corn Bran, to name but a few. But Henderson thinks such product proliferation is a fundamentally natural process.

"People are looking for different things," he says. "And the market is constantly being segmented into smaller and smaller subdivisions, where each seller in it is appealing to a smaller group of customers on a little-different difference or some different combination. These things are not static. They are constantly changing—in their boundaries and in the balances between them. The more stable the market is—like cereals—and the bigger it is, the more it gets subdivided into smaller and smaller groups."

This specialization may bewilder, annoy, or disgust you, but Bruce Henderson argues that it also protects you. The more specialized the market niches, the greater the opportunity for competition, he says, and the less chance that one company can completely dominate an industry.

"Look at IBM," he says vehemently, his voice a half-octave above where it started. "We thought that IBM was going to dominate the whole world computer market for a long time. But how many minicomputer companies were there with over a hundred million dollars in sales a few years ago, all growing at fifty percent a year? Plenty. Well, why was that, if IBM dominated the whole world?"

He paused momentarily and then fired again. "What the hell is a minicomputer anyway except a small version of what IBM has already been doing? IBM has more engineers, more money, more *everything*. Why can't it control the minicomputer market too?"

Perhaps IBM, for all its strength, has some inherent limitations. Perhaps "bigness" does not necessarily mean sustained domination.

"Let me tell you about Control Data," Henderson says. "It was started some years ago with eight engineers. They made the world's largest computer for the Atomic Energy Commission. And they sold it on price against IBM. And started a major business. How come? How was that possible?"

As it turns out, the answer was simple. The growth of the computer market required a tremendous amount of education, so IBM had to be in the education business as well as the computer-hardware business. It was in the business of supplying support to customers who really didn't know how to use the computers and didn't know how to debug them, service them, or anything else. All these services were incorporated in their price, their sales costs were twice as much as their manufacturing costs.

Those eight engineers at Control Data who had been making a somewhat similar type of product could sell it to the Atomic Energy Commission at 40 percent less than IBM because they didn't have to teach people there how to use it. And they were making only a few machines, so they didn't have much manufacturing expense or overhead.

So Control Data was an instant miracle of success until, guess what? It tried to sell large numbers of computers in competition with IBM. IBM then came back at Control Data with everything it had, including some cut-throat competition that landed it in court.

Yet IBM still was unable to compete with Control Data at the Atomic Energy Commission because it couldn't afford to.

In the late 1960s, IBM faced a similar problem with a company called Inforex. Inforex brought out a data-entry system with a video screen so operators could check—and correct—their work as they went along. This system competed with IBM's mechanical keypunch machines, the ones that turned out the "Do NOT FOLD, SPINDLE OR MUTILATE" punch cards.

IBM had hundreds of thousands of these machines out on lease. The machines provided the cash to subsidize the computer side of the business, which still wasn't turning a profit in the early 1960s.

Keypunch video technology was an easy technical step for IBM to take. But if it were taken, untold thousands of customers would terminate their leases on the card punchers and switch to video. IBM would be robbing Peter to pay Paul. Or, in business lingo, "cannibalizing" its own product, with one product eating into the revenues of another. So IBM stood pat, and Inforex became one of the hottest high-technology companies of the early 1970s.

Sometimes, however, IBM was the aggressor.

When IBM went into competition against Xerox in photocopiers, it made its own version of the most popular model in the middle of Xerox's product line and rented it to customers at a price-per-copy well below Xerox's. The problem for Xerox was that it had a pricing scale in which the price-per-copy went down as the machines got bigger. If Xerox tried to cut the price of its middle model, there would be no incentive for customers to trade up to Xerox's top model, which no longer would be significantly cheaper per copy. Consequently, if it matched IBM, Xerox would have had a large part of its total volume affected by this one price reduction. Its hands were tied. What happened? The new IBM copier took a major part of the new installations in the country.

If every business has its ecological niche, whether it be IBM or a convenience store, what does that tell us about the nature of competition itself?

Bruce Henderson looks to biology for the answer. Competition on the corporate battlefield, he says, is the economic form of Darwinian evolution.

"You can find no species on earth which coexists with another one, where both make their living in exactly the same fashion," he states emphatically. Just as in nature, it seems to be a law of business that no two competitors can coexist who make their living in the identical way. Each must have its own ecological niche, its own market segment. Thus little Leland Electric and giant Westinghouse could coexist because each of them dominated the market segment in which it made a profit.

Thus could competitors flood the computer marketplace, challenging IBM in an enormous variety of segments and carving out their own niches. Thus has Xerox been challenged, not only by IBM's middle-range machine, but by Savin, and more recently by the Japanese, led by Canon. As a result, Xerox diversifies in a search for new segments, and reexamines old segments in which it might be able to dislodge the current leaders by virtue of *its* competitive advantages: new ideas, new technology, money, reputation, managerial skill. IBM has the same strategy in many segments of the computer market.

But if the giants do not succeed in these efforts, they will become, in the Darwinian analogy, dinosaurs, stumbling toward extinction. And if the smaller species do not respond effectively to the new species that are attempting to invade their niches, they too will disappear, like so many organisms that have vanished from the earth.

Inforex, which poached on IBM's lucrative keypunch niche, found a dozen well-equipped companies entering the market soon after it. Each worked hard to improve the basic products, to redefine the market segment ever so slightly in a direction it was better able to serve. Inforex had the advantage of being first, but when a new generation of products began to transform the market, creating still new niches, Inforex found itself falling behind. Its new products simply did not sell well, even to old customers. By 1976, its stock, which had risen as high as $48 a share, was below $5. By 1979, it declared bankruptcy, some $60 million in debt. Today, it survives as a pared-down subsidiary of a onetime rival, Datapoint Corporation of San Antonio, Texas. Ironically, when Datapoint entered the market in the early 1970s, Inforex seriously considered acquiring it. But Datapoint proved itself a fitter species and turned the tables, buying up Inforex at $1 a share.

Every year there are many thousands of business bankruptcies in this country. "Extinction" is a continual process.

The Darwinian analogy has dramatically shaped Henderson's thinking in recent years. He even uses the term "Red Queen Syndrome" to describe the perpetual motion all business competitors must engage in merely to keep pace, the term coming from the "Red Queen Hypothesis" of biologist Leigh Van Valen, who used it to describe the constant evolution of a species to maintain its biological niche.

The Darwinian analogy has also led him to another important hypothesis about the nature of competition on the corporate battlefield—the culmination, in some sense, of all that has gone before. It is the hypothesis of "Hawks and Doves."

"Let's play a little game," suggests Henderson with a smile. "It's called 'Hawks and Doves' and there are two modes: you can play hawk or you can play dove. If you play hawk, once you start a fight, you go for broke. No holds barred. Anything goes. You never stop until one or the other of you is dead. If you're a dove, the rule is that you always avoid fighting if there's a high probability of major injury or loss. You withdraw rather than take the risk."

The final condition of the game is that you cannot tell by looking at a player whether he or she is a hawk or a dove. So, how do you decide whether to play hawk or dove?

"Well, let's say you play hawk," says Henderson. "What happens if you meet another hawk? It's simple. One of you is going to get killed. But what if you meet a dove? You would want him to *think* you're a hawk even if you're another dove, wouldn't you? Because then he would back away.

"Let's also assume that we have some payoffs or costs for winning or losing—since there's no point in fighting if there isn't *something* which is a payoff or a cost. And let's say the payoffs or costs are in terms of the Darwinian fitness factor. That is, the species with the best strategy will reproduce itself more often than the other species in the game."

Now, if you play hawk all the time, you will obviously lose. In Darwinian terms, that is, you can drive away the doves for a while, and create an all-hawk environment, but as soon as you do, it will be hawk versus hawk all the time, with blood and feathers flying. The hawks would kill each other off.

Enter a dove. In this all-hawk world, it survives by flitting off. It neither wins nor loses—but that's a lot better than the dwindling population of hawks is doing. Always playing hawk is a doomed strategy. In Darwinian terms, that means hawks will not be able to dominate by passing on their hawk-behavior genes to succeeding generations.

Similarly, if you just played dove all the time, any wandering hawk would have a field day, dominate the environment, and start passing along his or her genes until the environment got too full of hawks. So always playing dove is also a doomed strategy.

"Now, all my professional work," says Henderson, "has been to recommend corporate strategies in competitive environments. Is there any such thing as an appropriate strategy to play knowing what I've just outlined? Yes. In a game with these payoffs and costs, a *mixed* strategy of playing hawk and dove will give you the best outcome."

The businesses that survive on the corporate battlefield, like the species that survive in nature, are those which can adapt, developing new strategies as conditions warrant. If a species grows—each succeeding generation becoming larger than the last—it has a Darwinian fitness factor of greater than 1. (A factor of 1 means zero population growth; less than 1 means a decreasing population.) To Henderson, a Darwinian fitness factor of greater than 1 is the equivalent of a business that succeeds in increasing its total assets.

Henderson believes that if you can compute the payoffs and costs of business confrontations and accurately assess the odds of your competition pursuing the various hawk/dove strategies, your business will survive and grow. Your understanding of competitive confrontations will help you pick your openings and avoid fatal showdowns.

Say you're Texas Instruments, maker of semiconductor chips. Your industry is just beginning. You know costs per chip are going to go down as you make more and more of these new devices because of the "experience curve"—a concept which postulates that, due to experience, *every doubling in cumulative production yields a 20-percent cut in cost.* You also know that lots of competitors are starting out with you. What do you do?

Texas Instruments decided to price its chips as if it had already made millions of them. In consulting terminology, *it priced down the experience curve.* With a low price, its volume increased dramatically. And sure enough, it soon was making enough chips so that its production cost per chip was lower than its anticipated low price. It knocked dozens of competitors out of the world market.

Texas Instruments had computed the odds. It figured that if it played hawk first, it would discourage the competition from doing so. In other words, it figured it was up against many companies disposed to playing dove at that particular time. It wasn't a sure thing; one of the competition also might have played hawk—matched price—and destroyed the strategy. But the payoff of being the first to offer a much lower price outweighed the danger. Today, Texas Instruments is the nation's largest semiconductor manufacturer (No. 91 on the Fortune 500), doing $4 billion a year worth of business—in large part because of its hawkish pricing play, which was based on its assessment of the competition.

But then again, if Texas Instruments is ever faced with a small competitor seeking to carve off a piece of its business, it had better play dove, just as IBM did with Control Data, or it might find itself cutting its own throat.

Henderson cites the dangers of an all-hawk strategy: "I remember when I was first consulting," he says, "and two of the country's major gasoline companies got into a price competition in the Southeast. Each of the majors told its gas stations to undersell the gas stations of the competition—no matter what. The companies would guarantee a four-cent margin, regardless of the final price.

"You know what actually happened? By the end of the price war, an oil company truck would pull in to replenish its station's

supplies for free and, in addition, give the owner a check to preserve his profit margin. That's what a pure hawk strategy eventually leads to."

So price cuts are a gamble that the competition won't retaliate.
Price wars are usually price cuts that have gotten out of hand.
Occasionally they are bold hawk strategies in which a company
is sure it can outlast its competition. But if *both* companies are
equally confident—or reckless—both will lose.

Every smart corporation is forever playing a mixture of hawk
and dove strategies, depending on the situation. IBM takes on
Xerox with a hawklike entry into the photocopying market.
Xerox cannot afford to match the low price, and plays dove. Yet
when Inforex plays hawk with its new data-entry system to challenge the IBM keypunch, or Control Data plays hawk with a specialized mainframe computer, IBM, multinational behemoth
though it is, must play dove or lose a fortune in revenue.

"You're not going to have a hot fight break out where what
you lose looks like it's going to be more than you win," explains
Henderson. "You look back to the case of Leland Electric and
Westinghouse and you see that Westinghouse is not going to cut
its whole price level in order to intimidate a small company like
Leland where what Westinghouse loses is more than Leland's
total annual sales. On the other hand, there's the constant threat
of mortal warfare, the constant feeling out, the constant skir-
mishing along mutual boundaries."

The constant maneuvering for position . . . One business analyst has observed that in the competition between Gillette and
Bic in the disposable-razor market, Gillette should have begun to
test-market 5-cent pens when it learned that Bic was test-marketing a disposable razor. That way, it would have served notice
on Bic that *both* companies could suffer from an attack on Gillette's business.

And in the February 20, 1981, *Wall Street Journal,* a front-
page story read: "While John Deere [the farm-machinery manu-
facturer] is trying to make further inroads in construction equipment, Caterpillar [the construction-equipment giant] appears to
be coveting the farm equipment business by testing prototypes of
large farm tractors. Analysts doubt that Caterpillar plans any

major move into the farm equipment business, but one suggests Caterpillar may be trying to warn Deere against further invasions of its turf."

To come full circle, we need only return to the subject of Leland Electric and Westinghouse. Why *did* Westinghouse continue to make explosionproof motors if Leland could produce them and sell them more cheaply? The answer is that Westinghouse wanted to keep the pressure on. On the corporate battlefield there is always pressure, there is always competition.

This is true despite the concentration of ownership among fewer and fewer corporations. While that concentration may be politically distressing—or, to some, unacceptable—in terms of competition, the degree of concentration of firms within individual markets has actually been holding steady or dropping in recent years. The huge corporations are called conglomerates for a reason. They are composed of many different companies doing business in different markets. They are not growing by increasing their share of any one of those markets in particular.

Size is not necessarily the key to success and survival on the corporate battlefield—the key to competition. *Difference* is. A tiny twenty-four-hour convenience store can't compete with Safeway, but then Safeway can't compete with the convenience store either.

"It's not necessarily a fair system or a just one," says Henderson. "It has its tragedies and inequities, its wastefulness and God knows what else. Some businesses will fool consumers into thinking their products are better. People will lose their jobs. There are always casualties. In fact, there *must* be casualties, because that's the way the system works. It's the price of competition and change. And without change there's no progress."

To many this seems a heavy price—a price that social-welfare programs must help pay to avoid widespread suffering. Competition gets results—but at what cost?

The debate has been raging for centuries. But most of those who have seriously examined the issue, from Karl Marx to Andrew Carnegie, agree upon one thing: capitalism means competition, and competition means change—and uncertainty.

Faced with this unsettling state of affairs, companies spend a great deal of time and energy trying to achieve a position of *some* certainty—whether it be a dominant market share or a small, specialized niche—a position in which they can breathe more easily, if only for a moment.

CHAPTER TWO # Fortress
on the Charles

On the banks of the Charles River in Boston, there sits an institution totally dedicated to preparing the future managers of America for life on the corporate battlefield. It is the West Point of business schools—a ticket to both the front line and the upper ranks. It's where students learn how to compete and how to win.

Several years ago, in a burst of admiration, *The New York Times* called the Harvard Graduate School of Business Administration's master's degree the "Golden Passport." It was not hyperbole. The Business School's 1981 M.B.A. graduates received an average starting salary above $33,000 a year; their illustrious predecessors from the Class of '61 now count as millionaires more than one-third their number, and 41 percent are company presidents or chairmen.

Each spring finds the Business School's twenty-six interview rooms humming with the questions of corporate recruiters and the eager responses of their soon-to-be junior executives. As many as three thousand job offers will be made to H.B.S. graduates this year—and none of the students will be particularly surprised; after all, that's why they enrolled at the Business School in the first place.

The H.B.S. faculty is not averse to making money either. Full professors are paid as much as $75,000 a year, and some make as

much as $3,000 a day for consultant work. The school permits its
faculty members to spend one day a week away from their offices, consulting to corporations, because it helps to strengthen
ties to the business world, enhances the school's reputation, increases its power, and adds to the faculty's practical experience.

A casual tour of the Charles River campus will tell you all you
need to know about affluence, prestige, and the Business School's
pedigree. Consider stately Baker Library, named after George F.
Baker, the school's great benefactor, president of the First National Bank of New York (now Citibank). In the 1920s when
Baker was asked to subscribe $1 million of a $5-million endow-
ment fund, he replied that he would prefer to contribute the entire $5 million, if that was all right. The administration building
is Morgan Hall, named after J. P. Morgan, an early friend of the
school. Aldrich Hall is named after John D. Rockefeller, Jr.'s, fa-
ther-in-law.

Three exclusive programs form the core of the school: the
fourteen-week Program for Management Development (for rapidly rising thirty- to forty-year-old middle-management types);
the fourteen-week Advanced Management Program (for near-
the-summit forty- to fifty-year-old senior executives); and, most
important, the two-year M.B.A., or Master of Business Administration, program, for those just starting up the executive ladder.

The key to the Business School's educational technique—in all
its programs—is something called the "case method": an attempt
to simulate the corporate battlefield by focusing every class
around a case history in the life of an actual company. The
write-ups have the flavor of anthropology monographs, loaded
with basic facts and observations for the foreigner. But these are
monographs with a twist: a strong dose of drama, sometimes
even melodrama, added to engage the reader. They generally
end at a critical point in the story. Will Gillette president "Ralph
Bingham" introduce a line of audiotape cassettes for the company? Should giant Rockwell International bother with the
hand-calculator market? The Business School has produced
more than forty thousand such monographs in its seventy-three-
year history. That's forty thousand ways to demonstrate the
complexity of business.

As in real life, these "stories" at first seem to be unique to themselves and unrelated. What could the sad tale of a bankrupt computer company have to do with the marketing of a new toy or the relocation of a heavy-industrial plant? But the Business School does not believe in randomness. It sees patterns everywhere.

At 8:28 A.M. on a bright New England morning in early September, with the rest of Harvard University still weeks away from convening, Section C sat waiting nervously for the flamboyant, intimidating professor of marketing, Steven Star.

Its room, indistinguishable from those of the other eight sections, looked somewhat like a large air-raid shelter, with its windowless walls of whitewashed concrete. Three horseshoe tiers of desks rose to the back of the room, with two aisles along which the professor was free to roam. On the front wall, facing the students' desks, were five green chalkboards, three of which could ride up or down at the professor's touch of an electric switch. Professors at the Harvard Business School rarely use erasers.

They do, however, use a great deal of chalk. And never was this more apparent than in Section C's first class.

At 8:30 exactly, Professor Star, dressed in a suede sport coat and elegant soft kid boots, began to stride back and forth in front of the boards with a piece of chalk in his gesturing right hand. Before him sat his 80 students: 15 of them women, 20 from other countries, 7 nonwhite. Their average age was twenty-seven. They were paying $4,500 a year in tuition for the privilege of being one of 720 members of the Class of '78, chosen from more than 7,000 applicants. And some of them were beginning to think they had made a big mistake.

The students had been told to read a case in preparation for their first class. Without exception, they had read the case and had not known what to make of it.

The case concerned wax—specifically, the self-polishing paste and liquid floor waxes made by the Butcher Polish Company of Malden, Massachusetts. A small, high-quality, family-owned manufacturer, Butcher was putting its entire future on the line. The case focused on the scion of the Butcher family, Charles

Butcher II, as he attempted to chart a long-range course for the company. The goal: a tenfold increase in sales. The danger: a total collapse in the face of much larger competitors, Johnson's Wax and Beacon Wax.

Unfortunately for the beleaguered students, very few details escaped the case writer. For example:

> The Butcher company manufactured over 20 different wax products, each of outstanding quality, a factor which Mr. Butcher believed had been instrumental in keeping the company alive over the years. This quality was primarily due to the high proportion of *carnauba* used in Butcher waxes. Carnauba was an expensive ingredient since it was refined from a species of tree leaves grown only in South America. No direct substitute had yet been developed for carnauba, which produced an excellent wearing surface that improved in appearance with buffing and normal scuffing during use.

Now, you might think, as did much of Section C that day, that while the selling approach of a small wax maker may have some direct relevance to the aspiring corporate executive, the derivation of carnauba has none at all. But if the case method teaches one lesson above all others, it's that in business, you learn from experience, and from experience you learn that *everything* is relevant and interrelated.

This is certainly true of marketing (simply, what you do to bring a product successfully to market). Marketing entails not only market research and testing, but advertising research and testing, packaging, distribution, and finally, price setting. In a good marketing plan, everything must mesh, whether you're selling wax, dance lessons, cars, or cereal. And marketing is only one phase of doing business.

The case method is predicated on the notion that success will come to those who learn to recognize and handle the complexity of business—to those who ultimately can see the whole for all its parts.

But in the case of Butcher Wax, there were enough parts to overwhelm a mechanical engineer. The sixteen-page monograph on the company was crammed with information. In addition to the intimacies of carnauba and the company's growth target of 25 percent a year, Butcher's incredibly complex price schedule to wholesalers and retailers was reprinted; sales expenses were broken down by type and by year; recent advertisements were reproduced; sales figures for wax and polish—as against other grocery products—were chronicled in excruciating detail; an elaborate chart compared eleven major grocery items on the basis of "net profit per square foot of display space"; the competition's pricing was included; and the case ended with an eleven-point "Definition of a Butcher Salesman's Job," reprinted from an internal company memorandum.

The student's task was to make sense of all this information and integrate it into a plan of action: What sales strategy should Butcher pursue?

The case took at least an hour to read and understand. It took another hour and a half just to work through the maze of numbers and figure out what a retailer expected from wax sales, or what a salesman expected in terms of price. Then came the tough part: weaving all the information into a coherent marketing strategy.

A diligent person would require, say, two months of full-time study before attempting to develop such a strategy. Charles Butcher II obviously had spent a great deal more time than that. Yet the Butcher case had been distributed a mere twenty-four hours earlier, along with two other cases to be discussed in classes later that day. For Section C it meant an all-nighter, and a hopelessly inadequate one at that.

"Wax!" Star proclaimed at 8:31, and the students quaked. Each was certain—as certain as that a Harvard degree meant wealth and security—that he or she would be the first to be called upon, the first to expound on the case for at least ten minutes, the first to founder, flounder, stammer, blank out, never recover, flunk Marketing, flunk everything in sight, and never get that degree after all.

"Mr. Elkins!" Star boomed.

Charlie Elkins of Waco, Texas, froze in his seat.

"Mr. *El*-kins," said Star with a shade of contempt in his voice, "tell us about *wax*."

And as he ended his command, Star took the piece of chalk he had been holding in his right hand, snapped it in two, and flung one of the pieces against the far wall. Five seconds later, Donald Dax, whom the chalk had narrowly missed, slumped from his back-row seat to the floor, out cold—the victim of hyperventilation. While the two class members on either side of Dax revived him, the rest of the class paid scant attention—a function less of their indifference than of their strong sense of *there-but-for-the-grace-of-God.*

Charlie Elkins, meanwhile, stammered his presentation of the case: "The suggested retail prices of Johnson and Beacon waxes," he began, "are, uh, $.65 a pint, and, uh, $1.10 a, uh, quart . . ."

Star chalked up the numbers. So far Elkins had done nothing more than repeat the numbers on page 13 of the case, and he had taken his time doing it. While it wouldn't be fair to say that his classmates wished Charlie ill, it didn't seem that they were too distressed by his lack of poise. One student began to harumph disdainfully (not within earshot of Professor Star, however).

"Now, the case says that Butcher sells its wax for, uh, a retail price of $1.50," Charlie continued.

"Where does it say that?" Star snapped.

"Uh, let me see," Charlie said, thumbing through his case in panic.

Finally he found the reference. "Here, on page four. It says . . ."

"Yes, yes," said Star impatiently. His question had been merely a test. "One dollar fifty cents. Anything else?"

"Well," said Charlie tentatively, "I also figured out how much the dealers have to pay wholesale."

This had required some doing, since the numbers had to be computed from a set of data expressed in percentages. It was tedious, but obvious enough so that everyone in the class had done it.

"*How* did you figure out the wholesale price?" Star inquired.

Charlie began to mumble through the calculation while Star flicked the chalkboard switch to summon down the middle board to within his reach.

As Charlie read out the numbers from his notes, Star scribbled them on the chalkboard. But as the class watched him write, a strange dissonance became apparent. Charlie and Star were out of sync, like a movie with a sound track that lags a split second behind the action. Finally, the class came to a chilling realization. Star was writing down the numbers *before* Charlie said them. *He knew the numbers by heart. All* the numbers. He was not simply showing off; he was serving notice that he could not be conned—that he would know a false step when he heard it.

Charlie, who hadn't once glanced up from his notes, looked up innocently when finished, clearly worn out by the effort.

"So, Mr. Elkins, what do you conclude from your endeavors?" asked Star with an eerie mixture of courtesy and contempt.

"Well, I guess a dealer makes a lot more money by selling Butcher Wax than by selling either Johnson or Beacon."

Star wrote *"higher margin"* on the board.

"Is that important?" the professor asked. "Don't the dealers sell *more* Johnson and Beacon and thus make at least as much money?"

"I don't know," said Charlie anxiously.

There was a short silence.

"What do *you* think, Mr. Rein?" Star asked suddenly.

Bob Rein, who foolishly had thought he was safe because he had helped Donald Dax earlier, was caught off guard. As something of a specialist in bravado, however, he recovered quickly.

"I think it depends on the type of dealer, and where he's located," he answered.

Star moved to the clear board on the right flank, chalk poised. Rein took the cue: "I break it down two ways," he said.

Star drew a three-by-two tic-tac-toe outline—three rows, two columns—and wrote the names of the three companies to the left of the three rows. Then he waited.

"The first is the type of store," said Rein.

Star labeled column one *"type of store."*

"The second is geographical location."

Star wrote *"geog."*

"Now, when you look at the companies," said Rein as Star's chalk hand gestured at the rows, "you see that Butcher is strong with specialty stores where, proportionally, a lot of wax moves. Beacon and Johnson are not."

Star filled in column one with the words *"specialty," "mass"* (for mass market), and *"mass."* The collaboration between student and teacher was beginning to seem somehow inevitable. It was just the effect Star wanted.

"Geographically," Rein continued, now brimming with a confidence that bordered on *hubris,* "the case says that Butcher is strong in Philadelphia and northern New Jersey because of wholesalers' pushing the product. I think it's fair to assume it must be strong in other areas where there are loyal wholesalers."

Star filled in the top box of column two with *"where the loyal wholesalers are."*

"And Johnson and Beacon?" Star asked. Rein cleared his throat and said something about performing an investigation similar to that needed to locate Butcher's loyal wholesalers, but he was stalling for time. His run was over. Star wrote a question mark in boxes two and three of the second column.

"Now, Mr. *El*-kins," said Star, utterly astonishing Charlie, who thought he had done his stint for the year, "what should Butcher infer from what Mr. Rein says? Assuming, of course, that there's some truth to it."

Elkins looked helpless.

"Well," said Star, his voice rising as he scanned the room, "tell me this. Who's *buying* this stuff in the first place?"

Remarkably, this question turned out to be the most memorable moment of the class, surpassing even Donald Dax's fainting spell. After seventy-five minutes of increasingly intense, at times bullying discussion of the Butcher Company, there came the fundamental insight that before you decided on a sales approach, you had better know who is buying what you're selling. It was so obvious that no one had considered how important it was to ponder thoroughly.

As Star put it near the end of the class, "We don't seem to know who's buying the product or why, and if we don't know who or why, we're not marketing."

So who did use Butcher Wax? As Section C's sole Pakistani student suggested, it was janitors in high-traffic offices. As a black woman from Boston added, it was people with fancy floors they had a serious interest in protecting. And as the mellifluous, mustachioed Bruno Montmerle from Paris pointed out, it was people who thought of themselves as purchasers of "the very best," regardless of the product.

"Do such people actually *know* which wax is the best, Mr. Montmerle?"

"Perhaps," said Montmerle, unsure of himself.

"Do you agree, Mr. Trung?"

Ha Trung, the affable former finance minister of South Vietnam under President Thieu, looked startled. When he spoke it was obvious he was having some difficulty breathing.

"I do not think that this type of consumer knows much about the difference between waxes," he said slowly. "I think she buys the most expensive one because she thinks it must be best."

"What are we saying here?" Star asked, gesturing at the blackboards filled with numbers and ideas. "Ms. Yerby?"

"Different people buy different waxes for different reasons."

The professor beamed.

Thus did Steven Star draw out the essentials of the case:

1. that Butcher Wax was an example of a most essential marketing concept: *market segmentation*;
2. that market segmentation was the indispensable analysis of any product's consumers into their various groups: for example, the practical users vs. the vanity users, or the young vs. the middle-aged vs. the elderly; and
3. that one could segment a market using several different criteria: for example, with *demographic* attributes, such as age, geographical location, and income, or with *psychographic* attributes, which

group consumers by their *psychological* characteristics or life-style.

He further explained that market segmentation could be de-
picted by a triangle, horizontally divided in order to emphasize
the breadth of the mass-market segments at the base and the
narrowness of the "upscale" segment at the top.

Butcher appealed to the top segment—demographically, to the
specialists (janitors and industrial and commercial users) and
psychographically, to the "floor fetishists and snobs," to quote
Professor Star.

Consequently, the company's strategy was clear: low advertising expenditure, since it was hard to reach such narrow segments; heavy promotion money—for more salesmen, lots of free
samples, and gifts to store clerks—since sales depended on
dealers' pushing the product on the consumer (as opposed to advertising, which *pulls* consumers into stores); a high markup
"margin" for the dealers, to encourage them to push the product;
a narrow channel of distribution—paint and hardware stores—to
maximize dealer involvement; high-quality product (carnauba
was important after all); and, most important perhaps, a visibility
higher than the competition's.

At 9:50 exactly, Steven Star turned dramatically on his heel
without a word and strode out of the room. The students, still
dazed, looked at each other for a few seconds until there came
the collective sigh of relief.

One class down, 434 to go.

The underlying lesson of Butcher Wax was simply this: to run
any business well, one must heed certain fundamental rules
common to all businesses. These rules govern most business behavior—even behavior that to the uninitiated seems to be self-
destructive or muddled or gratuitously mean-spirited—and any
Business School student who wishes to graduate had better learn
them all.

The Butcher Wax case gave a taste of just how systematic business is—and how any disruption of the system should be avoided

at all costs. Minimize risk, maximize profit, goes the old business adage.

The most fundamental rule of all is that in running a business, you must minimize risk by coordinating its innumerable parts as well as possible. Thus did Section C begin to realize in its first marketing class that a sales strategy depends on dealer promotion as well as narrowly targeted distribution, an emphasis on salespeople as well as high quality and high price.

Butcher had to maintain a balance among all these elements. Putting all its money into promotion, for instance, might cause dealers to order more wax, thus prompting Butcher to produce more. But if the wax just stayed on the shelves as inventory, there wouldn't be much reordering after the initial stocking up, and Butcher could find itself with swooning sales and a glut of wax.

The opposite tack could be even more dangerous. Too little promotion money might turn off the dealers altogether, and that could kill the product. Traditionally in such situations, a company will lower price, but for Butcher, high price was an important part of the product's appeal. Lowering the price might do long-term damage to sales.

Every element of the marketing plan depended on all the others, and their smooth operation had serious implications for other aspects of the company as well. There had to be money to finance the dealer promotions (What if carnauba prices shot up and absorbed all available cash?). Capable people had to be recruited and kept happy in order to keep quality up and service the all-important dealers. Production machinery had to be dependable and properly maintained to turn out enough wax to keep the dealers adequately stocked.

Conversely, the case suggested, the other aspects of the company had to be kept in balance in order to sustain the marketing plan. "Neglect any of these," the case implied, "and a business is doomed."

It's this complexity which helps explain, among other things, why management jobs can be so specialized, why executives spend so much time in committee meetings (trying to explain to the right hand what the left hand is doing), why planning is so important, and why a company can get very sick very quickly even if many people still want to buy its product.

At the next class—Production and Operations Management—the same point was drummed in, only this time the subject was the production line, the product was steel, and the question was how to make it most efficiently in a giant company pseudonymously called Lowell Steel.

The variables in this case were dizzying: four raw materials (iron ore, coke, limestone, and scrap metal) were fed into two blast furnaces, which prepared the mixture for ten open-hearth furnaces, from which the molten liquid was tapped into ladles, ladled onto platforms, poured into ingot molds, and then, as ingots, milled or rolled by a variety of other processes into about fifteen different permutations of final product. After hours of work on the case the night before, the only lesson that seemed obvious was that Business School was going to be an intolerable ordeal.

But during the class, the lesson of marketing began to re-emerge. Ingots, furnaces, ladles—*everything* was systematic and interconnected. The same balance that had to be achieved in a marketing plan was also necessary for the cost-effective production of steel.

After Production class, the students of Section C streamed out of their bunker in Aldrich Hall and met the autumn air with the relief of combat soldiers on sudden furlough. They trooped over to massive Kresge Hall for lunch in the cafeteria and sat at one of the long Formica tables. Conversation flowed freely.

Former Finance Minister Ha Trung cheerfully explained to the people at his table that his given name was Trung, not Ha, but that it seemed to him a waste of time to initiate every professor into the vagaries of Asian usage.

"Just call me Trung," he said.

"What did you think of this morning's classes?" he was asked.

"I think it is very interesting," said Trung. "But I am worried about the next class. It is the Managerial Economics course, and the professor will expect me to be good with numbers and know all the answers."

Since every professor had the biographies of the entire section, Trung might have reason to worry. But the case to be discussed focused on a real estate broker; it did not at all speak to Trung's supposed expertise.

"Yes," Trung acknowledged, "but the important issue of the case is how to calculate the wisest financial decision. The professor will think that was my primary job."

"What exactly *was* your job, Trung?" a classmate asked.

"My primary job was to calculate the amount of budget deficit," Trung explained, "so that the American Government would know how much money to send to balance our budget."

That sounded like a fairly easy job.

"It was not so easy," said Trung. "There were many things to think about. As the cases this morning showed, one must learn many rules and procedures to keep the parts of a business—or an economy—running smoothly. One must approach it logically and scientifically."

Then he added, after taking a sip of water, "Of course, here we always manage to fit those parts together by the end of class. In my country we did not do so well. . . ."

In the M.B.A. program, students learn not only lessons of logic, analysis, and procedure, but also how to develop a killer instinct. Self-interest dominates the classwork, which features competitive games, and even colors student life, as the bright young initiates prepare—and are prepared—for life on the corporate battlefield.

One of their instructors is Professor Elon Kohlberg, a young Israeli mathematician who joined the Business School from Harvard's Economics Department in 1977.

He teaches a very popular—and, to the outside world, controversial—second-year M.B.A. elective called Competitive Decision Making, in which the class plays thirty competitive games in the course of the term. One-third of each student's grade is based on how well he or she fares in the competition. Competitive game playing—and winning—is very serious business here.

Underlying this course is a branch of mathematics called

Game Theory, invented in the 1940s by a brilliant German émigré working at Cornell University, John von Neumann. Game Theory is an all-encompassing method of analyzing human interaction which assumes that everyone looks out for his or her own interests: in Game Theory, every player is out to maximize his or her gain.

But defining and calculating "gain"—and how to maximize it—is no simple matter. Thus Game Theory must depend on another assumption: that you can translate all competition into competitive "games" and translate the games into numbers. By doing so, you can figure out the costs and payoffs associated with any given competitive strategy.

Here's how. Take Bruce Henderson's example of the two gasoline companies that played pure hawk. For simplicity's sake, let's depict the game as a two-by-two matrix: Brand X-On versus Immobil. At the outset, they are charging an identical price. Each has two choices: to cut price or to hold price. Again, to keep things simple, let's say that if one cuts price, it will do so by only a penny.

So the matrix will look like this:

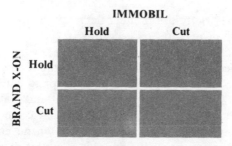

Now, what are the payoffs and costs? It's safe to assume that if both companies hold price (and act like doves), the competitive situation will remain unchanged and the payoffs (in the upper left box) will be zero for Brand X-On and zero for Immobil. We'll write it as 0,0—the first zero signifying Brand X-On's payoff and the second signifying Immobil's.

On the other hand, if both companies cut price (and act like

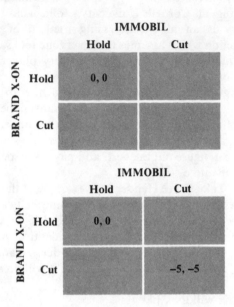

hawks) they will both lose money. Let's say the loss is −5 each. So we fill in the Cut/Cut box accordingly.

Now comes the hard part. How do we assess what will happen if one cuts price (acts like a hawk) and the other holds price (acts like a dove)? The assumption is that the price cutter will get enough extra business to offset the price cut and make a profit. Otherwise neither company would ever even consider cutting price. Since there is the risk of a price war whenever prices are cut, we have to assume that the rewards of cutting price, in terms of taking business from the competition and attracting entirely new customers, are substantial.

Let's say the company that cuts price gains 20 worth of new business, while the company that holds price loses 20 worth.

To read the matrix, remember that the first number represents the payoff or cost to Brand X-On; the second number, the payoff or cost to Immobil.

Now, you're Brand X-On. What do you do?

IMMOBIL

		Hold	Cut
BRAND X-ON	**Hold**	0, 0	−20, +20
	Cut	+20, −20	−5, −5

You look at your options in terms of the competition. First, what happens if Immobil unilaterally holds price?

Clearly, you are better off cutting; you gain +20.

Next, what happens if Immobil unilaterally cuts price?

You're still better off cutting, since if you hold, you will lose big: −20.

Now let's apply a little more very basic Game Theory. What if you are Immobil, not Brand X-On? You would analyze the situation exactly the same way, and cut.

But (and here's the lesson of the game) if both Immobil and Brand X-On cut, they both lose. If both had held price, however, neither would have lost a thing.

This is one of the games played in Kohlberg's class, and in Game Theory classes the world over. Its implications are fascinating. Even when cooperation would save both companies, self-interest seems to demand a strategy of attack. Since you can't trust the other guy to cooperate, the game teaches that you will go on the offensive, even though it will wind up hurting you. This is "Looking Out for Number One" with a vengeance.

There are an infinite number of such confrontations in business. Take major-league baseball owners and free-agent players. As a group, the owners repudiate the practice of bidding up the price for talent. But some owner always manages to break ranks and pay a huge sum in order to secure a ballplayer he thinks will help his team and lure fans.

For any given owner—let's say George Steinbrenner of the

New York Yankees—the Game Theory matrix would look like this:

ANY OTHER OWNER

		Never Bid	Bid
STEINBRENNER	Never Bid	0, 0	+20, −20
	Bid	+20, −20	−5, −5

Once again, you calculate the payoffs.

Obviously, Steinbrenner gains nothing—and loses nothing—if he never bids, and no other owner gains or loses either. It's the old hold price/hold price, dove/dove option.

If Steinbrenner does bid, he calculates that the players he bids for will eventually more than pay for themselves in increased attendance. So if he bids and no one else does, the payoff should be huge. He might even corner the market on talent.

"And what happens if I don't bid and someone else does?" Steinbrenner asks himself in a rare moment of introspection. "Why, those greedy bastards will buy up all the best talent and win all the games, and fans will no longer come to see the Yankees." So he fills in the Never Bid/Bid box with a big minus payoff for himself and a big plus for the owner who bids.

And if they both bid? Well, in that case no one's any better off in terms of talent than before, yet it has cost them both big money. It's a double loss. *But not as great a loss as when one side never bids and the other does.* Which brings us back to the central paradox of this common business game: there is a good outcome for both owners (in this instance, "Never Bid") in which they will retain their ballplayers without having to pay them more; yet it is in the self-interest of each to break ranks and bid, *regardless of what the other guy does.* If any other owner never bids, Steinbrenner makes far more by bidding than by never bidding. And if the other owner bids, Steinbrenner loses far less by bidding than by not bidding.

This, of course, is precisely why baseball-team owners maintained for more than a century a system in which players were bound to one team for their entire careers—to prevent such costly game playing. It is why in 1981 the owners provoked the longest strike in baseball history—an attempt to destroy free agency. And it is why the president of the Boston Red Sox declared after the 1981 season: "The only way we're going to survive is to subordinate self-interest and accept that we are twenty-six subdivisions of the same business."

It is also why Immobil and Brand X-On have learned to love OPEC (because it prevented game playing by keeping prices artificially high) and why most of the major airlines fought against deregulation (because regulation prevented game playing by putting a floor under fares so that price wars could not occur). Just watch how every time TWA, Eastern, United, or American lowers its coast-to-coast fares, the others quickly follow suit.

If Looking Out for Number One is inevitable in business without some help—OPEC, the government, illegal collusion among companies—the best strategy would seem to be to cooperate as long as possible, thus preventing needless losses, and *then* attack the other guy at the last moment, reaping large rewards. This may not be the most admirable behavior one could mention, but it is how the Harvard Business School students find themselves playing competitive games—in class and on the corporate battlefield.

One spring morning, Elon Kohlberg walked hurriedly into class, just beating the clock to 8:30, as was his habit. Trim, nattily attired, but with his tie not yet knotted, he began the class by distributing a one-page handout with the forbidding title "Interactive Decisions: Exercise #3."

"Select a fellow participant to work with you on the Exercise," the handout read. "Designate one of you as the 'A' player, the other as the 'B' player." It then laid out the following matrix:

B

	B_1	B_2
A_1	($5, $5)	(–$5, $10)
A_2	($10, –$5)	(–$2, –$2)

A

"In this game," the handout concluded, "assume you will play the game only once and that your goal is to do as well as you can for yourself. You are neither altruistic nor vindictive with respect to your competitor."

The class paired off, studied the matrix, jotted down their moves—either A_1, A_2, B_1, or B_2. The result of each pair's game would be determined by examination of the relevant square in the matrix.

"Don and Ali," said Kohlberg, addressing a cheerful young American and his Iranian buddy, who always sat next to each other and had therefore chosen to play this game together, "tell us your moves. Don?"

"I was the A player," said Don, grinning. "I played strategy A_2." Ali's eyebrows rose slightly, but did not alter his usual ironic smile.

"Why?" asked Kohlberg.

"Well, I thought Ali might figure that, we being friends, I would choose strategy A_1, so we could both come out ahead, with five dollars each. That meant he would play strategy B_1. If he played B_1 and I kind of tricked him by playing A_2, I'd get the ten-dollar payoff. And," added Don, "if my dear friend Ali chose to play me for a sucker with strategy B_2, figuring I'd be the nice guy and *he'd* get the ten bucks, well, we'd both lose. But losing two dollars is a lot better than losing five, I figure."

"Ali," said Kohlberg, relishing the moment, "what strategy did you play?"

"B_2, of course," Ali replied. "One of the reasons Don is my friend is that despite his apparently good-natured innocence, a clever brain is clicking there. I did not think he would go for the good deal, where we each would get five dollars. I thought he would play strategy A_2. To defend myself, I had to play B_2." He then smirked at Don.

"But you have both lost," declared Kohlberg. The smiles vanished from the two students' faces as one appeared on the professor's. "You have been logical, but you have lost. That is the most interesting lesson of this game: Rational behavior ends up hurting both players. Did anyone in the class play strategy one?"

A half-dozen students raised their hands.

"Were any of you playing against each other?" Kohlberg inquired. Two were: Ann and Bob, both members of the class's informal liberal caucus. They were rather smug about their choice.

"Why did you play strategy one, Bob?" asked Kohlberg.

"Because Ann and I sit next to each other, sometimes study together, and frankly," Bob admitted, "I'd rather run the risk of losing big in this little game than alienating her with strategy two."

"Ann?"

"I figured Bob was a really nice guy. The only risk was that he might have bent over backward to be nonsexist, but I thought he knew me too well for that."

"So you *trusted* each other," said Kohlberg. "Because the stakes of the game were small and the stakes of your friendship were higher. The real payoffs, for you, weren't in the matrix. What would you have done if the numbers were in thousands of dollars, and the game was for real?"

Neither Ann nor Bob answered. After class, they said they knew they would have done the same, no matter what the stakes. They hadn't said so in class because they thought people wouldn't have believed them.

Another student responded that if the payoffs, no matter how high, were always less than the value of their relationship, then they were the first perfect couple he had ever met, and that they ought to get married before the next class.

Kohlberg said simply that they were the exception that proves the rule.

"When people play this game in the laboratory, and it's a one-shot thing, then everybody chooses strategy two, once they understand what's going on. Of course, you have to make sure that what counts is the payoffs, and there's not some consideration of friendship or something else, because then the numbers won't represent the real payoffs to the players—you would have to add some number for friendship in.

"But what if the experiment repeats, and instead of playing the game once, you play it three times, five times, ten times, or whatever? If you were logical to an extreme, you would choose strategy two even if the game is played twenty times, because you know that on the last round you're going to attack, the other guy knows that too, so there is no goodwill to establish on the nineteenth move, because everybody knows that goodwill will disappear on the twentieth move. So you should do it on the eighteenth move, since you both know that the other guy is going to do it on the nineteenth, and so on, as the logic ripples back to the beginning. Logic, then, dictates that you should do it on the first move.

"*But,* if you choose strategy two too early, you will induce the other player to do the same, and both your payoffs will be rather low. The name of the game is not to beat the opponent, but to do well for yourself, and you would not be doing very well for yourself.

"On the other hand, if you choose strategy two too late, then the other guy will very probably attack before you, so on that one move you will be socked. You have to try to anticipate and attack just one move before the other guy would, and get the big payoff where you attack and he doesn't."

In other words, the question is not *whether* you'll turn on your opponent but *when.* Months, years, even decades of gentlemanly competition in an industry can swiftly deteriorate into savage warfare. From each other's behavior, Business School students learn, in effect, that warfare is inevitable, and the company that has "first-strike capability" and acts before the competition does will often prevail.

The Harvard Business School has other methods of bringing out the competitive instinct in its students. It forces them to compete for the attention of their teachers, since class discussion is a significant part of one's grade (in some courses, as much as one-half). No one wants to wind up like Dave Tucker. He sat at the very back of the classroom. He was short, and his arm didn't go up very high when he raised it. He was shy, so he wasn't very eager to raise it in the first place. He was unaggressive, so when someone else was called on, he dropped his arm—and his effort to talk—for the rest of the class period.

At midterm, Dave had a meeting with one of Section C's nicest professors.

"You don't talk in class," said the professor.

"I try," said Dave.

"That's not good enough," said the professor.

Dave flunked out at the end of the year.

It was not that any member of the section wished Dave ill. When he "hit the screen" (a Business School term for flunking out) he was the subject of heartfelt sympathy. Neither his fellow students nor his professors wanted him to fail. Any group of people spending so much time together are bound to develop strong feelings of friendship and respect.

Yet behind the group consciousness lay an irrefutable truth: ultimately, many of the classmates would become adversaries, competing against each other on behalf of their future companies, or for promotions within the same firm. The Business School's express purpose is to prepare its students for corporate life, and it does so thoroughly.

The pressure to speak in class, for instance, has a threefold purpose: first, to teach through participation; second, to keep noses to the grindstone through the threat of low grades and public humiliation if one is unprepared; and third, to temper the individual by driving home the omnipresence of self-interest. When push came to shove, America's future managers would be on their own—against one another.

Competition between students often surfaces. Individuals are at times sarcastic in response to their fellow students' comments in class. When small groups within the section take on one another, the competition can get nasty, and when, on occasion, subgroups from the various sections play one another, matters can get almost out of hand.

One particularly fierce competitive game was played not in Elon Kohlberg's course but in staid old Finance, taught by the always-congenial Professor John Meyer, who assumed the vice-chairmanship of Union Pacific in early 1982.

The ambiance of Finance was mild, given Meyer's gentle nature; his various dry formulas on the values of stocks and bonds; and his wry view of business. Once, in discussing the sanctity of a company's profit figures, he quoted a famous executive: "Give me the accountant *I* want, and I'll give you the net earnings *you* want." (That is, any given profit statement can be drastically affected, quite legally, by a good accountant.)

Yet it was in Finance that game playing became counterproductively aggressive. The objective was to negotiate the purchase of Company A by Company B. Groups of eight students from different sections met each other at a prearranged time and location. (There isn't much time for intersection fraternization in the first year of Business School, so few members of one team knew members of the other.)

Each pair of groups represented two companies. You were given ample information on your own company, but a good deal less on that of your partner-to-be. The idea was for Company A to bargain for as high a price for itself as possible, while Company B would bargain for as low a price for Company A as possible.

When Company B showed up at the student-union building two minutes late, it was greeted with icy stares from the Company A team.

"Who is your spokesperson?" a stern-faced woman asked. Company B team members mumbled something about how they had more than one, but finally designated Tom Fitzgerald. Another member of the Company A team silently handed Fitzgerald a note. He read it, then passed it around. It declared, in extremely neat lettering, that "IT IS NOT CONSIDERED PROFESSIONAL BEHAVIOR TO ARRIVE LATE FOR AN IMPORTANT NEGOTIATING SESSION."

This was an opening gambit, followed by various others, to get the B group, which represented the acquiring company, to fork over an absurdly high amount for the A company. (They were demanding a price roughly twice what Professor Meyer later said was reasonable.) But they were so carried away with their own negotiating swagger that they missed an opportunity to make a very good deal from their point of view. Their success in intimidating the B team only spurred them to new heights of demand, and ultimately, to no deal.

Elon Kohlberg plays a similar game in Competitive Decision Making—one that has gotten the Harvard Business School into trouble.

One player tries to buy an item from another. The seller is given the real value of the item to himself—say, $75—and a range of numbers—say, $100–$200—representing the real value of the item to the buyer. The buyer is given the item's real value to himself—say, $150—and a range representing the real value to the seller—say, $50–$100.

"Now, we have looked at a lot of historical examples of bargaining," says Kohlberg, "and it turns out that the most important determinant of final sale price is the *opening bid*. So if I start by asking for $100, and you say you're willing to pay $50, it's a pretty good bet that the final price will end up someplace in the middle."

You might say, "Why not just ask a very high price?" The problem with that is that too high a price might destroy your credibility, and that would be irreversible. Either you're not going to be taken seriously or you will have to come down drastically in price, or both.

"In order to model this situation," says Kohlberg, "we devised the *buyer-seller game*. The rule in this game is for me to submit an opening number and for you to submit an opening number. If our two numbers overlap—that is, if the buyer is willing to pay as much or more than the seller asks for—then there's a deal. If the numbers don't overlap, there's no deal. One-shot. That's one way we play, and it demonstrates that the numbers we start with very much determine the final outcome. Exaggerate and you get nothing. Personalities aren't involved; you don't talk. You just submit a number, which is run against the numbers submitted by all students on the opposite side [buyer or seller] from you."

This version of the game makes a point, but stirs no controversy. Not so with version number two.

"*Then* we play a version of the game where it's really people getting together in pairs," says Kohlberg. "They get together in the evening, each having been told separately, in secret, how much this thing is worth to him, and the range of what it's worth to the other guy. Then they have to haggle. If they can't reach an agreement, they both get zero. If they can agree, the payoff is the dollar number of how much profit each one makes—profit being the spread between the price each gets and its real value to him.

"Well, here we try not to play the role of policeman, telling the students what they can do and what they cannot do. Some go as far as taking their secret information—which is given to them in print—blotting it out, typing in a different number, then going ahead and telling the other guy, 'Well, look, my secret information says that the value for me is 120, so I have to sell it for that or more,' even though the value to him is really only 100. This is, of course, against the rules of the game, but they aren't enforced. If you get it by the buyer, you get away with it."

You don't have to be as devious as that, though. You can hint in all sorts of ways that you just can't take less than 120 because, cross your heart, that's as low as you can go.

"Here, a lot of people get hung up on questions of ethics and morality: Is it okay to do this? Or this?" says Kohlberg. "The Harvard professor who created the course, Howard Raiffa, is concerned with such discussions. I personally try to stay away from them. People who are twenty-five or thirty years old and who have lived in this society should know how to handle these issues themselves. I don't think I can tell them what to do one way or another."

Until 1979, the only people who ever got "morally hung up" about such issues were those directly involved with the course. Until, that is, *The Wall Street Journal* printed a front-page story about the game in January 1981.

The story was headlined: "To SOME AT HARVARD TELLING LIES BECOMES A MATTER OF COURSE." The subhead was explicit: "Untruths Can Improve Grade in Business School Class; Peer Pressure and Ethics."

The lead kept the theme going:

> BOSTON. Gerald M. Thomchick got the highest grade in part of the Competitive Decision Making course at Harvard Business School because, "I was willing to lie to get a better score."
>
> That's fine with Professor Howard R. Raiffa, whose course is designed to teach budding businessmen to negotiate in the real world. Like it or not, Professor Raiffa says, lying (or "strategic misrepresentation," as he calls it) is sometimes resorted to in business negotiations.
>
> Each week Professor Raiffa and his students play a game ...

The article goes on to give a fair, lively description of the course.

The dean of the Harvard Business School, Lawrence Fouraker, called the story "an injustice to a really fine institution," threatened to cut off free use of Harvard cases by the textbook subsidiary of the Dow Jones corporation, and said emphatically: "If newspaper boards of directors don't exercise some responsible editorial accountability, either the courts will have to take over or this country will rise up against the press and we'll have an American ayatollah running it."

Then came editorials in the *Christian Science Monitor*, the *Chicago Tribune* and the *Sun-Times, The Washington Post* and *The Detroit News*. The article was reprinted throughout the country. In a mass-circulation newspaper in Zurich, Switzerland, an article titled "Lying Can Be Taught" used the course as an example of decadence in American society and business, and implied that the main purpose of Competitive Decision Making was to teach future managers how to lie effectively.

Back in Cambridge, the Business School was flooded with

mail, two-thirds of it deploring the course. At the *Journal,* only articles on gun control and abortion had generated more letters.

"Unfortunately," Kohlberg says softly, "this article was done at the time Howard Raiffa taught the course, and he is a person concerned with ethics, really a deeply moral person; much more than I am"—he laughs self-deprecatingly—"or for that matter, anyone I know on the faculty. It was ironic that he was the one that was singled out and got all this flak.

"But I think it was very cynical of people who complained about the course. We see lying all around us. People get ahead by doing many unethical things. So what do you do about that? If your ethics are strong enough, you will forgo profits. And that's the way it is in the real world. Why should it be any different in a course that tries to simulate the real world?"

Kohlberg thinks people misunderstood and thought that students were *encouraged* to cheat and lie because they would get good grades if they did, when in fact, most of the games in the course are a matter of strategy and analysis. But he does admit that in a few confrontative games a student who cheats stands a good chance of doing better than a student who doesn't.

"Well, what can you do about this?" he asks. "One way is to take these games out of the course, but I think that's pretty cowardly. Another way is to police everybody, which I find both impractical and ridiculous. These are grown-up people. We're not going to try to sneak behind their backs to see what they're doing.

"One of the things Howard Raiffa says, which I disagree with, is that cheating isn't going to help, because if you cheat, you get a reputation as a person who cheats, and others will gang up on you in games of cooperation. And so the short-term gain in those games where you cheat is not worth it later on.

"I wish this were true, but I don't think so. We don't really have empirical information on who cheats; we can only guess. And I don't think the guesses are very good. But look at the people around you. There are many individuals that I'm sure you know—I certainly do—who became very successful because in the beginning they were, you know, 'not vegetarian,' as we say in Hebrew."

. . .

Kohlberg points to the important cultural differences between America and some other societies—differences that he thinks may partly explain why competition among individuals is central to business here.

"I think the students here are much more pragmatic than in other countries. I think it's a very pragmatic system. Form doesn't play such an important role in America as it does in other places such as Japan, or more traditional European societies.

"You're a much more pragmatic people. You want to get things done—get the damn thing settled. So the dance that precedes it, 'the rules,' need not be structured as beautifully as they are in more traditional societies, where they think the *way* the deal is reached is almost as important as the deal itself."

One game students play in Kohlberg's class is a union–management negotiation. Every day that the two sides fail to reach an agreement, they both lose a certain fixed amount of money because of the strike. So, in effect, they haggle over how to split the pie while the pie is shrinking.

"Though it's not really a question of cheating," says Kohlberg, "you can make statements like 'I will not accept anything less than X dollars and I don't want to talk to you until you agree to that,' and you can then leave the room. Things of that nature. That's not cheating; it's bluffing. You say something but you don't really mean it. If the other guy is going to stick to his guns, well, maybe you will change your mind. But saying that you will or won't do something in the most convincing way is considered by some people to be cheating. A lot of students get hung up in discussions like 'Is it ethical to make a statement when you know you're not going to stick to it? Is it *lying?*'

"I myself think it is a matter of the culture in which you operate. In this culture, everybody knows that when I make such a statement, it just means it's my opening position. There are other cultures where people expect you, if you make such a statement, to be telling the truth. You are honor-bound not to go back on it. I think arguments about whether or not this is ethical are meaningless in the abstract. They have to be analyzed in the context of the culture in which they take place.

"In American culture, I don't think it's cheating. It's the way people do business. They make very aggressive statements and everybody knows they will back off it if they need to because it's a very pragmatic system."

Kohlberg has his own hypothesis as to why businesspeople are so pragmatic in this country.

"Because you are on your own," he says. "It has always struck me that Americans are very lonely, particularly the businesspeople. You have to look out for yourselves and be more pragmatic, because you do not have the support systems of other countries—the family and friends you would know for all of your life."

With the family fragmented, Kohlberg observes, the job, the profession, becomes much more important here than in other countries. He says America is one of the few countries he knows where it's natural to move because your company tells you to (although this is beginning to change, as two-income families find themselves less mobile than households with a single wage earner).

In most other countries, one's birthplace, family, and friends are considered all-important, but for the managers of America it is individual success that is crucial.

Sometimes even Kohlberg is amazed at his students' attitudes. He tells a story about a Harvard case study involving an insurance company and a lawyer for a girl who has been severely disfigured in a car accident. The class follows the negotiating process through to the settlement of $200,000. But every time Kohlberg teaches the case, he tells himself that $200,000 is awfully small compensation for someone's face.

One year he decided to ask the students what they thought. After he had finished the case analysis, he said, "Doesn't anyone here just think we should give this poor girl more? Would someone like to forget about the negotiating process and just give her more money?"

Not one person raised his hand.

"It's a big insurance company. It can certainly afford it."

Still no one responded.

"In this particular case," he finally said in frustration, "can't we just be humane and say to hell with the negotiating process?"

One student raised his hand and was called upon.

"But, Professor Kohlberg," he protested, "that would destroy the insurance industry!"

CHAPTER THREE # The Competitive Edge

The American economy is based on one simple assumption: that we all are as fundamentally self-interested as the students of the Harvard Business School. Indeed, this self-interest is the very foundation of capitalism.

Examples abound. We take our money out of the savings bank, where it was earning 5¼ percent interest, and put it into a money-market fund—a pool of money invested in short-term I.O.U.s of banks, corporations, and the Federal government. This money-market fund pays a variable rate of interest that in recent years has rarely been less than double the savings-bank rate, and it appears relatively free of risk. Such a large number of us have made this investment transfer that in 1981 the "free-market" Reagan Administration in Washington felt compelled to pass a law enticing us to put our savings back into banks—in the form of high-interest, tax-exempt "All Savers Certificates." Those of us in the upper tax brackets who saw it as in our interest to transfer our money back did so.

This example illustrates a rather obvious economic principle: that all else being equal, we will—and are supposed to—seek the highest rate of return possible on our investments. Economists call such behavior "rational maximizing," and, it's nice to report, they give us all credit for knowing, and ultimately doing, whatever is in our own best economic interest.

"It is not from the benevolence of the butcher, the brewer or the baker that we expect our dinner, but from their regard to their own self-interest," wrote Adam Smith in the bible of capitalism, *The Wealth of Nations* (1776).

But this idea of economic self-interest—of working for profit, of competing with others for gain—is not much older than Smith's masterwork. It was alien to ancient and medieval society and still is to some Third World cultures. Before capitalism, the kind of individualism on which economic self-interest is predicated was virtually unknown. Each person had a place in the scheme of things, and there he or she would live and die. In ancient Egypt the pharaohs issued regulations making every profession a hereditary duty; in medieval Europe, feudal lord and serf were bound to the land and bound by their obligations to each other. The Catholic Church taught that "No Christian ought to be a Merchant"; buying cheap and selling dear was considered a sacrilege. Land and labor were rarely sold, and capital, although it certainly existed, was employed, if at all, in fighting wars of conquest, not in building factories.

But when the feudal system began to crumble by the end of the Middle Ages, the changes wrought were so profound that the political economy would seem almost the reverse of what it had once been. Land became a commodity to buy and sell, and serfs and apprentices became workers who sold their skills in the marketplace to whoever could pay the price. The bedrock of feudal obligations was replaced with the shifting needs of the new market system; social custom and the authority of church and state were being challenged by the laws of supply and demand. The self-interest of the individual was superseding the self-interest of the status quo.

Men of business began battling for raw materials and labor and markets, and as in any conflict, the winners moved quickly to consolidate their gains. The once socially isolated, politically vulnerable merchant was now becoming more powerful than many a prince; his "descendant," the captain of industry, would become more powerful than many a king.

True, the new system worked wonders. Led by a new moneyed class, it "created enormous cities," "greatly increased the urban population as compared with the rural," and "thus rescued a considerable part of the population from the idiocy of rural life." It "created more massive and more colossal productive forces than all preceding generations together."

Or so wrote Karl Marx in 1848 in *The Communist Manifesto*.

But ironically, this explosion of economic self-interest which had made possible the creation of the new moneyed class created for it a thorny problem: the larger and freer the marketplace in which people could pursue their self-interest, the harder it was to control that marketplace.

There were simply too many competitors rushing in. The "free market" was becoming downright unruly. The more wide open it was, the more anarchic it seemed to those on top, whether they had been there for a century or had just clawed their way up.

Karl Marx looked ahead, and saw this competitive anarchy as the seed of capitalism's destruction. "One capitalist always kills many," he wrote, describing the ultimate centralization against which the huge mass of working people would inevitably revolt. And although history has thus far shown him wrong, by the nineteenth century there arose a breed of men whose existence Marx had predicted. These men believed deeply that *their* self-interest would prevail, because bigger was better and biggest was best, and they had—or would have—the biggest companies and fortunes to prove it. Given that capitalism was now indisputably paramount both economically and socially, the most successful business strategy seemed to be the simplest: the best way to keep one's business fat and profitable was to make it the only business in sight.

When Adam Smith wrote, in 1776, about the self-interest of the butcher, brewer, and baker, he did not envision butchers like Armour, brewers like Anheuser-Busch, or bakers like ITT's Continental Baking. He meant small, independent businessmen of the eighteenth century, not the leviathans of the nineteenth and twentieth. Those companies' self-interest nearly choked the capitalist system and brought about a new era of government reform, a new age of corporate strategy. To understand today's corporate wars, you need to understand yesterday's.

Consider the Standard Oil empire. Exxon, Mobil, and the other Standard progeny owe their existence not to John D. Rockefeller's vision of industrial progress but to his mastery of the art of conspiracy, which he considered merely a logical extension of sharp business practice.

In 1858, at the age of nineteen, Rockefeller was a founding partner of Clark & Rockefeller, a new produce business which turned a tidy profit of $4,000 in its first year. He was a shy, reserved, humorless young man who had been working hard since he was a small boy. At the tender age of seven he was raising turkeys for profit; at ten, he lent a neighboring farmer $50—at 7 percent interest.

Whatever he was, John D. Rockefeller was not impetuous. In 1860 he visited the wild boomtowns of western Pennsylvania, a year after the first commercially successful oil well had been drilled in Titusville. Witnessing firsthand the fierce anarchy of the oil fields—the fires, explosions, the pioneer bellicosity of the drillers, and worst of all, the wildly fluctuating prices, with dry wells forcing the price up to $20 a barrel one week and gushers sending it down to $3 the next—Rockefeller came home to Cleveland with strict warnings to his friends to avoid investments in the hopelessly volatile oil business. Too risky, he said.

But a few years later, when Samuel Andrews, the owner of a small refinery in Cleveland and an expert on the extraction of kerosene from crude oil, came to Clark & Rockefeller looking for money to expand his operation, Rockefeller reconsidered. Refining, he realized, might just be the way to tap into the great flow of wealth from oil while avoiding the boom-or-bust kind of business he so abhorred. It would not matter to him if one well or another went dry as long as somewhere there was a gusher which needed a refinery. And it would not matter what the price of oil was, for the price of refining could always stay high.

In 1863, Andrews, Clark & Company was established, with

Rockefeller the silent partner. But Rockefeller, taciturn as he was, rarely stayed silent for long. In 1865, after Clark and Andrews began to bicker and he began to see how much money could be made quickly and easily from refining, Rockefeller bought out Andrews and was in the oil business to stay. Soon after, he was heard to shout with glee in his private office, "I'm bound to be rich! *Bound to be rich!*"

But becoming rich was one thing, rivaling Croesus quite another. The young Cleveland refiner had to be more than brilliant to accomplish that; he had to be a relentless, overpowering competitor. And so he was. He swiftly entered into a secret agreement with the railroad companies to destroy his competitors. Rockefeller knew that the railroads also abhorred the "anarchy" of oil and were looking for a way to smooth out the wildly fluctuating supply, which created a wildly fluctuating, unpredictable demand for their oil-carrying trains. The railroads thus agreed to rebate large amounts of money to Rockefeller and several other major refiners in other cities if they would guarantee a steady stream of oil shipments, which in turn would mean a steady, orderly flow of profits for the railroads. (Later, the smaller refiners were even charged extra fees, called drawbacks, which were passed on to the conspiring refiners by the railroads.)

The parties to the agreement all signed a pledge of secrecy:

> I, ———, do solemnly promise upon my honor and faith as a gentleman that I will keep secret all transactions which I may have with the corporation known as the South Improvement Company [their front organization]; that should I fail to complete any bargains with the said company, all the preliminary conversations shall be kept strictly private; and finally that I will not disclose the price for which I dispose of any products or any other facts which may in any way bring to light the internal workings of the company. All this I do freely promise.

With the huge rebates, Rockefeller could operate at a far greater profit than the other Cleveland refiners. He also could afford to undercut them. In 1870 he formed a new company out of the old, called it Standard Oil, and advised his competitors that they had best join him by merging with Standard. If they did not, he threatened, he would crush them. There were no exceptions. He even destroyed his brother's firm, for which his brother never forgave him. Money, John D. felt, was thicker than blood.

By the 1890s the Standard Trust controlled three-quarters of the oil business in the United States, and it was not until 1911 that it was broken up by the Supreme Court into thirty-four separate companies, including such giants as Standard Oil of New York (Mobil), Standard Oil of New Jersey (Exxon), and Standard Oil of California (Chevron). But Rockefeller, by then long since retired, had the last dry chuckle. When the stock of the new Standard companies was traded on Wall Street for the first time, investors stampeded to buy it, increasing John D. Rockefeller's personal holdings by almost $50 million ($500 million in 1982 dollars).

Sometimes a company was *born* a near-monopoly, as was United States Steel, America's first billion-dollar corporation.

This classic tale of not-so-free enterprise begins in the early 1850s when a clever, bold, and extremely ambitious eighteen-year-old telegraph operator named Andrew Carnegie went to work for a Pennsylvania Railroad executive in Pittsburgh for $35 a month. But when he had learned "how to get something for nothing," as he put it, by borrowing other people's money and investing it in other people's companies, and had grown restless with the Pennsylvania Railroad organization, he turned his attention, and small fortune, to the iron industry. He had seen how insatiable the railroads' (and nation's) appetite for iron was—for tracks, rolling stock, bridges, and machinery—and since his appetite for money and power was also prodigious, he and the industry made a fine couple.

Carnegie and his associates' first move was to invest in Kloman & Company, a small iron-axle business with a fine reputation for superior craftsmanship. Their second move was to take it over (earning founder Andrew Kloman's lifelong enmity), then acquire an interest in a foundry, build an iron-bridge company, and as Rockefeller had done, negotiate hefty rebates from the railroads (especially from his friends at the Pennsylvania).

Carnegie was another titan of industry who played the pioneer reluctantly. The Bessemer process for decarbonizing iron into steel, which revolutionized world industry, had become commercially successful in France in 1856, but it wasn't until 1872 that Carnegie, by then one of the country's great iron magnates, caught on to its possibilities. Perhaps it was the $28-per-ton protective duty on foreign steel and the growing demand by the railroads for steel rail that helped open his eyes. But once he made up his mind to enter the industry he moved quickly, building the J. Edgar Thomson Works, his first steel mill (shrewdly naming it after his largest prospective customer, the president of the Pennsylvania Railroad).

It wasn't until twenty-five years later, at the turn of the century, that the Carnegie Company faced its first serious competition: an audacious challenge from the finished-steel manufacturing trusts newly organized by J. P. Morgan and his allies. Holding companies like the American Steel Hoop Company, the National Tube Company, and the American Steel and Wire Company, which completely dominated their respective industries, began to make their finished products out of their *own* steel, not Carnegie's. More ominously, the Morgan-controlled Federal Steel Company had swiftly become the second-largest producer of steel in the country.

So it was to be a battle of giants, with Andrew Carnegie, the Titan of Steel, on one side, and J. P. Morgan, the King of Finance, on the other, with neither man accustomed to losing. A war of monopolists. "I notice," Carnegie coolly informed his chief aide in 1901, "that the American Steel and Hoop Company is taking only 3000 tons per month from [us]. That should be stopped, or we should go into making their products directly."

Carnegie was sixty-five years old at the time and had decided to devote himself to philanthropy, but this new threat to his empire galvanized him. It excited him. "It is a question of the survival of the fittest," he wrote heatedly to one of his partners. "For many years we have seen that the manufacturer must sell finished articles [as well]. One who stops half-way will be crowded out."

So Carnegie readied plans for the construction of an enormous steel-tube works on Lake Erie; and when the Pennsylvania Railroad, by then a Morgan ally, suddenly stopped paying the Carnegie Company the rebates to which it was accustomed, he also readied plans to organize his own railroad. He moved to buy small lines in Maryland, Pennsylvania, and New York, and even joined in a scheme to put together the nation's first truly transcontinental railroad line.

Morgan was appalled. He hated the "waste" of competition, especially between monopolists who should know better. Interlocking directorates and trusts were more to his taste. "Carnegie is going to demoralize railroads just as he demoralized steel," he declared in disgust to his associates. Only one solution seemed possible: if Carnegie could not be defeated, he must be bought out, and the various steel trusts combined into one gigantic new corporation: United States Steel.

After a series of secret meetings between Morgan and a Carnegie Company partner, the subject was broached to Carnegie himself. He pondered it for a day. On the one hand, he had enjoyed this new struggle immensely; but on the other hand, now that he had them where he wanted them, perhaps it was time to retire after all. He decided to sleep on it, and the next morning, after some more thought, summoned his partner and handed him a piece of paper to be delivered personally to J. P. Morgan.

It was Andrew Carnegie's price for his empire:

Capitalization of Carnegie Company: $160,000,000 *bonds to be exchanged at par for bonds in new company*	$160,000,000 [$1.7 billion in 1982 dollars]
$160,000,000 *stock to be exchanged at rate of* $1000/share *of stock in Carnegie Company exchanged for* $1500/share *in new company*	$240,000,000 [$2.6 billion]

Profit of past year and esti-mated profit for coming year	*$80,000,000* [$850 million]
Total price for Carnegie Company and all its holdings	*$480,000,000* [$5.15 billion]

The partner dutifully took the handwritten note down to Wall Street and handed it to Morgan. The financier glanced at it for a moment and without hesitation turned to the Carnegie man and said simply, "I accept this price."

It was all over. Carnegie's personal share of the sale was nearly $300 million ($3.2 billion in 1982 dollars). He had to build a vault in New Jersey just to hold all those U.S. Steel bonds. And Morgan, who eventually made millions on the deal, had the additional satisfaction of saving the industry from the ravages of unbridled competition.

Not every captain of industry, of course, was as ruthless as Rockefeller, Morgan, *et al.*; but a sober look at the history of our largest companies suggests that an unsentimental attitude toward the competition did wonders for combatants in the corporate battlefield of the nineteenth century.

Contemporary capitalism is quite different. As we enter the last two decades of the twentieth century, self-interest is said to have been raised almost to the level of a science, with the majority of citizens implicated in the calculations.

No longer is the corporation a swashbuckling expression of one insatiable industrialist ego. No longer is the corporate vision one of Napoleonic empire. No longer is the objective to crush or swallow one's rival, the cost be damned.

Today, the government is by far the biggest single economic player in our system. With its regulations and taxes, it affects every aspect of business behavior and prohibits most predatory business practices.

Today, corporate bureaucracy has replaced most individualism; competition is accepted, however reluctantly, and cost is *never* damned.

The underlying theme of modern corporate strategy is now

"cost/benefit analysis." The procedure is to evaluate every move by comparing its eventual costs with its eventual revenues. It is a mathematical regimen as far from the impulses of John D. Rockefeller as it is from those of Napoleon.

The modern corporation tries to reckon the costs of any expenditure or investment (adjusting for expected inflation), then subtracts the costs from expected revenues, and tries to choose that course of action which will maximize the difference. In other words, it is supposed to "rationally maximize" its investments by putting its money behind those products and services which yield the highest numbers on the bottom line of the cost/benefit calculation: the profit line.

Say a company is considering a new product which will require an investment of $1 million to develop and produce and is expected to return a profit of $200,000 a year for the foreseeable future. If the company can earn more than that $200,000 annual profit by investing its million dollars in something else (a different venture, modern machinery, a new plant, or even a money-market fund), it supposedly will not develop the new product unless there are additional benefits which will eventually show up on the bottom line.

Every major corporation has its own "rate-of-return hurdle"—the annual percentage an investment is expected to return. A $200,000 profit on a $1-million investment would mean a hurdle rate of 20 percent. If a company feels a new product can jump the hurdle, it will supposedly put money into it. If not, it won't.

In the days of the Rockefellers, Carnegies, and Morgans, of course, the first and foremost item on the business agenda was eliminating the competition. A company did not have to worry much about hurdle rates if it could completely dominate its market and charge whatever it wished.

But when that was no longer possible—when the excesses of the "robber barons" forced the Federal Government in the last quarter of the nineteenth century to begin regulating business — the Age of the Buccaneer ended and the Era of Scientific Management began. Today, business expansionists try to prosper in many markets, constantly entering new ones in their search for that rational, "scientific" ideal, the best possible rate of return.

The four-phase history of the corporate merger, for instance, is a good reflection of the radical change in business strategy over the last one hundred years.

Phase I was "Merging for Monopoly." When Morgan swallowed Carnegie's empire, when Rockefeller throttled the oil industry, the motivation was monopoly. From the latter part of the nineteenth century to the early twentieth, the great trusts were born, as companies bought out competitors in the same industry. The economist's phrase is "horizontal integration"—you buy up everyone beside you. In hawk/dove terms, it was an era of pure hawk.

Phase II could be called "Betty Crocker Grows Up." The archetype of this phase, which occurred in the 1920s, was the creation of General Mills, a consolidation of six independent flour mills which together could more effectively compete against giant Pillsbury. Betty Crocker (a 1921 advertising creation) and Wheaties were among the new company's assets.

There was a second type of merger in Phase II. With monopolistic mergers prohibited by government, there was a move toward "vertical integration," in which a company would acquire the firms above and below it on the production line. A steel company, for example, might buy a coal-mining operation as well as a plant that made specialty products out of steel. The acquiring company would be expanding from its steel-mill base in both directions—below (raw materials) and above (finished goods).

But in both cases—consolidation of smaller companies and vertical integration by larger ones—the result was not monopoly but "oligopoly." In economics, an oligopoly is a market dominated by a few key companies. Business was coming to terms with the new governmental restrictions.

Phase III was "Conglomeration." The years from 1965 to 1969 witnessed the rise of the modern conglomerate—companies that expanded by purchasing firms, often willy-nilly, in unrelated industries, usually by trading their own high-flying, highly valued stock for shares in the acquired company. Textron, a staid textiles firm based in Providence, wound up a purveyor of helicopters, rocket engines, eyeglasses, zippers, pens, golf carts, and silverware. Financial "ledger-demain" was often behind the conglomerate takeovers, but to many the trend seemed to lead to a rational rearrangement of American business.

Phase IV was (and is) "Merging for Growth." The stock-market decline of 1969 and the 1973–1974 recession ended much of conglomerate fever, but by no means stamped it out. As the economy picked up, so did the pace of mergers and acquisitions, with 1981 witnessing the largest corporate takeovers to date. Free-market economics sees such mergers as a rational response to the situation in which corporations find themselves. That is, the companies weigh (1) the need to expand; (2) the anti-trust constraints against buying out their competitors; (3) the considerable cost and expense of creating new products; and (4) the relatively low market price of many companies. At the same time, they are presumed to follow that course of action which most enhances the bottom line for the benefit of the stockholders, who own the company.

Growth by conglomeration is not necessarily a black-and-white issue, with conservatives in favor and liberals against. The noted liberal economist Lester Thurow, for example, approves of the latest trend. "Instead of prohibiting mergers," writes Thurow in his book *The Zero-Sum Society,* "firms should be encouraged to engage in different activities." That way, he says, they can reinvest their earnings—and the money they borrow as well—in products and services that bring a higher rate of return. If they're stuck with one old product—steel, for example—managers tend to pour all corporate funds into a dying industry with a low rate of return. But if a steel company were to buy a hot new computer firm, it could start phasing itself out of the low-yield steel industry and put its profits and borrowing power behind a highly productive, highly remunerative new technology, where the costs are small by comparison with the eventual benefits and the return on investment is considerably higher, even immediately, than that of steel.

Or so the argument goes, with pointed reference to Japan, which has followed this model, largely by government fiat, since the 1920s, with notable success from 1960 on. It is how Japan phased out of the aluminum industry, and how, when it finally loses its cost advantages in steel to countries with cheaper, more productive labor and equivalent technology, Japan will probably phase out of steel as well. Today the Japanese Government, in partnership with the nation's giant conglomerates, is fostering massive investment in computer semiconductors, industrial robots, solar power and other alternative energy sources—any new technology it deems likely to bring the highest rate of return in the future.

The most compelling reason for large companies to expand in several directions is simply to avoid the danger of putting all their eggs in one basket. The prudent corporate planner charts a course of diversification to buffer his firm against the collapse of any one product. *Any* return, after all, is better than an out-and-out loss.

This point can best be illustrated by the extreme case—the one-product company, which is always vulnerable. In looking at its long-range profit prospects, it would have to reckon the odds of an eventual downturn as fairly high. It might even want to forgo higher returns today by spending money to diversify, in order to protect its rate of return tomorrow and thereafter.

Gillette was a one-product company for decades. King C. Gillette, who founded it in 1901, had two obsessions. One was to reform humankind by organizing the world as one giant company in which each citizen owned stock. The other was a bit more realistic: to become rich. As a salesman for the Baltimore Seal Company, which made bottle caps, Gillette saw firsthand the great profit potential of disposable products. After six years of tinkering, he came up with the disposable razor blade, and went into production soon after. The first razor, accompanied by twenty new blades, was advertised in 1903; by the end of that year, Gillette had sold fifty-one razors at $5 each (that's $50 in 1982 dollars). In 1904, the company was granted a patent that legally protected for the next seventeen years "a detachable razor blade of such thinness and flexibility as to require external support to give rigidity to its cutting edge."

With an ad budget of 50 cents per razor set, the company began advertising in mass-circulation periodicals such as *Judge* and *Review of Reviews.* The ads promised from ten to forty shaves per blade. The pitch: "It takes but a moment to insert a new blade. You cannot cut yourself or fail to give yourself a smooth delightful shave. Think of the cleanliness, the comfort, the security from infection of shaving yourself and of the satisfaction of being free from the barbershop habit. Think of the waits you save—and the dollars."

By 1909, almost two million razors had been sold; more importantly, blades were selling by the tens of millions each year. The key ingredients of the runaway success were the idea, the patent, the marketing, the blade-making machinery, and according to Russell Adams, author of the Gillette corporate biography, a very efficient, extensive, and ruthless distribution system which kept the price of the razor set at $5 by threatening retail price cutters with legal action for patent infringement, and other unnamed harassments.

To King Gillette, marketing was as important as price-fixing. In 1912, two years after having sold two-thirds of his stock for $900,000 (while remaining on a $12,000 annual retainer), he wrote in a memo to his fellow board members that "the whole success of this business depends on advertising." Some years later, he wrote, "We must be the aggressor. We must be continually advancing and drive [our competitors] back at the point of the bayonet, and our ammunition must be money for advertising."

(He also wrote proudly that men like himself were "promoters," who, by creating "great noncompetitive corporate bodies," had become "the true socialists of this generation, the actual builders of a cooperative system which is eliminating competition, and in a practical business way, reaching results which socialists have vainly tried to attain through legislation and agitation for centuries.")

Gillette Safety Razor itself had certainly become a noncompetitive corporate body. By 1920 the company's reach was global. Some twenty million men used a Gillette razor and blades.

But in 1921 the Gillette patent ran out, and in the post–Robber

Baron era, that meant competition. For a one-product company, regardless of how far back it could drive its rivals when it had the competitive edge, true competition meant surprises.

In 1926, one of Gillette's competitors, Henry Gaisman, whose AutoStrop Safety Razor was marketed worldwide, asked the Gillette brass if they wanted to buy the patent for his *new, improved* double-edged blade, which was less likely to crack. Whereas the Gillette blade was held in place by three cylindrical shafts over which fitted three equally spaced holes in the blade, the new Gaisman blade would have more elaborately configured holes which would provide a tighter fit and could be slipped not only onto the shafts of his new razor but also onto those of the Gillette razor.

When Gillette turned him down, Gaisman decided to go it alone and began making plans to launch the Probak razor and blade.

Gillette counterattacked with a new razor and blade that fitted on a horizontal bar running across the razor's length. (The old holes would remain for reasons of sentiment and consumer recognition.)

But the new blade would not fit Gaisman's razor.

Meanwhile, either by coincidence or as a result of industrial espionage, Gaisman had, within a week of Gillette's design epiphany, altered his Probak patent to include a horizontal bar. In 1930, the new Probak blade hit the market and took it by storm. A new tempered edge *did* seem to make it a better product, while a headlong rush by Gillette to get out its own tempered blade resulted in poor quality control.

Gaisman's sales continued to increase, eating into Gillette's market share. The giant, after having just retooled at great expense in order to bring out its new model, was selling fewer razors and blades. The company's rate of return on investment began to erode rapidly. Even without the retooling, Gillette was in trouble. Executive salaries were high. Advertising costs were high. Its physical plant and its research and development were advanced and expensive. In other words, Gillette overhead was high, and remained fixed, regardless of volume. Thus when volume dropped, profit per item dropped, too—precipitously.

Finally, in late 1930, Gillette agreed to buy Gaisman's company with Gillette stock, in order to halt the potentially fatal decline. An audit of Gillette's books, however, revealed a company that had been living so high on the hog that it was now, in harder times, nearly destitute. By the time the buy-out was effected, Gaisman had amassed so much Gillette stock in recompense for his company that he had gained control of his erstwhile rival. His product—and a new production technique—supplanted those of the old Gillette Company. The former Gillette management was exiled, and King Gillette himself wound up in hock. He was forced to divest himself of all his remaining holdings in the company.

By 1931, only five years after Gaisman had first approached Gillette, and only ten years after Gillette's patent had expired, the Gillette Safety Razor Company was no longer the same company that King C. Gillette had founded in 1901. In a market it had created and totally controlled, it had been bested by a minor competitor.

The new Gillette Company, however, was never to make the same mistake. Its modern history is a tale of diversification, which began as soon as the Depression and war were over.

In 1948, Gillette acquired the Toni home-permanent company.

In 1954, an internally developed lipstick, Viv, was launched. That same year, the Gillette labs also turned out Foamy Shave Cream.

In 1955, Gillette bought the country's hottest ball-point pen company, Paper Mate, for $15.5 million in cash.

In 1957, the company introduced Hush, a women's cream deodorant; the hair spray Adorn; and a cough syrup called Thorexin.

In recent years, Gillette has bought into everything from pocket lighters to plant-food companies to Welcome Wagon International. It pushed its personal-products division—especially Right Guard deodorant and a wide variety of shampoos—while protecting its shaving flank with the 1967 purchase of Braun, the German electric-razor and small-kitchen-appliance manufacturer.

By 1980, blade and razor sales accounted for less than 35 percent of Gillette's total revenues of $2.3 billion. The company was no longer living—could no longer *risk* living—by the sword alone.

What Gillette did gradually, the entire tobacco industry did feverishly. In the 1950s, when the tobacco companies feared that an emerging link between cigarettes and cancer might eventually cripple the industry, they embarked on one of the most dramatic diversification campaigns in business history.

Their first move was to buy time—quite literally. Lobbying pressure was intensified, at considerable expense, by the American Tobacco Association. The association had so many politicians on its books that even the president of the Boston School Committee was on a $20,000-a-year retainer. It financed medical counterstudies; it sent out public relations flacks to dispute the danger of tobacco whenever and wherever they could. A British film about Marlboro Man–like cowboys who had cancer was squelched with the threat of an expensive lawsuit because it used old Marlboro TV commercials.

The industry's second move was diversification. In 1966, R. J. Reynolds bought control of Chun King Chinese foods, purchased Patio Foods the next year, and followed with the acquisition of the enormous Sea-Land Shipping Company in 1969 and the large Texas oil independent Aminoil in 1970. Reynolds finished the decade by gobbling up Del Monte. The company that brought you Winston and Camels now also brings you My-T-Fine pudding, Hawaiian Punch, Vermont Maid syrup, and Davis baking powder. Clearly, Reynolds diversifies good like a cigarette company should.

R. J. Reynolds' rival, Philip Morris, has branched out into soft drinks (7-Up) and beer (the huge Miller Brewing Company). American Tobacco, which was selling 9 out of every 10 cigarettes in the United States in 1900, is now called American Brands, and sells Jim Beam bourbon, Hydrox cookies, Jergens hand lotion, Swingline staplers, Titleist golf balls, Master locks, and Mott's applesauce and juice. For extra protection, American bought the Franklin Life Insurance Company. The Liggett Group has J&B Scotch, Grand Marnier liqueur, sporting goods, Pepsi bottling plants, and Alpo. By 1982 it was selling the nation's number one Scotch and the number one dog food, but none of its cigarette brands was in the top twenty.

Diversification is arguably the chief modern means of protecting a corporation's rate of return, and it seems an inevitable corporate strategy—a way to make good money chase after better returns, and a way to protect corporate flanks.

But diversification is not the only way modern companies sustain their return rate—and themselves. "Product proliferation" is another—a way to diversify the product line itself. The laundry-detergent industry is a master at this; of the twenty-four major brands, Procter & Gamble alone produces eight, each in at least two and as many as four sizes. The same sort of thing occurs in many "mature" consumer industries—from cereals to automobiles to cigarettes. A dizzying array of products helps protect such companies by reducing the chances that any competitor will develop a truly novel, thus potentially highly successful, thus preeminently dangerous rival product. It erects an entry barrier by monopolizing that most valuable asset of the retailer—space. Product proliferation can also limit the damage of a product failure. When one brand of cereal fails, a half-dozen others can take up the slack.

The Philip Morris Company's 1971 takeover of the Miller Brewing Company is a good example of both diversification and product proliferation.

In 1970, Miller had sales of approximately $200 million. It brewed five million barrels of beer and was the nation's seventh-largest brewer, selling the nation's seventh-most-popular beer. But Philip Morris was a master of marketing. Its stated diversification objective was to buy "quality products," redefine them in the marketplace, and sell the hell out of them. Philip Morris kept Miller's brewing people, but installed its own financial and marketing executives. It was relying on what businesspeople call "synergy"—a felicitous combination of two businesses in which the whole is greater than the sum of its parts.

The company's first step was "repositioning" Miller High Life, the so-called "champagne of bottled beers." Repositioning means changing the public perception of a product, thereby changing the product's position in the market. Philip Morris felt that Miller High Life was positioned as a "country-club product," explains one of Miller's executives. The problem was that the country club is not the natural habitat of the high-volume beer consumer in the United States. This is a country in which 80 percent of the beer is consumed by 30 percent of the drinkers—drinkers who are eighteen to thirty-four years old and are blue-collar workers, college students, or entry-level professionals. Consequently, Philip Morris's strategy for Miller was to reposition the beer to attract that group.

The ad campaign was ready to roll by 1973: "Miller Time"—a way to reward yourself after accomplishing something, anything, whether it was a hard day's work in a fishing trawler or a hard day's night on the rock-'n'-roll bandstand.

The key to the campaign, which remained unchanged for almost a decade, is, according to Miller Vice President Al Easton, "maintaining the quality image—the beer as a reward—while positioning it to anyone: the bridge worker, the guy in the steel mill. We have stuck with that theme religiously."

Part two of the Philip Morris strategy was to develop a product portfolio for Miller—a "family of brands." In other words, product proliferation. The first new product was a brilliant way to increase the company's rate of return. Up until 1974, brewers were increasing their profit margin by selling so-called "premium" beers, which differed from their workaday brethren in name and package only—that is, they cost little, if any, more to produce, yet sold at a premium price. But in 1975, Philip Morris introduced a new approach to improve profit margins: Miller Lite, a beer no more expensive to produce than Miller High Life, yet special (lower in calories because it had a lower alcohol content) and thus more expensive. The company also defined a new segment of the beer market—those people worried about their weight and/or wishing to drink more without "feeling as full." Miller Lite became the most successful new beer ever.

The company then added the classic German beer Löwenbräu to the product portfolio (a premium price for a premium beer) in 1975, reformulated Löwenbräu for the American market in 1978, reformulated Löwenbräu Dark in 1979, and introduced a malt liquor called Magnum in 1980. It is now planning to launch a new "super-premium" called Miller Special Reserve. By 1981, Philip Morris had moved Miller all the way from seventh to second among American beer companies.

Can a company proliferate but not diversify? Levi Strauss and Company is betting that it can. It rode the most durable fashion trend in the history of the clothing industry to its current status as the world's number one clothing manufacturer. But with five hundred million pairs of jeans now in the American wardrobe, and with new competition from the fashion segment of the industry, Levi's has had to proliferate quite a bit to sustain its growth and, most recently, to maintain its rate of return.

There have been Levi's slacks in all colors, boys' wear, a "Gals' " division, Activ-wear, polyester suits, socks, and belts. But it has all been pretty close to home base. The emphasis has been on what the company already can do well. Levi's rejected suggestions for a ceramic planter in the shape of a human behind (with a red Levi's tab affixed) and a denim-upholstered mousetrap. It also rejected the notion of modern diversification.

"I don't think any of us wants a conglomerate-type thing," Chairman Walter Haas, Sr., told Levi's corporate biographer Ed Cray in the late 1970s. "We're not going to try to buy a chewing-gum company or a real estate company. The idea is to build on our strength—starting with the name and what that connotes." (Quality, tradition, and social responsibility were what Levi's name connoted to Haas.)

By the early 1980s, Levi's was beginning to proliferate "up the marketing pyramid" (the same pyramid that Professor Steve Star of the Harvard Business School taught his class).

"We make shirts, hats, socks, belts, skirts, blouses," says Menswear marketing manager Steve Goldstein, "and all of them are in moderate price points." ("Price points" is business jargon for prices.) "But if we want to grow, we're probably going to have to go to upper-moderate price points, and somewhat higher taste levels for our products."

Fortunately for Levi Strauss, it's a manufacturer of clothing, one of society's essential needs, so the company has a way to go before it runs out of room in which to product-proliferate. Less fortunate, perhaps, are the likes of the Polaroid Corporation, another company that views its *raison d'être* as providing something that is of unique value to consumers. Polaroid faces competition from Japan's 35mm and electronic cameras and Kodak's instant ones. In general, the company is entirely too dependent on the instant-photography business. If Polaroid hadn't recently begun extending its reach into every phase of the photography business—industrial, commercial, and scientific—it might well have been courting instant disappearance.

The evidence is overwhelming. A company may diversify or proliferate, but it must, in any case, offer a diversity of distinct products. This realization became a canon of the corporate strategic liturgy with the introduction of the "product portfolio" concept in the 1960s. The concept was formulated by Bruce Henderson's Boston Consulting Group as a result of its work with the Mead Paper Company. It has become one of the most popular examples of corporate strategy ever devised.

The strategy can be summarized as a two-by-two box, representing a company's portfolio of products. Each of the four squares within the box has a pictogram, and each pictogram represents a product or product line.

In the upper left quadrant is the Star, a product whose share of

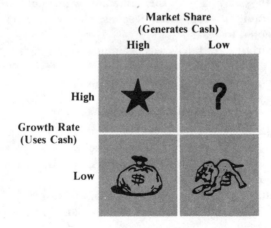

the market is growing rapidly. It needs a great deal of cash for raw materials, for new factories, for new workers. It also brings in a great deal of cash.

Below the Star is the Cash Cow. This is a product which already dominates its market; unlike the Star, it doesn't need much money for expansion, and brings in far more cash than it spends. A Cash Cow, then, is every company's dream.

Next to the Star, in the upper right quadrant, is the Question Mark, a product with an uncertain future. Like the Star, it has considerable cash needs, but its future is uncertain. A company must decide whether to risk money in the hope that the product can become a Star.

The Question Mark could, of course, become not a Star, but a Dog. The Dog, which lives in the lower right quadrant, is a "cash trap" which costs more to keep alive than it returns in revenues. By definition, it's a losing proposition.

According to the product-portfolio strategy, a company would then have to identify the Stars, Cash Cows, Question Marks, and Dogs in its product portfolio, and develop a separate program for each. Put as simply as possible, the idea would be to "feed" the Star (give it as much cash as it needs to grow), "milk" the Cash Cow (take the Cow's cash and spend it on other products that need the money more), kill the Dog (shut it down or sell it off), and try to figure out the "answer" to the Question Mark (will it become a Star if you feed it enough cash or will it become a Dog?). The strategy is based on a historical insight: Most successful products have a life cycle in which they travel through each of the four quadrants. They begin as Question Marks, turn into Stars, mature into Cash Cows, and finally, when they're milked dry, end up in the kennel with the other Dogs.

What is true of products and product lines, according to modern corporate analysis, is also true of entire industries. Just as the product portfolio has profound implications for a company's return on investment, so too does the "market cycle" for an industry's return.

Most markets are thought to have a life cycle. They begin with a period of slow growth, then suddenly take off and grow mightily until they reach a plateau of little or no further growth known as "maturity." It's a pattern that has been followed by everything from automobiles to zippers.

The process is often pictured as a graph, with the horizontal axis representing time passed and the vertical axis representing the size, or dollar volume, of the market.

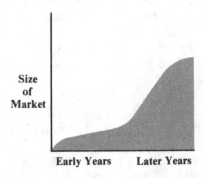

Size
of
Market

Early Years   Later Years

The flat early years are marked by a variety of efforts—often entrepreneurial—to develop products for the still-small market. The rate of return here is usually more pipe dream than cold cash. As John Maynard Keynes pointed out, business pioneers are motivated far more by a drive to achievement and by irrational optimism than by "reasonable calculation." If those who start businesses, he wrote, are left "to depend on nothing but a mathematical expectation, enterprise will fade and die."

But if the market takes off, the alchemy of capitalism transforms optimism into profits, and those who enter just before or at the takeoff point will be enjoying rates of return well in excess of ordinary mathematical expectation. To put it another way, they'll be raking it in.

Bonanzas do not go unnoticed in any economic system. The occasional specialist may be able to corner a lucrative market (witness the oil-well sucker-rod producer who attended Bruce Henderson's anti-trust seminar), but in the world of business as usual, new markets bring new neighbors, and very quickly. As the market approaches its plateau, however, an inevitable "shakeout" occurs, and one company after another quits the market in question—or bites the dust.

The Bowmar Brain was a classic victim of shakeout. It was among the first of the electronic pocket calculators, produced by the Bowmar Instrument Company, which had been supplying precision mechanical counters and electromechanical systems to the U.S. Armed Forces and the aerospace industry.

With the development of the tiny semiconductor chip and the miniature light-emitting-diode display (LED), Edward White, president of Bowmar, spotted the potential for a mass-market consumer product and decided to enter the calculator market with a pocket-sized model featuring LED display numbers. When he couldn't sell the idea to any of the twenty or so companies in the consumer calculator business at the time, he decided to go it alone. Production began in 1971.

In the years 1963 to 1971, Bowmar's stockholders earned a return of approximately 3 percent after taxes. But as soon as the company began to produce the Bowmar Brain, sales—and profits—took off. In 1971, revenues were $13 million; by the end of 1972 they had more than doubled. After-tax earnings zoomed from $333,000 to more than $2 million. The rate of return became a stunning 30 percent after taxes.

But the pressure was on. There was pressure to expand in order to meet the seemingly insatiable demand and prevent competitors from filling the orders first and beating Bowmar to the rush of new business.

There was pressure to produce in greater volume in order to get production costs down. According to the so-called "experience curve," for every doubling of production volume in manufacturing, the cost per unit drops about 20 percent—as workers become more adept, machines become more efficient, and the manufacturing system is continually improved. In the pocket-calculator market, that meant prices would be coming down fast. (It's why prices can come down fast on any new product that achieves sudden popularity—from color TVs to Rubik's cube. The type of calculator Bowmar sold for $240 in September, 1971, went for $110 by June, 1973. Bowmar had to increase its production capacity exponentially or lose out to competitors who were making more calculators, cheaper.)

There was also the pressure to invest in research and development to reduce costs further and increase the capability of the calculator, because the competition was doing the same.

And finally, there was the pressure to find financing for all of the above.

What happened to Bowmar? It couldn't grow fast enough. Nor could it afford to price low enough, quickly enough, to keep pace with the competition, which included Japanese companies and Texas Instruments. The latter was a primary manufacturer of semiconductor chips for Bowmar and hundreds of other companies. It specialized in chips, not consumer products. But when the pocket-calculator market took off, TI found itself in an enviable position. With sufficient resources to manufacture the LED calculators itself and price them *below cost,* it figured it could generate so much volume that the experience of mass production would bring its calculator cost back down below its price. Pursuing this strategy, TI soon had the lion's share of the business.

Bowmar simply did not have the resources to follow suit. It spent all the money it could on manufacturing, but with its competitors now producing in greater volume, it couldn't produce as cheaply as they could. Its sales dropped off. Meanwhile, it had financed its growth with borrowed money, money it had intended to pay back from future growth and profits. But the competition was squeezing profits. Bowmar was overextended, and its creditors demanded payment, forcing the company into Chapter 11 bankruptcy.

(Bowmar eventually worked out a debt-repayment plan with its creditors, and by 1982 it was back on its original track, a modest company making high-tech devices for the military and aerospace industries, and doing quite well at it. But its escape from "Brain death" had been a narrow one.)

Small companies are not necessarily the only victims of a shakeout. North American Rockwell (1980 sales of $7 billion) was also ousted from the hand-calculator market. And RCA, General Electric, and Xerox all lost millions of dollars on the manufacture of computers during the 1960s. Their investments yielded such low—in some cases negative—rates of return that all three giants were desperate to get out of the business, much as they tried to hide the fact. (A popular joke at Xerox at the time had the top management of Xerox and RCA meeting to discuss the acquisition of each other's computer operations. Only after the meeting had begun was it understood that both sides were trying to sell.)

In the economy of the 1980s, however, many U.S. markets are long past the shakeout period. Common economic wisdom has it that they have settled into a state of competition in which mature markets are generally dominated by a few major players. As tastes and the overall fortunes of companies change, the number and rank can vary, particularly now that there is so much competition from abroad (in automobiles, for example), but in general, most mature markets are oligopolies.

Once attained, oligopolies tend to feature stable competition, with few shakeouts, little basic change in the relative size of the competitors, and steadily, if slowly, rising prices. Price wars are quite rare. Though each company makes a large effort to maintain its market share, great leaps forward are unlikely, since all the major producers are already taking advantage of economies of scale—the cost savings that come with producing in great volume. And since the market is saturated, and thus growing slowly, if at all, no further cost advantages can be gained through the experience curve, which depends on dramatically increasing production.

Improved technology *can* reduce costs, of course, and is a battlefront even in mature markets. In 1978, Philip Morris was installing machines that could manufacture eight thousand cigarettes per hour at a time when the industry average was five thousand. Yet Philip Morris isn't likely to lower the cost of cigarettes commensurately in an effort to increase its market share. Cigarette smokers do not seem to be "price-sensitive"—that is, likely to make choices on the basis of price—so any technological advance would more likely be used to improve the company's rate of return than to lower price and court retaliation by the competition.

If price cutting is not the battleground of mature markets,

what is? The modern corporate answer is often: Marketing. The stakes are nothing less than profitability—and survival. If a market is mature (stagnant), one company's market-share gain will be another company's market-share loss, and marketing seems to be the chief means of making such gains.

Because there's so much at stake, marketing in mature markets often becomes a matter of statistics first, intuition second. Many companies feel there is too much money involved to take unnecessary chances. When Gillette introduced its Daisy women's razor in 1974, for example, it attempted to leave nothing to chance. Every aspect of the product, from the weight of the handle to the color of the plastic, was subjected to statistical scrutiny.

It all began with a 1973 market study which projected that American women would spend $75 million on "wet-shaving equipment" in the next year, while they would spend only $63 million on eyebrow pencil and shadow, $59 million on hair-color rinses, $55 million on mascara, and $14 million on rouge. Wet shaving, then, seemed to represent a desirable market. (Gillette's Safety Razor Division also calculated that of the 83.6 million women over thirteen years of age in the United States, 18.7 million did not remove hair from their legs or underarms, leaving 64.9 million women who did. Of the latter, a mere 15.8 million used electric razors and 2.6 million used depilatories.)

Next came a 2,500-woman market survey (by comparison, the Gallup and Harris polls use a sample half that size). In home interviews, with no mention of Gillette, women's shaving habits and preference for various razors and blades were determined. The study discovered, among other things, that of all "past-month hair removers—underarms and/or legs," employed wives were 67 percent more likely to use "depilatories, waxes, etc." than students. You can imagine the enormous amount of data that was gathered and analyzed.

Intensive interviews were then conducted with a smaller sample. The women were asked such questions as "If someone else changes your blades, please explain why you don't do this yourself. Give all reasons."

And there was this question:

Think about your feelings and attitudes toward shaving. Then look at the grooming functions listed below. Consider your feelings toward each of these and compare them to your feelings about shaving. Which one is most similar to your feelings about shaving? Check one of these and then explain why your feelings toward shaving and this other grooming function are similar.

____Applying Make-up   ____Eyebrow plucking
____Bathing   ____Brushing teeth
____Pedicures   ____Hair care
____Manicures

They are similar because:

Next came an intensive survey of handle versus nonhandle razors, ranging in weight from 5 to 64 grams, using several configurations of the twin-blade Trac II format with varying degrees of blade sharpness.

And the result of all this? A 13-gram throwaway called the Daisy, with a nonreplaceable Trac II head on a curved neck at the end of a handle with daisy designs pressed into it.

To succeed with the retailers, a separate Gillette study had determined that the Daisy had better be the fastest mover of all female wet razors out there. That meant an intensive marketing campaign. A product without marketing is not unlike an army without weapons, so Gillette quickly came up with seven different "positioning concepts" and tried them out on sample groups of consumers. The actual marketing of the product would be based on one of the following:

"Blind spots" (curved handle for closeness and safety)

"Daisy loves me" (product name: safer than older razor)

"Twin-bladed shave" (closeness demonstration, as in men's ads, where first blade tugs hair so it's supposedly primed for the second one)

> "Bows to a woman's needs" (new design just for
> women)
> "A girl shouldn't have to" (convenience of dispos-
> ability, no blade changing)
> "Wouldn't hurt a thigh" (smoothness, safety)
> "Under 50 cents" (price)

When the results of the new study were in, "Wouldn't hurt a thigh" had won. Next, a "feminine" package was readied, and four medium-sized cities were chosen as test markets for the women's wet shave market as a whole. In each of the cities a range of prices, displays, cents-off deals for stores, newspaper coupons, and three different TV commercials were tested. In addition, Daisys were given out free at movie theaters and as part of a package of cosmetic products sold at university bookstores. Meanwhile, a two-day meeting of the Daisy test-market sales force was held in Chicago, at which promotional material about the razor was distributed, and the offer of an AM/FM radio was made to all salespeople who met their quotas. And back at the factory, an entirely new production line was being built on the assumption that the product would "go national."

It did, and has been an extremely successful product ever since. But that doesn't mean the interviews, questionnaires, and commercials have ended. They haven't. If companies believe that good marketing puts them ahead, they also believe it helps keep them there, and Gillette is no exception. Every day, it gives blind shave tests to hundreds of factory workers at Gillette world headquarters in Boston. The products are the competition's as well as Gillette's. The record keeping is fastidious. A timer ensures uniformity of conditions; a computer monitors a number of variables, including blade contact with skin. At the same time, dozens of marketing slogans, concepts, packages, and ads are being tested. It is a never-ending process.

Businesses are always changing or refining their market strategies. In 1979, Coca-Cola notified its agency of twenty-four years' standing, McCann-Erickson, that it wanted a new theme for Coke. From all of McCann-Erickson's worldwide offices, the agency's creative directors were summoned to New York to produce a presentation for the Coke representatives from corporate headquarters in Atlanta. Reputations could be made or broken at the presentation, which was to run around the clock until all those present had put forth their ideas. McCann-Erickson itself was on the line, since the Coke account represented a major portion of the agency's yearly business and Coke could, if no one at McCann came up with a good enough theme, take its business elsewhere.

The team, which included McCann executive vice-president Al Scully, saved the day with a presentation that retraced the advertising of Coke since its inception. Scully had isolated a common element throughout: the Coke drinkers were invariably smiling. It was true in 1900, and still true in 1979. No overblown product claims were necessary, Scully maintained. The new Coke theme need do no more than make it clear that Coca-Cola provided a little extra enjoyment in people's lives, that all one had to do was "Have a Coke and a smile."

On such modest insights are fortunes made—and maintained.

It all seems preposterous until you realize that in a large mature market, the difference of just one percentage point's worth of market share can mean millions of dollars. Furthermore, much of that money is likely to be profit, since it is "marginal revenue." The company is already paying for its overhead, so additional sales involve only the new costs associated with extra production. In manufacturing, those costs generally average no more than 50 percent of a product's wholesale price; in industries such as airlines, hotels, network television, and movies, there are almost no new costs associated with extra sales. The plane and hotel cost nearly the same to run full or empty; the TV show or movie costs the same, whether it shows to vast multitudes or one family in Norwalk, Ohio.

Since the products sold in most mature industrial markets have long since undergone their basic physical evolution, any battle for market share must be waged with "intangibles"—image, packaging, distribution—and among the lesser players, with price. Intangibles constitute the domain of modern marketing. They're expensive, but no major player feels it can afford to pass them up. It's another of those business situations in which it might behoove all established players to desist, but they won't—or can't—for fear of what the other players will do.

Thus Coke and Pepsi slug it out, as do the TV networks, Hertz (owned by RCA) and Avis (owned by Norton Simon), Miller and Budweiser, the aspirin vendors, the insurance companies, the airlines, and just about every other company in a mature market with time-tested products. No one denies that the merchandise in these markets often seems interchangeable, if not indistinguishable. That's exactly why marketing has become the major method of differentiation. It makes sense for a company to spend $20 million on advertising, say, if every 1 percent of its market is worth $50 million in sales with a marginal profit of $20 million.

As long as consumers respond to advertising, companies will advertise. Consumers Union regularly discovers on the basis of sizable samples that products ranging from stereos to margarine are virtual commodities, with so little product differentiation that sometimes even brand loyalists can't tell their favorites from the competition. Clearly, it's the "image" of a product and the set of psychological associations the image arouses that count. Consequently, marketing often *becomes* the product.

Advertising people are quick to point out that if extraproduct attributes were not of value to consumers, we would all purchase generic products. Aspirin, *haute couture* dresses, toys, appliances—almost every successful product around—are copied ("knocked off") as soon as they prove capable of making money. Yet a vast segment of the American public—almost all of us—continues to pay extra for the intangibles of products, be they "designer" jeans, "macho" cigarettes, "feminist" cigarettes, "upwardly mobile" beer, or anything else on which significant advertising money is spent.

But how does a company decide *which* product to advertise heavily—or which businesses to take over, or which new products to develop, or which factories to build?

In this "era of rational management," it supposedly decides by the numbers. The profit that a given investment will return to the company is literally—and figuratively—the bottom line.

When a firm uproots itself and emigrates to another state, a political hue and cry goes up. Workers rightly claim that they are being abandoned. Local politicians decry the loss of tax revenue. And city planners worry about more urban decay.

But such concerns do not show up on the balance sheet, nor do they affect the company's rate of return on investment. Lower wages do. Tax breaks from municipalities, states, and countries do. Lower utility costs do. These are the elements of economic decision making by the modern corporation.

When the Advent Corporation left Cambridge, Massachusetts, for Portsmouth, New Hampshire, chairman of the board Peter Sprague was under siege to explain the move. He did so this way:

> The process of decision making that a businessman goes through may sound heartless, but it's fairly logical. We considered plant sites in Puerto Rico, in Mexico, in Texas, North Carolina, Maine, Massachusetts, and New Hampshire. And it was a very simple process. We looked at the state's attitude toward business, the cost of labor, the cost of a square foot of land, the tax situation for our employees and for the company, the cost of Blue Cross, the cost of Workmen's Compensation, and we filled in squares for each area. And then we looked at them and saw how they compared. And then we threw in some other factors that are less quantifiable— the need to be near a city, the importance of keeping our own people together—and we finally made our decision. It was not done by whim, and it was not done casually. The process was very logical.

For the past few years our country has been in the throes of what *Business Week* dubbed "the second war between the states." South Carolina woos businesses with job-training programs, Pennsylvania goes them one better by helping Volkswagen build an automobile plant at a cost of several hundred million dollars, Colorado sweetens the pot for high-tech, and so on. A state that drops out of this game does so at some economic peril. Not only may it be unable to attract companies planning major expansion, which would provide significant numbers of new jobs, but it may also be in danger of losing the major companies it already has.

Of course, what South Carolina can offer cheaply, Ireland can offer even more cheaply, particularly if the major cost component is labor. And Malaysia can underbid Ireland, so that a move there might outweigh the problems created by its greater distance and job-training problems.

The bidding for industry on the basis of cost goes on worldwide, and has gone on since the Industrial Revolution began. If, after taking everything into account, a company can produce more cheaply in Bilbao, Spain, than Chicago, Illinois, and produce the same amount of revenue, why not invest in Bilbao, and earn a better rate of return?

Critics charge that this blinkered focus on the bottom line eliminates some crucial factors from a company's line of sight. The American Asbestos Textile Corporation (AMATEX) of Norristown, Pennsylvania, for example, has a manufacturing plant just outside Juárez, Mexico. In 1977, the Arizona *Star* reported that "asbestos waste clings to the fence that encloses the brick plant and is strewn across the road behind where children walk to school."

The Mexican plant was built in 1973. At about the same time, AMATEX's six-year-old asbestos mill in Pennsylvania was shut down. Mexico not only had cheaper labor, but very little pollution regulation, whereas the United States had the pre-Reagan Environmental Protection Agency controls, which added considerably to the costs of working with asbestos and other dangerous substances. In Mexico, the rate of return was presumably much better.

The environmental costs, however, may have been greater, to both the Mexicans and, just possibly, those north of the border, when the wind was blowing in that direction. But in a world of competition *for* business, it is hard to see who will ultimately impose environmental costs upon private industry. Consider that

New York State welcomed back the Hooker Chemical Company, a firm that was charged with polluting the Love Canal section of Niagara Falls, because, in the words of State Comptroller Edward Regan, the new office building Hooker intended to construct was "absolutely vital" for downtown Niagara Falls, would generate jobs and new taxes, and would "anchor the downtown Niagara Falls redevelopment."

The comptroller approved a $13-million building loan to the company, at less than 12 percent interest. There was no local opposition to the loan, and according to Regan, "labor leaders and others made it clear that they were extremely concerned that if Hooker didn't get this it could cause the erosion of Hooker's employment in this area."

This type of economic influence can be seen in every part of the globe. Yet it's not as if companies mean to cause harm (although some companies will knowingly continue to cause harm if it is in their economic self-interest). It's usually much more impersonal than that. In the search for a better rate of return, other factors often don't find their way into the equation.

The cost/benefit credo of modern management means that companies fill in the numbers whenever they're faced with a decision: how much to pollute (or spend on pollution control); where to build a new factory; whether or not to spend millions (or these days, possibly billions) in acquiring a new business.

We discussed the history of the corporate takeover earlier in this chapter, but even more illustrative of modern managerial techniques is the method of acquisition—how a company evaluates the purchase of another.

The General Cinema Corporation, like every other company, tries to acquire "by the numbers." GC is a conglomerate best known as the largest motion-picture exhibitor in the United States, with nearly a thousand screens. It is also the nation's number one independent soft-drink bottler, the manufacturer of Sunkist orange soda, the owner of a TV station in Miami and radio stations in Chicago, Philadelphia, and Boston. It also invests in the production of feature films.

In 1980, General Cinema was ranked 362nd on the Fortune 1000, up 200 places from 1975. Its dramatic growth has been

based on the acquisition of stable companies already well established in their markets. Only Sunkist has seen substantial expansion since its acquisition.

How, then, does General Cinema actually evaluate a company
for acquisition?

First it asks itself:

1. Is the company really available?
2. Does it fit in the General Cinema "family"?
3. Is its management likely to remain, and does GC
   want it to?
4. Is it "clean"? ("Some companies are clean, some
   are dirty," says a GC executive. "We have a
   hard-and-fast rule that we won't get into anything
   messy." No litigation, no controversy, period.)

Then GC puts together a financial fact sheet, which it calls a
"quick look-see." It lists:

1. The ratio of fixed to current assets (i.e., the ratio
   of machines, buildings, and such to ready sources
   of money—mainly cash and inventory). This suggests how much capital it takes to run the business.
2. The historical growth of revenues. This suggests
   how well the company is likely to perform over
   time.
3. The rate of return, computed several ways.
4. A comparison of three sets of numbers: first, the
   "book value" of the company—how much the
   company is worth in its own accounting terms
   (book value is the total assets of the company
   minus all debts); second, the "market value" of
   the company (how much it would cost to purchase all the company's shares at the current
   stock price); and third, "after-tax cash flows" (literally, the amount of cash generated per year
   after payment of taxes).

The financial fact sheet gives GC a sense of whether the company in question is overvalued or undervalued. If it's undervalued—a bargain—then GC asks itself if it can add something to the running of the new company. "We have to bring something to the party," says one of General Cinema's line executives, referring to the concept of synergy. "Besides our financial resources, that is. Creativity, know-how, management expertise. Historically, companies that have brought nothing to the party have often failed with acquisitions."

If, after that, the company still looks good (historically, no more than 5 percent of the companies GC considers have made this first cut), the really serious quantitative analysis is performed, in which GC will carefully project the new company's earnings out over ten to fifteen years, across a range of operating assumptions. GC calls this "modeling the company fifteen years forward," on the basis of all recorded historical data. Specifically, it looks at exactly how much cash it figures the new company will generate after paying its taxes, and measures that figure against 10-, 15-, and 20-percent rates of return. With high inflation, a potential acquisition had better project forward at a considerably higher rate of return to stay in contention.

(General Cinema projects relatively far into the future because it is interested in stable businesses with proved products in established markets. If it were assessing a high-tech acquisition, it might model over only three or four years, since the market is changing so rapidly.)

When the serious cash-flow calculation is done, GC has a number: the amount of after-tax cash the new company would generate in fifteen years, according to GC's best estimate. It now takes that number and subtracts from it every penny the company currently owes, as if it were buying a debt-free company. Finally, it computes the amount of money it thinks it could get if it sold the acquired company fifteen years from now. From all this it determines how much the company would be worth to it. "It's a pure cash evaluation all the way," says a GC executive. There is little stress put on the value of buildings and equipment, or the value of corporate expansion for the sake of sheer growth.

How can GC have the temerity to project a company's profits

fifteen years into an uncertain future? Its analysts begin with a linear extrapolation: if after-tax cash flow of the company in question was $1 million in 1975, $1.1 million in 1976 (i.e., 10 percent higher), $1.21 million in 1977 (another 10 percent), and so on, GC will begin its projection with the assumption of 10-percent-a-year growth. Since GC's "hurdle rate," however, is 15 percent or greater, this company isn't looking very attractive at 10 percent a year.

But GC then adjusts the projections with the help of outside consultants in an attempt to determine how GC's ownership might affect the operating profits. What will GC bring to the party? And how much will the party wind up being worth?

The obvious way to improve earnings is to cut costs. Can the company's current management be trimmed, with GC people taking over much of the responsibility? Can the sales force or distribution network be cut back? This is the negative side of so-called corporate synergy. On the positive side, GC may feel its experience will enable it to boost, say, a soda company's sales, even if they've been flat for years.

There is another class of companies that do very well, but are not likely to be improved by General Cinema's management. For example, GC took a long look at Binney & Smith, the company that makes Crayola crayons. "It's a fine company, with a monopoly in its market," said the GC executive, "and everyone else looking for acquisitions has analyzed it. But what could *we* do to improve it? Develop new markets? That's not our specialty. Piggyback the name to new products? That's not our specialty either. Oh, we've come up with a few harebrained schemes for new little market niches—but not enough to make the acquisition worthwhile. It was a nonstarter."

GC also looked at Orkin, a company that exterminates termites and other pests in homes and apartments. Again, it was a successful company, but Orkin was not right for GC. There were not enough "entry barriers" to this business; a new competitor could buy a fleet of trucks and take on Orkin without prohibitive expense, GC decided.

On the other hand, Toys 'R' Us, the successful retail toy chain, looked extremely secure. For anyone to compete with it at current financing and real estate cost, and then try to match its name recognition as well, would be extremely expensive. But Toys 'R' Us didn't want to sell, and the majority of its stock was so closely held that what the major stockholder didn't want wouldn't happen.

In these—and all other—acquisition analyses, General Cinema ultimately reduces the variables to numbers. The established market position, the synergy, the potential competition are all supposed to be reflected in the cash-flow projections. If the fifteen-year, after-tax number represents a 15-percent or better rate of return, GC's analysis dictates pursuit of the company.

All in all, then, General Cinema is: (1) a diversified company which (2) grows by acquisition and (3) focuses its acquisition instincts on the Cash Cows of Bruce Henderson's product portfolio, thus (4) winding up in mature markets with mature products because it (5) buys companies that have survived the shakeout, companies which will then (6) produce more revenue if combined with GC.

Each of these factors affects the way General Cinema writes its "equations."

Other companies consider other factors. In 1981, a number of oil and mineral companies were involved in intense corporate takeover struggles. Would-be acquirers began making open offers for the stock of target companies at prices substantially in excess of the going stock-market price. The offers expired in a few weeks, so that the owners of the sought-after stock would have to "tender" (agree to sell) their shares within a fairly short time. The idea, of course, was to induce enough shareholders to tender at the premium price to give the acquirer control of the company it was pursuing. Usually the price of the stock would rise even further when bidding developed between two or more would-be acquiring corporations.

How could so many sophisticated companies place significantly higher values on a company's stock than the great mass of supposedly rational investors in the stock market had? The answer the acquiring corporations give is that they calculated their rate of return on a different basis than the investment community. A company was worth more to them than to the general public, for a variety of reasons.

Let's take the battle for Marathon Oil of Findlay, Ohio, in 1980 the nation's thirty-ninth-largest industrial company and seventeenth-largest oil company. On November 1, 1981, Marathon Oil was selling for $66 a share. Multiply that by the approximately 60 million total shares of Marathon, and you get a company worth about $4 billion on the open market.

But Mobil Oil of New York, number two on the Fortune 500, looked at Marathon differently. According to Mobil, the cost of purchasing refineries, oil leases, and reserves equivalent to Marathon's would have been well in excess of $4 billion. So it made an offer of $85 a share for Marathon's stock, the offer to expire in ten days. Multiply $85 a share by 60 million shares and you get an offer of $5.1 billion for what that morning had been, at market value, a $4-billion company.

On the day of the Mobil announcement, Marathon's stock shot up, but not to just under $85—the logical maximum one would pay if one were planning to resell to Mobil and pick up a little profit, minus commission. Instead, Marathon stock went to $88 a share. Investors, particularly a group of Wall Street stock traders known as "risk arbitrageurs," were buying up the Marathon stock in the expectation that another company would bid even more for it, now that Marathon was being evaluated as a return on investment for a huge company rather than one for institutional or individual investors. A huge corporation like Mobil, once it owned Marathon, might be in a position to try to improve Marathon's earnings. It could conceivably cut costs and exploit potentially valuable resources that Marathon had been unable or unwilling to tap, perhaps because it had inadequate finances or overcautious management or simply because it had assessed differently the value of its resources. Unproved oil fields, for example, can look like a sure thing to one set of geologists and an impossible long shot to another.

These, at any rate, were Mobil's justifications for a higher-than-market bid. But could Marathon be worth even more than $5.1 billion? U.S. Steel thought so. By late 1981 U.S. Steel had amassed $2 billion in cash and a $3-billion line of credit from its banks. Not many banks would have granted that credit for expansion in the steel industry. If, on the other hand, U.S. Steel was going to buy a "safe" company ... So when Marathon's management went looking for an alternative to "predatory" Mobil, there was U.S. Steel with all that acquisition money.

But why would U.S. Steel want Marathon? What made the nation's seventeenth-largest oil company so valuable to the nation's largest steel company, a firm that fifty years earlier was far and away the world's largest corporation?

Management-by-the-numbers suggests that U.S. Steel would compare Marathon's rate of return with its own. Since rate of return is the ratio of profit (after tax) to total assets (all the material wealth of a company), it suggests which firm is making more of a profit per investment dollar.

For 1980, the rates of return were Marathon 7 percent and U.S. Steel just over 4 percent. (The average for all U.S. manufacturing companies was 11 percent.)

In other words, making steel was not the same thing as making money. To call the steel market "mature" would have been charitable; "doddering" was more like it.

Since Marathon's rate of return was better than U.S. Steel's, the steelmaker would arguably want Marathon more than Mobil would. (Mobil's rate of return in 1980 was 10 percent.) Admittedly, Mobil's expertise should give it the edge in squeezing profits out of another oil company, which would suggest that Marathon was worth more "synergistically" to Mobil. On the other hand, Marathon's worth to U.S. Steel as a way to diversify out of the moribund domestic steel industry might be even greater. As long as the final price was low enough to improve the corporate rate of return, U.S. Steel would ostensibly be making a good deal. And if oil prices shot up again in the future, the return would be that much better.

As it turned out, U.S. Steel made an offer of not $90 a share, or even $100, but the equivalent of $105 a share, increasing the total value of Marathon from the $4-billion market value of November 1, past the $5.1-billion value of the Mobil offer, to $6.3 billion. Moreover, Marathon's management, frantic to repel Mobil, which presumably had plenty of oil executives of its own ready to step in and replace Marathon's, agreed to sell its much-prized oil and gas reserves in Texas to U.S. Steel if Mobil outbid the steel company, thereby making Marathon far less attractive to Mobil—or any other company, for that matter. (This deal was later ruled illegal, as was Mobil's continued pursuit of Marathon, the latter on anti-trust grounds.)

So what *is* Marathon worth? Value, it seems, is in the eye of the beholder. Whether a company is acquiring another firm or launching a new product, it must calculate the costs and the benefits of each venture, no matter how nebulous, until it has some idea of what its return on investment might be. It then should compare that return with its present one—its "hurdle rate"—and if the projected rate is the same as—or better than—the present rate, the company should, according to its own logic, proceed.

The emphasis is always on *quantifying*—turning into numbers as many factors as possible. Market share, cost/benefit analysis, return on investment—these are all expressed as numbers in an attempt to render the decision-making process as scientific as possible. Gone is the buccaneer style of the old robber barons; "rational management" has supposedly replaced it. The total warfare that raged on the corporate battlefield of the nineteenth and early twentieth centuries has been supplanted by a much less disruptive strategic warfare. Companies now follow mixed strategies, playing hawk one moment and dove the next. They diversify to protect themselves against frontal assaults; they grow, in part, to protect themselves from acquisition by those seeking to diversify. And, according to the theory of modern business, they do it all by the numbers.

Does that mean, then, that today's corporations are models of rationality? Have we finally arrived at the day when business decisions are made on a purely scientific basis?

No, not quite.

Bob Moore, currently acting dean at Babson College, was once an IBM financial executive who worked on the planning of the computer System 360 before it was built. That system revolutionized the computer industry in the 1960s; it helped make IBM what it is today. Its importance to the company cannot be overstated; it was much faster, cheaper, and more flexible than anything else around. It was the prototype of the so-called third-generation computer.

But back in 1964, IBM was trying to decide if it made sense to create this new family of computers. Part of Moore's job was to pull together all the figures, including how much it would cost to develop the machines, which the company's engineers had not yet even designed. One of the senior engineers in charge of the team responsible for designing the tiny integrated circuits around which the computers would be built worked with Moore in putting together the estimated cost and time schedule for their development.

Months later, when the colossal project was under way, Moore returned to the engineer to seek help in cutting costs, which were growing by leaps and bounds.

"What happens if we reduce your budget by two million dollars?" Moore asked.

"Nothing," said the engineer.

"I mean, what will it cost the project in terms of time or quality of the product?" Moore asked.

"Nothing," answered the engineer.

Moore was perplexed. "Then why shouldn't we do it?"

"If you do," said the engineer, "you'll simply increase the probability of failure beyond its current level."

As it turned out, Moore ended up giving the project an *additional* $1 million. "When it came right down to it," says Moore, "I was betting on people. That's what you're always really doing. Who is giving you the most reliable information, and then, who can do what they say they can do? Ultimately, it's a gut call. You can quantify all you want—and believe me, people do. But you can never replace the need for a judgment call."

"Yes," says the General Cinema executive, when the question is later posed to him. "After all the quantification, I think acquisitions are made on the basis of vision, not numbers."

Judgment calls? Betting on people? Vision? Perhaps rational management is not so rational after all.

CHAPTER FOUR **The Corporate Stumble**

Several years ago, at the Harvard Business School, Professor Robert Glauber posed this dilemma to his Finance class: At a board meeting of the Kennecott Copper Corporation, a director is faced with what he feels is a self-serving, financially unsound move by the company's management, which has decided to make a takeover bid for another firm, Carborundum.

The reason? Kennecott's managers want to spend the mountain of cash generated by the sale of the company's coal subsidiary, a purchase of years past. Why are they in such a hurry? Because the company is a sitting duck for an opportunistic corporate "raider." With Kennecott's stock selling at a low price, the raider could gain control of the company relatively cheaply and then force the distribution of the company's cash to the shareholders (including the raider).

Given Kennecott's rather poor performance, the odds are high that the current management would be fired should Kennecott be taken over. So Kennecott tries to make itself less attractive to the would-be raider by using all its cash to buy Carborundum, at a price *several hundred million dollars* above what most observers think is Carborundum's actual value. Once the purchase goes through, Kennecott will be rid of its surplus cash and burdened with an overvalued acquisition. Seeing this, the raider will, it is hoped, give up.

How, asked Glauber, should a member of the Kennecott board vote on the Carborundum takeover?

"With management," responded the students.

Glauber was appalled. Not one of the eighty students supported the position that a director should insist on a course of action that maximized return—and thus reject the company's seemingly profligate bid for Carborundum.

Not one student suggested that a director resign from the board. Not one so much as suggested a strong protest.

"But I was probably appointed by the chairman, who wants to go ahead with the purchase," said one student half-apologetically when pressed by Glauber.

Explained another student: "I'd never win if I cast a dissenting vote, since the board is made up of the chairman's choices. So why oppose them?"

"I think a 'no' vote will ultimately hurt the shareholders I'm supposed to represent," rationalized a third. "Expressing 'no confidence' in management could hurt the stock price."

"But then why do people sit on boards of directors?" Glauber asked finally.

For the business contacts, agreed the students. And also for the power and ego. (And to help the capitalist system function as it's supposed to, of course.)

Afterward, Glauber was genuinely upset.

"This is the second year I've tried to get my class to deal with the Kennecott issue," he complained. "But they won't do it. They act as if they're already on the board. It's crazy. People blame the business schools for creating Machiavellian managers. But we don't mold their characters. These students are co-opted before they get here."

Glauber's Harvard Business School students—and the managers they become—will always be trying to maximize their own self-interest. When it coincides with the interests of their company, everything will be fine. But when it doesn't, both the individual and the company will have a problem.

In the uncertain world of business, it is human fallibility that often wreaks the most havoc, "rational management" and "quantitative decision making" notwithstanding. Those among us who are vociferously pro-business may think of corporations as profoundly rational organizations, and those of us who are adamantly anti-business may think of corporations as the incarnation of Big Brother, but in truth, the two groups believe the same myth: that big businesses and their executives know exactly what they're doing.

If Professor Glauber's students are the future managers of corporate America—and they are—then many of our top executives are predisposed to the same conflicting goals, fear, and self-interest as, say, anyone who cheats the I.R.S. and then complains about higher taxes—meaning most of us. These are not omniscient and omnipotent people. They are simply human.

Managerial self-interest increases the uncertainty of the corporate battlefield, which in turn fosters more managerial self-interest. It's a vicious circle. If the future of a company is uncertain, it follows that the future of the average manager is uncertain as well. Business downturns or changes in top management, shifting corporate priorities or technological advancements, mergers or acquisitions can all jeopardize a manager's position. Consequently, many executives feel that they must always look out for themselves. Just as the uncertainty of the economy promotes short-term corporate thinking (a company can hardly make reasonable long-term plans if it doesn't have the slightest idea what the future will bring), uncertainty also aggravates the problem of managers thinking short-term when it comes to their professional—and emotional—commitment to their firms. Small wonder that many managers put their personal interests first. It may not be "rational management," but it is understandable.

According to rational-management theory, boards of directors are the agents of *stockholders,* not managers. Their function is to oversee management on behalf of the "true" owners of the company—those who own its stock. The Kennecott case, however, shows how wide the gap between theory and practice can be.

"When it comes to a takeover, there's generally no one on the board who represents the shareholders," says a former finance man who advised on the investments of one of America's wealthiest foundations. "The directors are either in management's pocket or they're bamboozled by the bright young investment bankers from Wall Street who perform a four-hour dog-and-pony show on why the purchase is economically sound and in the company's best interests. The typical board member, meanwhile, has spent no more than half an hour looking over the documents on the plane to New York from his vacation home in Tallahassee."

When the Kennecott board agreed to acquire Carborundum at twice market value, the vote was unanimous. (Six of Kennecott's seventeen directors did not attend the critical board meeting, however.)

The Carborundum purchase generated far less loyalty among the Kennecott stockholders. "Management was widely considered to be supremely inept," wrote *Fortune*; many shareholders were "enraged." The stage was set for a confrontation.

Enter Curtiss-Wright, a conglomerate on the lookout for undervalued companies. C-W believed in buying substantial shares of such companies at depressed prices, replacing the management, and trying to turn around the fortunes of the company—and the value of the stock. If C-W couldn't gain control, it might at least frighten the target company into a merger of convenience with a *third* company, at a higher stock price. C-W could then sell its shares to this third company at a substantial profit.

C-W began buying Kennecott shares on the open market—discreetly, so as not to push up the price—and when it had acquired 9.9 percent of the total, it made known its intention to oust Kennecott's top management. C-W assumed that Kennecott's board members and management had so discredited themselves with the Carborundum deal that C-W could appeal directly to its fellow Kennecott stockholders. It nominated a new slate of directors which, if it won, would owe allegiance not to current Kennecott management, but to C-W. C-W's campaign platform was based on the sale of Carborundum and a distribution of the proceeds to Kennecott stockholders.

During the campaign, C-W Chairman T. Roland Berner launched a personal attack on Kennecott's chairman, Frank Milliken, charging him with incompetence and characterizing him as inadequate. Berner even asserted at a press conference that Milliken knew that he was not up to the job. (The attack was so personal that one of Kennecott's directors felt compelled to write and distribute to the Kennecott board a several-thousand-word memo defending Milliken's character. It even cited Milliken's heroics as an undergraduate athlete at MIT.)

The votes were cast at Kennecott's annual meeting. After several weeks of tallying, Kennecott management announced that it had narrowly defeated the dissident slate, 12.5 million shares to 11 million.

C-W challenged the results, claiming that some shares had been improperly voted because of biases of certain individuals within major shareholding institutions. The votes did not reflect the "true wishes" of those institutions, C-W insisted. A struggle for the "true vote" ensued.

One of the targets of the C-W effort was the foundation for which the former finance man worked. As far as he was concerned, C-W deserved the foundation's votes.

"Kennecott management had completely screwed things up," he says, "so I thought, Why not give the Curtiss-Wright guys a chance?"

With this controversy over the vote, a new meeting—and election—was ordered. Just before the new meeting, however, an op-ed column appeared in *The New York Times*. It was written by T. Vincent Learson, a member of the Kennecott board and former chairman of IBM. Learson argued that C-W's "challenge" to Kennecott represented an ominous trend in American business. Curtiss-Wright, and the various institutional shareholders inclined to side with it, were profiteers, "willing to sacrifice the long-range growth and profitability of Kennecott for immediate cash gains."

Learson concluded with a flourish. "The distinguishing characteristic between barbarism and civilization," he wrote, "is the ability to plan for the future." By implication, the institutional investment community was not acting in the best interests of the nation.

Several days after Learson's piece appeared in the *Times,* copies appeared on the desks of the foundation's board members. The lobbying effort was in full swing.

And it worked. When the new election was held, the dissident slate lost again.

"It just wasn't worth it for me to use any political capital fighting a battle like that," says the former finance man. "Like any big institution, our stockholdings were diversified, so Kennecott didn't represent a major portion of our portfolio. In the end, the financial interest just wasn't as important as the Old Boy network, the corporate status quo."

Kennecott's stock price, already low, plunged even deeper when C-W failed to gain control of the board. C-W began to buy more shares. Chairman Milliken was dumped and a truce was effected. But it soon fell apart.

Then Kennecott went on the offensive. It began buying up shares of Curtiss-Wright, threatening a countertakeover. C-W tried to thwart the effort by repurchasing its own stock. The conflict had become a street fight, with "maximization of profit" taking a back seat to the real issue: managerial power. Finally, in 1981, after almost four years of combat, Curtiss-Wright and Kennecott agreed to sell their respective shares back to each other. Curtiss-Wright had made $18 million—after taxes—on its "investment" in Kennecott stock.

(The story ends with a rather ironic twist. In the summer of 1981, Kennecott was swallowed up—not by Curtiss-Wright, but by Standard Oil of Ohio [itself controlled by British Petroleum]. Sohio paid $62 a share for Kennecott's stock—stock which just previously had been selling for only $25. As a division of Sohio, Kennecott lost money in 1981, and its prospects for the next few years did not seem much better. Hundreds of employees were let go, including almost all of Kennecott's top management.)

In the case of U.S. Steel and Marathon Oil, the steel company's stock also dipped after the acquisition. Whatever the oil company may eventually be worth, investors didn't think it was worth the $105 a share U.S. Steel paid, particularly given the low oil prices of 1982. A detailed analysis of the merger by the Kidder, Peabody investment firm, made before the deal was consummated, summed up the stock market's opinion: "The real winner . . . is the Marathon shareholder. If the merger goes through, U.S. Steel's financial condition will be considerably enfeebled; its ability to spend money for steel modernization will be eroded; and the operating cash flow position of the combined company will be weakened." Marathon, that is, would cost more in interest payments and maintenance than it would throw off in operating profits. "It will be absolutely necessary," Kidder's analysts stated, "for the company to borrow additional funds and/or sell some of its own assets or Marathon's to make up for the cash flow shortfall of the combined company." In other words, U.S. Steel's rate of return after Marathon would go down, not up.

Takeovers of this sort raise an interesting question. If the stockholders of U.S. Steel had wanted to invest in an oil company, wouldn't it have made more sense for them to buy Marathon stock themselves, for the pretakeover price of $65, rather than the $105 a share that the U.S. Steel Management paid with "their" (the stockholders') money? What, after all, did the stockholders get for this dramatically higher bid? A "synergistic" combination of companies that will make Marathon 60 percent more productive, justifying the 60-percent premium in stock price? Perhaps, but it's not likely. How much expertise can a steel company bring to the oil business?

For the management of U.S. Steel, however—or for any management that tries to acquire another company outside its area of expertise—there are other considerations. U.S. Steel had to do *something* with the $2 billion in profits it had amassed. It didn't want to funnel the money back into steel, because the industry was in terrible shape. And it certainly didn't want to give the $2 billion back to the stockholders by increasing dividends or buying back stock, because there's no incentive to do so—no extra power, greater glory, or corporate rewards. Moreover, it wouldn't help the *company,* only the stockholders. The management of

U.S. Steel didn't want to preside over what it feared might be the declining years of the company. No management would. Rather, it wanted to increase its domain. By hedging against the possible collapse of the domestic steel industry, U.S. Steel management tried to increase its chances of long-term survival, regardless of the short-term economic consequences.

The U.S. Steel managers' deepest concern, we assume, was their own professional welfare, as well as the economically dubious goal of corporate immortality for their company.

As for Marathon's top managers, they got to divide up $30 million in stock options exercised at the time of the sale. They also assured their continued employment, since U.S. Steel had no oil executives with whom to replace them. "They had their cake and ate it too," says *Wall Street Journal* mergers-and-acquisitions reporter Tim Metz, who followed the deal closely. "If they had accepted the higher Mobil bid, they still would have gotten the money from the options, but it would have been 'Goodbye, boys.' "

Many major institutional investors also agreed about the inadvisability of the Marathon deal. They sold their U.S. Steel stock, thus driving down the price to the point where U.S. Steel itself became a candidate for takeover. Months after the Marathon deal, the steel company was again pleading with the Federal Government to restrict "unfair" steel imports.

The record of huge corporate acquisitions does not do the acquisitors proud. In the spring of 1982, *Fortune* magazine made a careful study of the ten largest conglomerate deals of a decade earlier and concluded that "investing in unfamiliar businesses is unduly perilous."

Social scientist Herbert Simon won the Nobel Prize in Economics for, among other things, arguing that instead of "maximizing," modern managers "satisfice." That is, they satisfy a minimum performance level—whatever it takes to insure their tenure at the top. What they try to maximize is not the return to stockholders, but the return to themselves.

When they diversify their companies, they are protecting their own careers against the decline of any one line of business. Their companies' stockholders, after all, could diversify all by themselves—and at much lower prices.

It's not difficult to see how such behavior can devolve into economic irrationality. A 1982 survey showed that fully 40 percent of the Fortune 500 considered themselves likely targets for takeover attempts. Add to that every company that is planning or executing one, and you have accounted for a significant portion of management time and money that could otherwise be spent on running a business or making it more productive.

Management is not alone in this. Just imagine that you are the investment banker advising U.S. Steel on the soundness of its bid for Marathon. The true value of a corporation is, as we've seen, an elusive and controversial matter, susceptible to all sorts of value judgments. This is particularly true in the oil business, where the price is quite volatile and no one can say for certain how much it will cost to turn reserves into revenue. Of course, if U.S. Steel's investment banker, Goldman Sachs, suggests the steel company bid high for Marathon, it doesn't necessarily mean the bank did so because of self-interest, even given that investment bankers are paid as a percentage of the total deal. Yes, Goldman Sachs stood to make $10 million in cash if the bid for Marathon prevailed, and only $1 million if it failed; and yes, the investment banker for Mobil was in precisely the same situation; but that certainly doesn't prove that an investment banker's professional evaluation of a company's worth to its client is based largely on greed. It does suggest, however, that if you were an investment banker for an acquiring company, you might just find yourself developing some very persuasive arguments for the financial soundness of a very high bid.

Numbers, after all, are often quite arbitrary. "Garbage in, garbage out" is what they say in the computer industry: that is, numbers are only as good as the assumptions behind them. This means that all quantitative judgments are a function of qualitative choices, no matter how concrete the numbers themselves seem. This also means that the whole notion of "cost/benefit analysis," which underlies "rational" management, may be somewhat suspect.

American semiconductor corporations in Malaysia, for instance, pay factory workers there a tiny fraction of American wages. It all seems very cost-effective. But the numbers change when you compute in the cost of the outbreaks of mass hysteria that have become prevalent in these factories. Assembly-line workers see the apparitions of evil spirits in their microscopes and fall screaming to the floor, setting off a wave of panic in the factory, which in turn leads to a shutdown. Before the plant can be reopened, an exorcism ceremony must be performed by a local *bomoh* (a licensed healer).

Cost/benefit analysis is another way of saying you manage by the numbers. But what if you leave the most important numbers out? In the early 1970s, the Ford Motor Company did a cost/benefit analysis of a redesign of the Pinto automobile's gas tank. The Pinto had become controversial because of a number of fatalities which may have resulted from the explosion of its gas tank in rear-end collisions.

Ford's analysis, contained in an internal memorandum reprinted by *Mother Jones* magazine, assumed 180 burn deaths, 180 serious burn injuries, and 2,100 burned vehicles per 12.5 million Pintos. The conclusion, based on the National Highway Traffic Safety Administration's own figures of $200,000 "cost" per death and $67,000 per injury, was that an $11 improvement in the gas tank would not have been worthwhile in economic terms. Ford calculated $49.5 million in benefits (saving lives and preventing injuries and damage to property) and $137 million in costs (the cost of modifying the tank in 12.5 million cars and trucks).

This famous instance of cost/benefit analysis (and the $200,-000-per-life figure) is not only chilling, but of dubious economic value. Clearly, Ford made an egregious miscalculation. It didn't factor in the cost of lawsuits brought against it by accident victims and the immense negative publicity generated by the controversy.

The legal expenses have run into the tens of millions and are climbing, the Pinto has been discontinued at enormous cost, and Ford's reputation has been tarnished at a perilous time for the company.

. . .

If cost/benefit analysis can mislead a company, so too can the "science" of market research, upon which so much of modern market decision making is based. Gillette's Daisy razor sold well, but it also ushered in the era of the disposable razor, which has meant increased competition and lower profit margins. Most new products do not even survive, despite the vast research and subsequent marketing efforts that go into them. In 1973, for example, two New York entrepreneurs attempted to start a yogurt company wholly on the basis of consumer research. They tested and tested, and finally debuted in New York in 1976 with New Country yogurt, which claimed a 5-percent share of the market after only a year. But by 1979, it had dropped 2 percent and was fading with the changing market. Their research could not predict consumers' changing tastes.

Nor can market research predict how retailers will react to a product. Levi Strauss and Company created a high-quality, low-priced men's suit in 1980 and got a very reassuring response from its extensive consumer testing. But when the company began to sell to the trade, it found itself hamstrung by the traditional Levi's association with casual clothing. Retailers envisioned the suit as a competitor to polyester clothing, not as a less expensive alternative to classier attire. The suit, which was already a good buy, had to be reduced still further in price because the retailers felt they had to display it next to other low-priced clothes. They also had doubts about its chances in the marketplace, so not enough were ordered to give the line a fighting chance. Although consumers liked the suit, the retail trade, with its own perception of self-interest, did not.

There are no guarantees of success. The product-portfolio matrix, with its dogs and cows, may be a helpful way of looking at a company, but it doesn't tell which products to make. And the consultants who peddle business insights such as the matrix have their own self-interest to look after. They market themselves with their insights and business-school pedigrees. But once on the job, they may pay as much attention to the power relationships at a client firm as they do to any "objective advice" they are being paid to give.

Moreover, yesterday's strategy may not work today. Philip Morris succeeded in boosting the sales of Miller beer, but its purchase of 7-Up in 1978 has done little for that renowned soft drink, despite the same infusion of marketing talent and money that made Miller number two. And while Gillette's strategy of diversification was quite logical, the company has bought any number of losers which it has been forced to sell off. In 1981, the company's blade and razor revenue was down to 33 percent of Gillette's total, but it still accounted for fully 71 percent of the company's profits.

All across the corporate battlefield, the latest acquisition wave is touted as an exercise in shrewd business strategy—diversification come of age. But most of the acquisitions of recent years have been of divisions or companies that larger corporations are actively seeking to dump. *Divestiture* has now become a major part of the corporate scene, as firms sell off acquisitions that didn't provide the expected rate of return.

No industry is immune from the uncertainties of the corporate battlefield—not high tech, agribiz, or manufacturing, not even oil.

Probably the most hated and feared of all businesses today are the oil companies. They always seem to come out on top, often reaping dazzling profits. With their huge size, they suggest not a bloated bureaucracy, as that of similarly large institutions might, but a united, purposeful nation-state shrewdly looking out for its interests. They have an image of near omnipotence: the Seven Sisters, a sorority loyal only to itself—a Mafia of sorts, whose only mistake is getting caught. To many people, the oil companies seem to know *exactly* what they are doing, always maximizing their profits with rational (if Machiavellian) planning.

But consider their recent dabbling in another energy source. In the 1960s and '70s, after having amassed unimaginable wealth, the oil companies had begun to look far into the future and had read the obvious: the source of their riches would inevitably dry up. They needed an alternative; and so they chose . . . uranium.

Why uranium? "Because many of them were just trying to keep up with the Joneses," explains Wesley Cohen, economics professor at Carnegie-Mellon University, where for years a group of thinkers, led by Nobel laureate Herbert Simon, has argued that the corporation is not necessarily a paragon of rationality.

Cohen devoted much of his doctoral dissertation in the Yale economics department to corporate investment in the uranium industry. As part of his research he filed a request under the Freedom of Information Act. He wanted corporate-planning documents of the oil companies, documents subpoenaed by the Federal Trade Commission as part of a routine but comprehensive investigation into potential monopolistic practices in the uranium industry. Cohen got a rare glimpse into the planning mentality of the oil majors.

"How would you think the world's most powerful group of companies analyze their growth?" asked Cohen. "Liberals suppose they do so malevolently, spotting new energy sources and buying them up to stifle their development. The economics profession, on the other hand, supposes they rationally plot the future, evaluate their options, calculate the returns, and proceed with the most attractive alternatives. A careful look, however, seems to indicate that both sides are wrong."

For example, Cohen learned that Sohio (Standard Oil of Ohio), in its "Nuclear Energy Review" of July, 1969—a report submitted by its industry-analysis department to top management—prefaced its recommendation that the company enter the nuclear power business by referring not to the world's energy needs, or to the internal imperatives of the company, but to the other oil companies.

In the report's preface, it is explained that the report had its origins in an earlier study of the synthetic-fuels industry. "In that study," relates the Sohio report, "a survey of the activities of [our] major domestic competitors indicated heavy involvement by many in one or more aspects of the nuclear industry." What's good for the competition must be good for Sohio. Hence, a thorough report on Sohio's opportunities in nuclear energy in 1969. Hence, in 1976, Sohio begins construction of its first uranium mill.

An internal document of Standard Oil of California dated

February 11, 1974, concerning the nuclear-fuel industry states SoCal's impetus in no uncertain terms: "The boom in uranium exploration is already here. It has been signalled for the past year." But SoCal's "signals" were amazingly weak. In addition to such ones as "decreased availability of drill rigs and loggers" and "increased concern by the Atomic Energy Commission over the 1980 uranium supply situation," SoCal picks up most of its indicators from the other oil companies.

The document reads:

> Signal two: Increased activity by majors, Exxon in particular. Industry rumors indicate that Exxon Minerals has been proceeding since at least mid-1972 on the basis that uranium prices were going to increase drastically. Conoco, Mobil and Gulf are very active.
>
> Signal three: Increased hiring of geologists and expansion of staff, including Exxon's recruiting goal of 100 summer students for 1974 vs. 80 in 1973 for minerals field jobs.

Think of it. Standard Oil of California bases a major and costly diversification on rumors about what Exxon thinks uranium prices are going to be, and on Exxon's recruiting goal for summer students.

"When you read as much of this material as I have," says Cohen, "it becomes clear that the supposedly all-knowing oil companies have no better idea of the future than the rest of us, and moreover, can base their predictions on data we'd be ashamed of. Can you imagine admitting to your boss, even circuitously, that you were suggesting a major course of action just because your competitors seemed to be pursuing it? The planning documents are full of such reasoning. Despite the fact that the nuclear-fuel industry was by no means dominated by the oil companies. Despite the fact that none of the oil majors had turned a profit in nuclear. Despite the fact that no oil company had enough experience in nuclear or uranium to draw any conclusions at all about the future.

"It's somewhat akin to noticing that the Joneses next door

seem to be putting up a fence, and then putting up your own. Except that these aren't suburban households we're talking about, but huge oil companies."

Several years ago, the Senate Judiciary Committee, headed by liberal Senator Ted Kennedy, began an investigation of the oil companies' penetration into the uranium and coal businesses. The staff began with something approaching a presumption of guilt, ascribing to the petroleum sisterhood a modicum of malfeasance and a great deal of savvy. With the election of a Republican majority in the Senate in 1980, the committee passed from Kennedy's hands, and the investigation was shelved. But the staff had already reached certain informal conclusions. Chief among them, it appears, was the feeling that the oil companies weren't too smart after all. Their corporate planning was a hodgepodge of guesswork, shaky reasoning, and herd instinct.

What happened to the majors' move into uranium? They almost all did it, and most are getting bombed. It turns out that U.S. uranium deposits are very expensive to remove from the ground. Far cheaper foreign deposits are now underselling them.

Even though there was great uncertainty in the uranium industry, the oil companies never saw it. They believed one another's apparent optimism. Theirs was the low-risk strategy of following the competition. In their planning, they trivialized the problems of health and environmental hazards in uranium extraction, and perhaps more significantly, they trivialized the effect of environmental factors on the nuclear-power industry as a whole. Finally, like everyone else, they overestimated the future demand for electricity. Since nuclear generating plants provide the demand for uranium, this was a huge mistake. The mishaps and licensing problems surrounding nuclear power plants have greatly restrained the demand for uranium. The nuclear industry is dormant now, and may soon be moribund.

Perhaps you think the uranium fiasco was an isolated case. Then you definitely will be interested in the story of Exxon and its entry into a young and booming industry.

By the mid-Seventies, Exxon was rolling in money and looking for new lines of business to hedge against the uncertainties of oil. But what could Exxon buy or start that wouldn't be picayune when compared with its main business—oil—which has generated more wealth than that of all but a few dozen countries?

Why, the industry of tomorrow: telecommunications. Exxon began several years ago to buy up high-tech companies and in 1981 merged them into one subsidiary called Exxon Office Systems, Inc. Who could possibly compete against a company with such enormous resources?

Howard Anderson, president of the Yankee Group, is one of the nation's foremost consultants on telecommunications. It's his company's business to watch the Exxons of this world take on the AT&Ts, the IBMs, and the Xeroxes. He makes a great deal of money explaining these companies to one another and to prospective competitors and suppliers.

He laughs at the mention of Exxon Office Systems.

"The idea was good, I'll admit," he says. "The oil companies were too dependent on fossil fuels. So they said to themselves, 'What's going to be the *next* oil industry?' Their answer? 'The information industry.' "

So Exxon looked around and asked itself, "Who, besides the giants, succeeds in this business?" And here the answer was small entrepreneurs. It's how almost all the high-tech firms began.

"Exxon bought a bunch of the hottest entrepreneurial companies and began to force-feed them with money," says Anderson. "If it had to bury a few, it would bury a few, but it assumed the winners would pay for the rest. And in the process, Exxon would get a piece of all the possible new technologies, instead of having to bet on just one.

"The last element of the Exxon strategy was not to wait for product development, for the products of the future. Instead, the motto was 'Buy market share today.' In other words, Exxon tried to build a broad customer base right away by coming in with current products—nothing too fancy, nothing much better than anyone else's.

"It sounds like a good strategy, doesn't it? Unfortunately, developing an entrepreneurial company is an uncertain art. You have to understand the company and the people well. And you can never be sure of the future. The gestation period of a new company is unknown and unknowable."

Finally, says Anderson, "you need a lot of guts to make it in this industry. You can't pull the plant up by the roots all the time just to see if it's growing. J. Paul Getty once told of a meeting he had with the top management of the Seven Sisters. His company was a midget compared with theirs. But while he was personally worth a billion dollars, they were working stiffs earning two hundred thousand a year. They were afraid for their jobs, accountable to everyone. It was amateur night.

"Exxon's foray into the information business was highly vulnerable. Top management was continually being replaced by new teams that didn't understand the necessary commitment. Meanwhile, Exxon would suddenly decide it needed all available funds for wildcatting. Five years of hard work in telecommunications could be destroyed overnight."

The results of Exxon's plunge into the industry were disappointing, to say the least.

Anderson sighs. Partly, it's his natural sense of the dramatic. Partly, it's because he has seen it before.

"You have to invest in product development," he says. "That's the key to the technology business. It's like storming a medieval castle. You start with the flamethrowers—your basic products—and they start a fire inside the walls. But if you don't follow up with foot soldiers—a second round of products which can't be denied—the flamethrowers get it through the heart when the castle counterattacks—and the siege is over. To enter a market like this, you need the precision of a Rommel, the technical backup of a Krupp, the commitment of a Speer, and more luck than the Germans had, thank God.

"Exxon's strategy was beautiful in its conception and bungled in its implementation, because that's usually how the world is."

One need not feel compassion for the mighty, of course, but one should at least acknowledge when they have fallen—flat on their faces.

One of Exxon's biggest mistakes may have cost it $600 million. That's what *Fortune* estimates Exxon had lost by late 1981 on its 1979, $1.2-billion purchase of Reliance Electric.

Exxon had paid an enormous premium for Reliance (almost twice Reliance's market price of $40 a share) because it wanted an electric company that could mass-produce its "alternating-current synthesizer," an energy-saving device it had developed to raise the efficiency of most electric motors. Exxon thought the synthesizer was just about ready to bring to market, and Booz, Allen & Hamilton, the consulting firm, advised the oil company that unless it introduced the device in a big way, imitators would soon overtake it. So Exxon rushed ahead and bought Reliance.

There was one small flaw in the plan. Exxon based all its calculations on a false assumption: that its device could be produced cheaply enough—by Reliance or any other firm—to make economic sense. As events soon proved, it could not. The Exxon synthesizer was neither a technological breakthrough nor cost-effective. It was a total bust.

Exxon would have been happy to let it go at that, but the Reliance story soon took an even worse turn. Reliance, on the eve of its acquisition by Exxon, had made an acquisition of its own. It had bought the Federal Pacific Electric Company from UV Industries for $345 million. What Reliance (and Exxon) didn't know was that Federal Pacific had cheated for years on tests of its circuit breakers by Underwriters Laboratories. (Without UL certification, the circuit breakers would have been unsalable.) Federal Pacific was found out in late 1979, after it had become Reliance's subsidiary. In 1980, the company lost UL certification on all its circuit breakers (which had accounted for $100 million in sales the year before) and faced a $200-million recall.

According to *Fortune*, Reliance would have had to earn $375 million in 1980 to match the rate of return on Exxon's energy operations. In Reliance's best recent year, it earned only $65 million. In 1980, it lost $42 million.

This was one takeover in which the taker was taken.

All businesses, from Exxon to Al's Widgets, share another huge problem: they must try to predict the future. With virtually every product, the lag between an idea's inception and its corporeal reality is long enough so that businesspeople are forced to divine the environment into which their products will be thrust.

But as virtually every oracle from Delphi to Dixon has demonstrated, divination is no piece of cake.

The television industry is a perfect example, as the experience of Maury Carr clearly demonstrates. Maury (whose name has been changed) went to Hollywood at the age of twenty-five and carved out a successful career as a television writer. But he knew, as all Hollywood writers do, that the real money in television is not in writing, but in developing your own series, so in the early 1970s he came up with an idea for a show titled *O'Hara* and wrote the pilot.

O'Hara was a detective who had just quit the overly stressful New York City Police Department and gone to work as the chief of police in a small Vermont town. At first his life had little excitement; the high point of his day was the arrival of yesterday's copy of the *New York Post* by Greyhound bus. But then a dog was found dead on Main Street, and when O'Hara investigated, an apparently simple case of houndicide turned into homicide.

O'Hara was taken under the wing of one of the many independent Hollywood production companies and then discussed with the networks. It made it all the way to step three or four of the review process. Unfortunately, there are about seventeen such steps, depending on who's counting. *O'Hara* was headed for the same fate as the dog on Main Street.

Maury professed no surprise. He explained, in his native Brooklynese, that any series idea is an incredible long shot. He described, as he imagined it, the desk of the then president of NBC, Fred Silverman:

"He must have piles of series ideas lying there in front of him, with every human situation a person could think up: a man, a woman, and two kids living on a houseboat; three midgets running a newsroom; a million monkeys trying to write *Hamlet*. You name it, Silverman's got it in front of him on his desk. In that crowd, *O'Hara* isn't likely to stand out."

It was also the wrong time for another ugly hero. There had been a bunch of funny-looking cops at the time—Columbo, Kojak, McCloud—all "off-center" heroes. Both Charles Durning and Jackie Gleason were contacted about playing O'Hara. But by the time O'Hara made it past the first couple of hurdles, a trend toward glamorous actors was emerging, with *Charlie's Angels* and *Starsky and Hutch.*

O'Hara was part of an earlier trend which, around the networks, was called "a reverse *McCloud*," since McCloud was a small-town cop in New York, and O'Hara was a New York cop in a small town. In general, that theme appealed to them. "A fish out of water always works," they would tell Maury reassuringly. "Like *The Beverly Hillbillies.*"

"*O'Hara* was hot for about a year," explains Maury, "but by the time people were taking it really seriously, the shift had come. Someone had sensed a new trend. Oahu was in, Vermont was out."

But then one day several years later, Maury received a call from the head of the production house. It had just talked to the horror novelist Stephen King, who was receiving an enormous amount of publicity in the wake of the movie *Carrie,* which was based on his book of the same name. King had several other best sellers, some of which were slated for, or already in, movie production. For a sizable percentage, he was willing to lend his name to a television series (any television series) made by the production house.

Now, Stephen King had no track record in television, but both horror and King were hot at the moment. If King was hot, then he was "bankable" (salable to a network). His name alone was worth money, in that it might induce a network to buy a pilot, even though the series would not go on the air for at least a year, probably two, and by that time, for all anyone knew, the public would be clamoring for sex comedies.

At any rate, the head of the production house had an idea he wished to bounce off Maury. Did Maury remember *O'Hara,* lying fallow all this time?

Maury did.

Well, how about using the same characters, the same setting as *O'Hara* with one little difference: when the chief of police's investigation culminates at the climax of each episode, it will turn out that the crime has a supernatural explanation, as horrible and Stephen King–like as possible?

"You want to know how crazy this business can be?" asks

Maury. "I told them to go ahead. I knew that the series had a better shot with Stephen King's name than without it, despite the fact that he had never done anything in television other than switch channels, that he wouldn't be really involved, that the horror-and-supernatural genre hadn't taken hold on television, and the series idea was totally ridiculous. But everyone was playing the future. Stephen King was *going to be* hot on television, so he was hot, and the production houses went after him."

Since the future is unknowable, businesses desperately search the present for clues. What will the public want in two years? Maybe what it is beginning to want today. Who would know best what the public wants? Other companies. So businesses watch one another, looking for trends and then often following them with herdlike instinct.

"The people in the television and film business are full of platitudes," says Maury. "They sound intelligent—a lot of them are Harvard- and Yale-educated, with a sprinkling of M.B.A.s—but the degree of self-delusion is very high. No one will admit it's a crapshoot.

" 'Nobody wants to see a show about a mean mother,' they'll say. Then a show with a rotten mother is a hit and they all put rotten mothers in their shows.

" 'Don't do sports pictures' is an industry rule. But I know a guy from United Artists who, after seeing *Rocky,* decided that the rule no longer applied. 'Let's do sports pictures,' he said. Can you imagine? He actually thought the success of *Rocky* was due to its being a sports picture. He thought he had discovered a new trend.

"In the past ten or so years there have been only two very successful Westerns, and one of them was *Blazing Saddles* [the other, *Butch Cassidy*]. So studio heads decided that people don't want to see Westerns. Television executives wouldn't give the most distinguished writer in the world five minutes to pitch one. After the disaster of *Heaven's Gate,* Sherry Lansing, the president of Fox, said flatly, 'We'll never do another Western.'

"But there's no doubt in my mind that if someone breaks through with a Western hit—say, a Lucas or Spielberg—then everyone who says you can't make it with a Western will be scrambling to produce one."

As Hollywood mogul Sam Goldwyn once said, "Forecasts are dangerous, particularly those about the future."

No matter how wise an executive is, he still must face the vagaries of the real world. The Greek philosopher Heraclitus compared life to a river, and declared, "You can never step in the same river twice." It is true for business as well. The marketplace is in constant flux; the only certainty is change. In the past thirty years, supermarkets have replaced groceries, discount stores have replaced "five-and-dimes," shopping malls have replaced downtowns, fast-food outlets have replaced diners, jet planes have replaced ocean liners and railroads, television has replaced network radio (after network radio replaced vaudeville), Xeroxing has replaced mimeographing, 33s have replaced 78s, stereos have replaced phonographs, calculators have replaced slide rules, ball-point pens have replaced fountain pens, and computers have replaced a good number of people.

In their heyday, the railroads seemed omnipotent; network radio, everlasting. And today we still assume that our largest and most powerful corporations are somehow beyond change, beyond failure.

Yet size is no guarantee at all. In 1917, *Forbes* magazine began covering American business. It introduced an annual tally of the country's one hundred largest industrial corporations (utilities and financial institutions excluded), in which *Forbes* ranked the companies by their assets—the total wealth that the companies controlled.

Sixty-five years later, *Forbes* has proved hardier than most of America's major corporations. The number one company in 1917, for example, was U.S. Steel, almost five times the size of the number two company, Exxon (then called Standard Oil of New Jersey). U.S. Steel was also, by far, the most profitable company in the world. But by 1982, it ranked seventeenth in assets among industrials and, as we've seen, was struggling to find a new line of business.

Industrial number three was Bethlehem Steel, which by 1982 was no longer in the top fifty.

Number four was Armour, the meat packer. By 1982 it was a middling division of the Greyhound Corporation, having been purchased in the 1960s when it was in dire financial straits.

Number five was Swift, another meat packer. It became the foundation of the Esmark conglomerate; in 1980, Esmark sold Swift—it had become a drag on Esmark's profitability.

Number six was International Harvester, which was on the rocks and flirting with bankruptcy by 1982.

Number seven was DuPont, which by 1980 had dropped to twentieth place, but then rose to sixth place by merging with an oil company (Conoco).

Number eight was Midvale Steel & Ordnance, which was acquired by Bethlehem Steel in 1923.

Number nine was U.S. Rubber, now Uniroyal, which by 1982 was not even in the top two hundred in assets.

Number ten was General Electric, still number ten in 1982.

These were the blue-chip stocks of their generation—the long-term investments that Americans have always been exhorted to make. Their performance, however, suggests that an investor might be better off with a shorter time horizon—and a keen understanding of the indeterminacy of modern business.

In the previous chapter, you'll remember, we sketched the growth of a new market as an S-like curve:

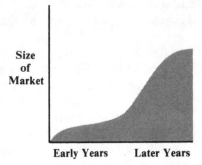

Size
of
Market

Early Years　　Later Years

But a more complete picture of a market over time would look like this:

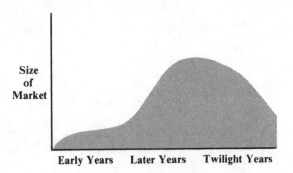

Just about every market, and every product, has a similar life cycle through which it moves. The time spans vary enormously: the Pet Rock crested within a year and died soon after; horse-drawn carriages lasted for many centuries. But in the long run, everything comes to an end. That is the only certainty in the uncertain world of business, and all the numbers in the world can't change it.

CHAPTER FIVE # Better Safe than Insolvent

If life on the corporate battlefield is as uncertain as the frequency of the corporate stumble suggests, it stands to reason that businesses usually will do everything in their power to make it less so. Most companies simply do not like taking chances; they are so intent upon minimizing risk that "risk aversion" has actually become the modern era's managerial imperative. The motto of modern management is "maximize profits," but the *modus operandi* is "minimize risk."

The more a company has, after all, the more it has to lose. Although it may have started by taking risks, success almost invariably breeds caution: "Don't tamper with success." "Don't break up a winning team." "Don't ruin a good thing."

Most companies become increasingly conservative as they grow. They begin to hire managers who are disinclined to take risks, who in turn hire subordinates at least as cautious as they are themselves.

How do cautious executives manage? They amass armloads of market research before proceeding with a new product because, even if they suspect the research is useless, it may help cover their flank if something goes wrong.

They prefer to reposition an old, reliable product as "new and improved" rather than develop a product that actually *is* new and improved because it's less risky than spending millions on something that is untested in the marketplace.

They produce *Superman II* and *Rocky III* because they seem to be safer bets.

They diversify and proliferate, willing to sacrifice the promise of enormous profits from innovation for the reality of a relatively low-risk, if unexciting, return.

They unceasingly weigh costs against benefits as if the precision of mathematics could somehow impose order on an ever-changing world.

Such managerial caution is understandable, of course; possibly inevitable; and certainly endemic. Yet it is also completely antithetical to our national self-image. Here, any deep aversion to risk is unacceptable behavior. We are in love with the idea of risk. Our heroes are the risk takers, the dice rollers, the winners-take-all. Not for us the prudent, the nervous, or the fretful. Even businesspeople want to believe in the gutsy risk taker as the standard-bearer of the American economy. But in truth, the risk taker is the exception, not the rule.

Consider the supposed paradigm of derring-do: the venture capitalist. Venture capitalists are the people who finance new companies for a living. In return for their cash investments in these companies, they get sizable blocks of stock—the more cash, the more stock. If the companies take off, the venture capitalists can sell some or all of the stock and make a bundle; but if the companies crash on the runway, it's a total loss.

Even the term itself—*venture* capital—conjures up danger and excitement: those daredevil financiers still willing to risk everything on a long shot, staking their careers on fresh, innovative people—rejuvenating the economy, making the system work with their independence and courage! People John Wayne would have been proud of; people Milton Friedman points to triumphantly.

But alas, venture firms operate just as other businesses do. They want to make money, not lose it. They want the odds firmly on their side. Since they're in the business of backing innovation and entrepreneurship, they face even more uncertainty than most firms. And that makes venture capitalists very careful. They have to be. It's venture capital, remember: not *ad*venture.

Just ask Charlie Waite, a Boston-based, three-piece-suited venture capitalist at the top of his profession. He's come out ahead by being cautious, not reckless.

A very energetic man in his early fifties, Charlie was once a close associate of General Georges Doriot, venture capital's Grand Old Man and the president of American Research and Development Corporation (ARD), its Grand Old Firm. For the past twenty years, Charlie has been a partner of Greylock, one of the country's most prestigious venture firms, whose original investors were some of the biggest names in American business.

In the spring of 1980, when Charlie was introduced to an M.B.A. finance class at the Harvard Business School (where Charlie once taught, and to which he returns frequently to give one of the school's rare M.B.A. lectures), the professor intoned, "Today I introduce you to Charlie Waite, who knows much more about venture capital than any of us are ever likely to know."

For the Business School this is strong praise indeed.

With the undivided attention of the eighty students in the room that balmy morning, Charlie quickly launched into his by-now-famous address, pacing back and forth, his ruddy face taking on more color as he leaped from thought to thought. It was as if he felt some compulsion to impart the sum total of his experience in the eighty minutes of class time—to save the students from making some terrible mistakes—and his intensity swept them along.

"We do four things at the firm," he began. "First we locate investment opportunities—companies in which to invest—and that takes about five percent of our time. Then we evaluate deals—how likely are they to succeed? That's another twenty-five percent. Third, we work with the companies we've invested in, which means working on the board of directors, listening, advising, becoming a friend, and that takes the rest—and by far the most—of our time.

"And finally," he said with a smile, "when we've done as much as we can, we distribute the shares we own in the company to our investors or sell our position. At a substantial profit, hopefully."

As the class laughed appreciatively, Charlie skipped a beat and then plunged into his central theme—how to make that "substantial" profit: by playing the odds as conservatively as possible.

"We evaluate all our deals," he explained, "on the basis of the people involved, the products, the competitive structure of the industry, and the future of the market. But the people are the most important element. Unfortunately, they are also the toughest to judge. I remember what Doriot said to me once: 'Charlie,' he said, 'I'm sixty years old and I've been sizing up entrepreneurs for twenty-five years. When I started, my record was fifty–fifty. And today my record is still fifty–fifty.'

"So with people, you've really got to check up on them; keep calling people you know, people they know, until you find the one perfect source—the person who can give you the real lowdown, with no frills, no strings attached. If you've still got confidence after that, if the risk seems minimal, then you can make the deal. *Probably.*"

Charlie paused, milking the audience like a pro.

"But you can never know for certain that it will work out, can you? That's why you often start with *gut feelings.*"

Now, that's a phrase you don't hear much in the vocabulary of modern management. When a few glances were exchanged at the back of the room, Charlie pounced.

"Yes, gut feelings. Now, this may sound strange, but I have a very positive bias towards Chinese. It's not that Chinese are necessarily better businesspeople, or smarter, or more reliable. It's just that we've invested in four Chinese entrepreneurs and we've made a slew of money with them. So if a Chinese guy comes in the door tomorrow, he's going to get a warm reception."

What about evaluating the product and the market? the class wanted to know. Charlie explained that there too he was always looking to minimize risk. He wanted new (but tested) products that had a long lead on the rest of the market. The less competition the better.

"I love the United States and its system of competition; it's great—for other people," he declared. "I, however, want to compete with the smaller, weaker guys. So if you want my venture capital, give me a situation with soft competition because the product is so far ahead of the field; a company that can become substantial, reaching twenty to thirty million in sales; and, most importantly, the best person in the world to run that company."

"So what do I do if I have an idea?" a particularly vexed student asked. "Do I have a chance if I haven't got the money myself? Suppose I came to you with the Pet Rock idea. You'd turn me down, right?"

"Of course," said Charlie. "You don't make money backing chancy things like that. If you were the guy who already did the Pet Rock, then maybe I'd listen to you."

As Charlie explained, venture capitalists consider only 10 percent or less of the business prospects presented to them, and will invest in only 1 to 3 percent, of which electronics, computers, telecommunications, medical technology, and anything to do with oil dominate. They're most interested in fields with dramatic technical change, with a constant demand for new products, with rapidly growing markets. Companies that can become big. If a vice-president of Honeywell with a great track record wants to go into business for himself with a new minicomputer, he'll get the money for it, but if someone comes into Charlie's office with a new toothpaste or a cheaper light bulb, he'll be told to come back after he's sold a million of them.

The venture-capital industry as it exists today began after World War II, when capital-hungry companies sprouted up to exploit the new technology developed for the military during the war. And high tech is still what the venture capitalists know best. They feel *safe* with it. Forget the better mousetrap, Charlie was telling the students; come up with the better semiconductor.

It is a lesson the most ambitious of them will remember: Better safe than insolvent.

A week after the Harvard lecture, Charlie sat in his conference room working the multibuttoned console phone that put him a fingertip away from the thirty or so companies in which his firm had a stake. Over his shoulder was a giant picture window with a view of metropolitan Boston as far away as Route 128, a beltway near which much of America's high-tech industry has been built: Digital Equipment, Data General, Wang, Prime Computer, Teredyne—multimillion-dollar success after multimillion-dollar success. And Charlie's firms have had a hand in more than a few of them.

His office is subdued, a bit old-fashioned, an unobtrusive play of natural wood and quiet carpeting. It has the feeling of old Boston money that has kept pace with the times.

This morning Charlie was anything but quiet and subdued, however. He was trying to juggle a trip to the Coast, a visit to his undergraduate daughter's lacrosse game in the Midwest, and a crucial partners' meeting in Boston. After several futile attempts, he gave up and resumed the discussion he had begun at Harvard.

"You have to understand how many traps there are to fall into, how many danger signals I look for when I start to consider a deal," he said, pointing to a pile of papers before him. "I frequently have people who come in here with three partners—a marketing, a technical, and a financial guy—and they sit around the table and none of them ever gets to talk except the president. If you ask the vice-president of marketing about something and he starts to open his mouth but the president answers the question, I get very nervous. Even if the president answers the question brilliantly, I'm not happy, because he'll try to run the whole show himself, and won't be able to attract and keep outstanding people. It's a definite danger signal.

"I look for other things. Did he go to a great college, for instance? I'd rather see someone who got his engineering degree from Cornell than from Northsouth Louisiana State. It's not that I have anything against Northsouth Louisiana State: it's just that I *know* that Cornell has a great engineering school, so the odds are better.

"How did the guy do at Cornell? Was he at the bottom of his class or at the top? Was he a great football player? Has he done well at his first few jobs? I figure that the people who start off doing well in life tend to continue to do well. Not always—sometimes they get in trouble or get lazy or whatever; there's always some risk, unfortunately—but usually. And that's important.

"I look at the home life. Has he been divorced three times? Not that that's good or bad, but an unstable home life has got to take up a lot of his time, and that's bad for business. I'm not saying that because a guy has an engineering degree from North-south Louisiana State and has been divorced a couple of times he's not going to make it; but I am saying that I might decide he's too iffy to back."

Again, Charlie goes with gut feelings. He goes with what has worked for him in the past—and avoids what hasn't.

Charlie illustrated the point with The Great Musical Instrument Fiasco—his very first venture-capital deal at ARD, more than twenty-five years ago, and his first cautionary tale:

"I'll never forget when this sales vice-president of a leading musical-instrument company came into the office with options to buy five small instrument firms. He wasn't happy where he was and wanted to be the top man of his own company. He also was a hell of a salesman, and he sold us on the idea. So we got a group together of three other venture investors and we put in one million dollars."

The five companies were "narrow-line": one made woodwinds, another stringed instruments, and so on. The idea was to put them all together and hire a more competent sales force to sell a broader line of instruments. Not that it was a new concept. Another very successful company like it had just gone public— Chicago Musical Instruments—and its stock price had soared; everybody was talking about it; so when its twin brother came along, ARD grabbed it. And it was a *disaster*.

"The guy who ran the business didn't understand his own profit-and-loss statement," said Charlie. "He didn't understand that if you did one dollar of sales and spent a dollar and eight cents to do it, you were losing money. And the damn business was in Elkhart, Indiana, which was impossible to get to. The only good thing I remember about it was a nice hotel there which made great milkshakes, but even I don't like milkshakes that much," Charlie said, putting his hand to his ample stomach.

"And then there was the major midwestern bank, which financed the company, and made things even worse. You see, it was a very seasonal business, a student-oriented business, so we were selling instruments to stores in the spring and early summer, and the stores wouldn't sell them to the students until the fall, at the start of classes.

"If you're going to succeed as a musical-instrument company, do you know where your product has to go? Into the attics of America. Because that's where lots of instruments go that are bought by parents for 'musical' children who take five fall lessons and never play another minute. If the musical-instrument industry had to rely on sales to real musicians, it could never survive. It's a crazy business.

"So from October 15 on, you made instruments every day, and piled the damn things up in inventory until it was spring and you could ship them to the stores. But you didn't collect your money until the fall. We invested in December and the bank bankrolled all the inventory and all the receivables for nine months and you didn't have the slightest idea where you stood in this business for almost a year. But the bank kept telling us it was all right: we didn't know the business, but they did, they said; we didn't understand the cycle, but they did, so we shouldn't worry.

"When we finally realized what was going on—how much the guy was spending—we were horrified, and really began to put pressure on him to slow down or to find a buyer for all our stock. Incredibly, he was such a good salesman that he found new investors, and we were able to sell without a loss. He convinced them that we didn't know what we were doing, and of course, they could talk to us if they wanted to, but his advice was not to bother, they wouldn't learn anything from us. So they didn't bother, and the guy convinced the bank to invest more money as well. Within two years the company went under and everyone, including the bank, lost a bundle. And even though we got out in one piece, I felt burned. It was my first deal and almost my last. A sixteen-month nightmare."

Years later, he said, someone called him with a proposal to buy another instrument company. It made piccolos and flutes. Charlie groaned and told the caller to forget it. But the man was insistent. The president, who ran the company, had just had a heart attack and wanted to sell out. The company made an exquisite product; more to the point, it made a huge 33-percent profit before taxes. It wasn't a large firm—doing business of $6 million or $7 million a year—but its manufacturing process was so good that no one could compete with it without spending a fortune.

Charlie didn't want to look at it, but he felt he had to. His firm then spent six months doing the numbers, but the deal fell through anyway and the company was snapped up by someone else. It subsequently made a very tidy profit. Charlie, however, does not let this bother him one bit. He still remembers those long, dreary days in Elkhart, Indiana. If another musical instrument deal comes across his desk, he might just throw up his hands and go have a $1 milkshake down the street—in civilized downtown Boston. That way, at least he would know exactly what he was getting for his money.

There are many other, almost legendary, war stories that gray-haired venture capitalists pass down to their fresh-faced juniors to foster a much-needed sense of caution.

One concerns an early deal which was made with the participation of several other major venture firms. The deal involved the start-up of a tuna business shortly after World War II. Someone had decided that since tuna like warm water, and the water was warm around a particular island in the South Pacific, the island would be a perfect place to catch, dress, and can tuna. A highly respected army officer-turned-businessman who had served in the area was to lead the project; a famous consulting firm did a lengthy study of tuna habits and the South Pacific; and the venture capitalists were all very enthusiastic. The only problem was that no one had bothered to find out if the tuna liked the waters around *this particular* island. As it turned out, they did not. The investors were finally put out of their misery when a typhoon blew down the wharf and the cannery.

A later misguided venture involved a shrimp company off the Texas coast. It sent out its fleet, caught the shrimp, packed them in boxes, and shipped them off. There was one small difficulty, however. For reasons never fully understood, only half the catch would make it to shore. One rumored explanation was that the fleet's captains, just before reaching port, would anchor and take off half their cargo to sell on the sly, dividing the ill-gotten gains later amongst themselves. As Charlie put it, "It's always hard to turn a profit with fifty cents off the top of every dollar."

Of course, admits Charlie, this business-by-gut-feelings-and-caution doesn't always work well. Just consider The Midway Airlines Saga.

Midway provides low-cost air service to a number of Mid-western cities within one hour's flying time of Chicago's Midway Airport. When the proposal came to one of Charlie's partners, his first response was negative. Airplanes, helicopters—anything that flies—are not beloved by venture capitalists. With its enormous fuel costs and operating expenses, and government deregulation, the aviation industry seems too uncertain to them.

"Airlines historically have been a no-no in our business," says Charlie. "We've looked at light-aircraft companies and companies that provided helicopter service—we've looked at them all, and we've concluded it's just too tough to make money that way. United Airlines makes a hundred million dollars one year and loses it the next. It's even worse with the small companies. Most of them are started by guys who just want to fly. If they can't get a job with one of the big airlines, they say to themselves, 'What this state needs is daily air service between Hyannis and Lowell. There are thirty-one thousand people in Hyannis and eighty-six thousand in Lowell, and *some* of them must want to fly back and forth.' But the guy won't run it like a business. He won't understand what you have to do to make a profit. And the flights won't be on schedule and there will be a bad thunderstorm and someone will fly the plane into a building and you can forget the company.

"It's just a bad business."

Midway, however, was being set up by one of the people who had helped turn around Hughes Airwest (an impressive feat). So Charlie's partner decided to check it out.

After considerable work, the firm decided the venture was

problematic for a wide variety of reasons. It required too much money to get off the ground; it had so many investors that Charlie's firm wouldn't be able to work closely with management; and it seemed particularly vulnerable to future competition because of deregulation.

Finally, Charlie's partner called a friend in Chicago who knew the venture. The friend said it didn't have a chance. "Midway's the wrong place for that service," he said emphatically. "First, because of the lack of connecting flights, and second, because it's no more convenient than O'Hare."

Charlie's partner turned down the deal and promptly forgot about it.

Six months later, Charlie had lunch with one of *his* friends, who asked if Greylock had looked at Midway Airlines. Charlie said no, and asked what the deal was. His friend told him and, a few weeks later, sent him some material in the mail. It looked promising, and Charlie brought it up at the next staff meeting.

"Are you kidding?" the partner said. "We shouldn't spend time on this. I turned it down months ago." Charlie shrugged, and that was that.

Several months passed, and Midway Airlines finally got off the ground with millions of dollars of pure venture-capital financing. And it stayed off the ground, carving out a modest niche at the expense of the industry giants, almost all of which were reeling from the price wars of the late 1970s and early 1980s and the competition from smaller rivals such as Midway.

But did Midway Airlines change Charlie's basic philosophy? Did it induce him to loosen up a bit about airlines? Not a chance.

"Sure we missed on Midway, but what about the turkeys, the ones you don't read about, which we also missed, saving ourselves a fortune? Like that company in Columbus: Executive Jet Aviation. They had Curtis LeMay as vice-chairman of the board with a whole bunch of Air Force bigwigs. The idea was to have a fleet of jets to fly executives around the country, instead of packages. *Tons* of money poured in.

"It was a complete mess," he says triumphantly.

"Remember, most of the people in our business have focused on technology, because that's where the rates of return have been, that's where the guys have made their money, that's what they're comfortable with. It feeds on itself. If one of our people left to join another venture firm or go out on his own, I'd expect him to do what he's learned in the past. Given how well we've done, you would expect him to try to duplicate our success. He might add a little twist—a particular electronics niche, say—but I'd be awfully surprised if he would suddenly change direction and start backing chain stores or ice cream–manufacturing companies. Why should he? He doesn't know anything about them. And the track records are pretty lousy.

"*You tend to do what you already know.* It's that simple."

CHAPTER SIX # Lonely Are the Brave

When television executives tend to do what they already know, it hardly comes as a shock. But when venture capitalists also tend to do what they already know, it's cause for alarm. If even venture capitalists are cautious, it does not bode well for the innovators.

Just ask Henry Kloss, innovator *par excellence*. Kloss is a visionary engineer-*cum*-entrepreneur, the father of high fidelity and wide-screen television; a man who knows how to envision and build dramatic new products which improve the quality of life and provide the basis for new, vital businesses. Not only does Kloss conceive products that consumers truly want, but he commits himself to selling them as inexpensively as possible to reach as many people as possible.

Now, one would assume that Henry Kloss would be the model of Economic Man: the risk-taker-turned-dynamic-corporate-leader, the executive who can infuse vitality from above, by encouraging his employees to be innovative and by bringing out brave new products in a world he will have had a hand in changing. You would think our economy would genuflect before such a person, would lay capital and responsibility at his feet, would seek to increase its much-maligned productivity by sticking with those of his ilk. Is not Henry Kloss typical of those mas-

152

ters of applied science who can take scientific ideas and translate them into products that please millions, employ thousands, and make investors rich? No one would deny it.

Yet in the winter of 1981, Henry Kloss, the creator of three multimillion-dollar companies, was working in the basement in a recently abandoned factory, trying to make a go of his fourth business. His capital was all the money left over from his share of the last company he had sold, plus some funds from close friends. At fifty-two, with a track record unequaled in the high-growth industry of home entertainment, Kloss still had to start from the beginning. The businesses he created, the businesses he approached, even the entire home-entertainment industry were leery not only of his entrepreneurial personality and *modus operandi,* but also of his innovation.

Henry Kloss sat in a rocking chair on the sun porch of his large, rambling house and talked of his trials and tribulations. With his longish white hair trailing down his neck; a large, open face dissolving into a double chin; and eyes that sometimes seem fixed on some distant horizon, Kloss looks the part of the eccentric inventor, and his tendency to swallow the ends of his sentences and trail off into silence does nothing to contradict the image. But Kloss is anything but absentminded, and he is concerned with what goes on outside his workshop as well as inside—especially the finer points of company building.

He got into business in 1950 the way most people do—to make enough money to get by. While he was studying physics at M.I.T., he also worked for a young husband-and-wife team who were making modern furniture. At the same time, some bright young people from M.I.T.'s acoustic lab came up with what they thought was a great idea for a new loudspeaker. It wasn't great or even good, as it turned out, but it did become rather popular. Since the students didn't want to make their own speaker cabinets, Kloss offered to make them for them. He built the cabinets because he happened to have woodworking equipment; because he happened to need money; because he happened to be in a community of people at M.I.T. who wanted to buy speakers in the first place because they were interested in high fidelity, which most people weren't. And because the speakers were not sold at retail, Kloss then decided he might as well buy speakers instead from a Midwest manufacturer, put them in his cabinets, and sell them through mail order. Again, just because he was trying to get by.

Thus, at the age of twenty, did one of the great pioneers of audio find himself in the industry. But a few months later, he was drafted and stationed in Fort Monmouth, in New Jersey.

"Every night I would grab the ferry from Hoboken to New York City to see a play or take an adult-education course," Kloss recalled. "One of those courses happened to be about high fidelity—I was selling speakers, after all—and one night the instructor, Ed Villchur, happened to confide to the class that he had an invention for a really *great* way to make a speaker but he couldn't tell it to anyone, it was really secret. 'This is for the big boys,' he said—the big manufacturers of audio equipment. Later in the term, however, he did reveal the secret to me—the proper way to make a low-frequency speaker—and I said immediately, 'You're right—that's the way to do it.' Believe me, it would have been obvious to anyone who knew anything about acoustics that he had hit upon the answer. So I said, 'I have this little company in Cambridge; let's go make this thing.' But he shook his head and said again, 'No, this is for the big boys.' "

University and Lansing were the big names in the loudspeaker business in 1950. It took a large company to make the huge speakers of the day, and Villchur, no entrepreneur himself, figured the giants of the industry would jump at a chance to become even larger by revolutionizing their product in terms of its size, cost, and quality. So he went to University, Lansing, and the best of the smaller producers, Bozak, and they all turned him down. Finally he came back to Kloss and said, "Okay, let's go make this thing."

This "thing" was the acoustic-suspension speaker, *the* breakthrough in high fidelity. Up until that time, speakers had been unable to reproduce the bass tones properly. Not only did bass tones rumble and buzz their way through the speakers, but they also adversely affected the higher tones, distorting the entire spectrum. Everyone in acoustics understood the source of the problem: the paper cone that responded to the electrical signal and emitted the actual sound was suspended within the speaker cabinet by elastic. The stronger the electrical signal, the greater the strain on the elastic. The greater the strain, the tighter the elastic, the less able it was to reproduce the bass tones accurately. The trick, then, was to find a method of suspension that would retain an even level of elasticity no matter how strong the electrical signal. Villchur's solution was to use an elastic body of *air.* Air was already present in the loudspeaker cabinet, so all he had to do was figure out the right amount of air to maximize elasticity, and construct the cabinet accordingly. And since the right amount of air wasn't very large, the speakers could be much smaller than those currently in use.

In 1953, Edgar Villchur, Henry Kloss, and two of Kloss's friends—Malcolm Low and J. Anton Hofman—joined together to form Acoustic Research (AR) of Cambridge, Massachusetts. Villchur had the idea, which he patented, and got half the company for it. Kloss had the woodworking equipment to make the cabinets, a loft in Cambridge, and some business experience; Low, Kloss's Army buddy, had $2,500; Hofman, Kloss's neighbor, another $2,500. The three of them split the remaining half of the company.

Villchur, who lived in Woodstock, New York, and worked part time, was made president. Low and Hofman (who also worked part time at first because he was teaching physics) handled sales and finance, respectively. Only Henry Kloss, vice-president and general manager, worked full time and drew a salary—a few dollars an hour in the beginning and finally, in 1957, $13,000 a year.

Though the four partners were manufacturing the best speaker in history, that didn't mean the world was going to beat a path to their door. "*No one* approached us with an offer to invest or buy us out," Kloss recalls. The resistance to change ran very deep.

"Ed's idea from the very beginning, in his magnanimous, liberal way, was that AR, which was going to do endless research and generate great ideas, would liberally license other companies to make our products, because it was the proper thing to do, because the world should have these things as readily as possible.

At the first, dramatic introduction of the speaker at the New York audio show, it did come to the attention of Heath [the maker of Heathkits], but the licensing agreement that followed was on a very small scale. Most of the other companies weren't interested at all.

"It was a great tempering of Ed's liberalism."

In 1957, with annual sales at $750,000, the partners found themselves arguing constantly. Villchur, still in Woodstock, didn't think Kloss, Low, and Hofman were doing a very good job running the business in Cambridge. Kloss, Low, and Hofman didn't think Villchur knew what he was talking about. Meanwhile, AR was still operating on a small entrepreneurial scale with a product that should have made it an industry leader, if only the capital had been there. It was a time of considerable frustration. Each side was convinced that the other couldn't exist in business for very long on its own. When Villchur adamantly refused to sell his half of the company, the other three reluctantly decided that they would have to be the ones to leave. After Villchur scraped up $53,000 to buy them out, a new company, KLH (for *K*loss, *L*ow, and *H*ofman), was born. It was agreed that KLH, as well as AR, would have the right to build Villchur's speaker.

As Kloss explains, "Here one had the right way to make a low-frequency speaker and the determination to do things right; a company without an absentee half-owner; a company committed to exploiting what it knew it had, to perfect it and then go into broader fields, to expand into radios and phonographs as well." Which KLH did, making a profit by the end of the first year. But while it was able to finance its growth out of profits for quite a long time, no company grows very quickly that way. High-growth businesses—computer firms, for example—demand a great deal of debt and equity money to finance new plants, production equipment, and research and development. In the preboom era of audio, before the Beatles and their record-buying generation transformed the industry, KLH might have been able to dominate the market had it been able to grow. But it simply did not have the money.

By the end of the decade, Villchur's patent was declared by the courts to be in the public domain. Any of the major audio companies could then have emulated KLH's superior loudspeaker with no penalty. But none did. The small company's continuing existence became testimony to the competition's deafness to innovation.

After six years of steady, unspectacular growth, KLH was doing $7 million worth of business a year. The partners finally realized they would need more capital to expand. First they went to their bank, but the bank did not want to extend as much money as KLH needed. So KLH went to a number of venture capitalists, but there too the company met resistance. To venture firms, KLH was in an industry that wasn't yet large enough or well enough established. Because they saw KLH as such a risky proposition, they demanded a huge chunk of the company in exchange for their investment.

At the same time, the L and H of KLH—Low and Hofman— were losing interest in the business. And so in 1964, a few short months before the audio explosion, KLH was sold to a much larger company, Singer Sewing Machine, for a respectable $4 million.

Although Kloss had reservations about the sale, he soon saw that it might have its advantages. "This was a time when conglomerates were particularly fashionable," he remembers. "Singer bought us with the hope that we would form the base for their entry into home-entertainment electronics, and I stayed on with a three-year contract as president, chief executive, and product designer with the hope that Singer's huge resources, their sixteen hundred stores, their production efficiencies, their access to large suppliers would allow me to do things that hadn't been possible at KLH."

Here at last might be the chance to do things on a grand scale, with Singer's name and money and Kloss's products and expertise. Without taking any risk—because KLH was a prospering company in its own right—Singer could make a fortune selling audio equipment in its sewing centers.

But, says Kloss, "the problem was that Singer couldn't sell high-fidelity equipment in their stores. So while we still did very well in the outside market, few of their stores participated, and the thing that was going to be my consolation for selling KLH—the excitement of making products for hundreds of thousands of people—obviously was not going to happen."

. Singer could have gone into home-entertainment equipment in a big way without its stores, of course, but Kloss says it never occurred to the company, even though with KLH it was in the right business at the right time—the mid-1960s—with the right talent and the right position with the public. KLH had gone from $7 million to $17 million in the three years Kloss stayed on, and he was seeing an awful lot of records being sold and a great new interest in music. Plainly, the component high-fidelity industry was going to boom. But, he says, "it didn't even come up for discussion at Singer that there would be a market outside their stores that they should go after."

With all the stories then about the children of the postwar baby boom reaching adolescence, one might think that Singer would have been as aware as Kloss of the commercial possibilities. Levi Strauss saw it coming; it cashed in on this market and became the world's largest clothing manufacturer. But Singer remained tentative and lost. In fact, it lost big. By 1980 the former powerhouse had sold KLH and was financially on the rocks.

But at least Singer fared better than the erstwhile "big boys" of audio. Of the companies that had had a shot at acoustic suspension, only Lansing (JBL) is still a major factor in the industry. The others had spent too much time looking over their shoulders.

Henry Kloss, however, never stopped looking ahead: "Here it was 1967 and I was assuming that the audio business would revert to the majors—to RCA, GE, Zenith, and Magnavox—since they were the most efficient producers and distributors of total sound systems; since it was becoming very easy technically to make good equipment; since the acoustic-suspension patent was public; and since surely they would see that the market was going to be very large. So after three years with KLH-Singer, one looks around and doesn't see anything important or new to do with audio, or any big effort on the part of Singer to capture more of the market, and one decides to leave."

It was time for Kloss to move on to something new: television. Here, he thought, was an industry as technically undeveloped as audio had been in the 1950s. Here was the newest, hottest, most broadly applicable part of an industry he felt he knew: home entertainment. Yet Henry Kloss never watched television. He didn't even own a set.

But perhaps that was an advantage. Because he never watched it, he held no preconceptions which might have constrained his thinking. To Kloss, television sets seemed far too small. He knew from the technical literature that wide-screen projection television was theoretically possible, so he decided to do for television what he had done for audio: help pioneer a new age.

"One day I read an article in a popular engineering magazine by this chap in Bermuda who proposed a color television set with three two-inch-diameter tubes with a very small picture inside that could be projected *outside* by a mirror—in other words, a plan for a projection color television which projects the image on a very large screen some distance away; this instead of the usual television with one picture tube that you look at directly. Now, I had known about projection television—the idea had been around since 1933—and was interested in the article's claim that the set would only cost three hundred dollars. Color televisions were much more expensive in those days, and three hundred dollars was very cheap. As it turned out, assumptions about projection television were completely wrong and it was impossible to build a model based on his ideas, though someone did try to carry it to completion, and it was a big failure and a lot of people lost money. But the idea of projection television was very attractive to me. It seemed a very efficient way to do things. For a given amount of electricity you could get much more light out with a projection television system than a direct-tube system. And it seemed to me a given that having a bigger picture would have to be an improvement."

This was to be Henry Kloss's very own business, with no partners, no disagreements, and no one to insist on selling the firm. With the $400,000 he had left from the $1.2 million in Singer stock he had received as his share of the KLH sale (the other $800,000 had been eaten away by taxes and Singer's precipitous stock decline at the end of the go-go era), Kloss formed the Advent Corporation to build his video dream. Or as he explains it,

"One had an interest in making products better; in doing something that, well, caused other people to do things in the right way; in seeing how one could change the way people did things. I also liked very much the idea of making products the easiest possible way, so one looked for things that were *least* well done. And there was television—an obviously important medium— which was being done by the same companies that had blown the whole audio business, so I assumed—and I'd say the circumstantial evidence was overwhelming—that they were not doing all they could with television."

Kloss also assumed that the sheer inventiveness and quality of his product would eventually secure its success, so for the first two years of his new company's life, at great cost, he was willing to devote himself almost entirely to the development of projection television. He wasn't going to worry about other companies this time and he wasn't going to worry about investors. But he was going to have to worry about running out of money.

In 1969, with the money almost gone, Kloss noted a curious opportunity. A key prediction about the audio business had not come true: the business was *not* reverting to the majors. They had waited too long, proceeded too cautiously. They were being done in by all those years of making lower-quality products. So Kloss decided a good way to make money to support the television R&D would be to go back into audio and make speakers. The speaker business permits a rather low entry cost—which is why there are about 350 loudspeaker makers today—and so all he needed was a relatively small amount of investment from the outside.

"I had done AR," says Kloss, "I had done KLH, and I finally had a working model of the projection television and could put a picture up on a screen, so naturally I expected that when I went looking for venture capital, they would say, 'Fine, what do you need?' The numbers were there—the bookkeeping had always been very good; there were all the short-term and long-term projections; and I showed how the speaker business alone would justify their investment, with the projection television as a kicker."

It wasn't that Kloss had become a believer in the investment community; he just thought he could finally overcome its aversion to risk by coming up with a safe deal. "As a result," he says, "I didn't give them the kind of fancy presentation they're used to. I didn't go out to lunch with them; I remember making it clear to them I didn't want to waste time, that I wanted them to call me back after two weeks and tell me what they thought, whichever way it went, and there was agreement on that. But nobody called me back. It seems it isn't the custom for them to call back; it's customary for them to be badgered and pursued. But I wouldn't do that. I knew that if I called I would get some negative response and my job would have been to knock down each of their objections one by one until there were none left. They always seem to look first at the negatives."

Once again the professional investors were too wary to get involved. No venture capitalist would touch the project; no bank would finance it. Kloss was forced to sell twenty shares for $25,000 each to friends—$500,000 in all. With this new money, Advent was able to produce a speaker. It quickly became a huge success.

The company also made a cassette tape recorder with Dolby noise reduction, a quantum leap in sound reproduction which no other company had had the daring to use. But that got Kloss involved in yet another frustrating situation.

He had heard of a new product that Du Pont had developed: chromium dioxide recording tape, which could store more energy than traditional magnetic tape. According to Kloss, Du Pont had been trying to get the big users of tape in the music industry to buy it; but the fact that it was better tape was no incentive for the companies to pay a premium price—there was nothing in it for them because there was no demand for the tape—at least, not yet—because it wasn't on the market, because there was no demand, because there was no market. You get the idea.

Advent got involved because its Dolby tape recorder and its speakers were of such high quality that the listener could more readily hear the improvement. The difference was dramatic, but only if one used all the components. Consequently, in order to prove itself in the marketplace, the tape had to be generally available to people with good equipment.

Advent first tried working with Memorex on the introduction of the new tape as a consumer product; but, Kloss laments, "working with such a large company was hopeless. They were far too slow to act and it was taking forever, waiting for decisions from the appropriate levels of the company, waiting for information to get to all of them and be digested—all this despite their good intentions."

Finally Kloss discovered that he could get the tape directly from Du Pont and market it himself. So it was Advent that wound up introducing the tape to consumers—not Memorex, not Du Pont: "We had to be the ones to show Du Pont, 'See, here's something of value people want.' And all we had been trying to do was make our equipment sound better. We never thought we would have to go into the tape business to do that!"

For the next few years Advent concentrated on the audio business, until it was ready to plow back its profits into the further development of projection television. But in 1974, just as Kloss was nearing completion of his first commercial version of the set, the Advent 1000, the company came to the attention of a local investment banker who was willing to underwrite (guarantee) the sale of a portion of the company's stock. As an established audio success, Advent finally was a safe investment; with the projection television system it also had the lure of a potential bonanza.

Kloss figured that some more capital couldn't hurt—once again costs had been higher than expected—and agreed to a public offering of the company's stock. Twelve percent of the business was sold, netting $1.4 million; the company received a considerable amount of public attention; and Kloss was able to finance further refinement of the Advent 1000.

His beloved projection color television system went on the market in 1974, and in the first year sold 2,600 sets—with a loss of $2.5 million. It looked like a disaster to some, but to Kloss it was simply a matter of pricing down the experience curve.

"Nothing we had done on the set had been secret," he explains. "We had shown it to everybody who was interested all along the way. And since it was obvious that the majors in the television business could make the sets a lot easier than we could, we just assumed that they would, that we would quickly have competitors a couple of legs up on us with their production efficiencies, and if we were going to stay competitive we would have to quickly get some economies of scale or be swamped. I pushed for a goal of ten thousand sets a year, which turned out to be absolutely ridiculous—we didn't even come close—and a price of twenty-five hundred dollars, which turned out to be much too low, but I thought that if we kept the price low enough we would discourage anyone else from coming in."

Advent did discourage competition, but it cost a great deal. It is sound strategy to price down the experience curve as long as you have enough money to sustain you and you're under no illusions about the size of your costs.

Advent, however, had relatively little capital, and was being misled by its accounting method. Many, if not most, accounting decisions are judgment calls—assumptions. Advent assumed that the labor costs that went into experimenting with the first batch of sets would be covered by the return from the first year's output. Kloss concedes it was a big mistake. The costs should have been treated as research-and-development and written off over many years, so that it would not take too much of a toll on first-year profits.

"I should have been paying closer attention to our accounting," Kloss says now. "That really caught up with us at the end of the year and we showed a big loss. But we did prove that there was a market there, and we had learned, finally, how to make the sets efficiently enough at the price. But by then we had run out of cash, and our bank was frightened. It wouldn't lend us any more money and was even threatening to foreclose, beginning to talk about how much money it would get if we were liquidated—closed down and sold off piece by piece. The bank had just had some big losses on a few other companies and some near misses, you see, and it was furious that we were losing so much money. We said it was an investment in the future and a short-term thing, but the bank saw it as a chronic thing. We tried to explain. It was summer, we said, and no one buys televisions in the summer, but the bank wouldn't listen. It panicked. There was no real communication."

In June, 1975, an Advent board member contacted Peter Sprague, the young, adventurous venture capitalist who had invested heavily in National Semiconductor in its early days and had become chairman of its board; who had just bought the ailing, legendary British sports-car manufacturer Aston Martin; who had taken control of Design Research, the upscale home-furnishings firm; and who had, among his other entrepreneurial credits, a chicken farm in Iran and the movie *Steppenwolf.* Sprague, clearly a dyed-in-the-wool risk taker, was told that Advent's bank was about to call in its loan: would he be interested in investing in the company?

Sprague was intrigued by projection television. He also was intrigued by any investment that might bring a huge return. That was almost always the case with a promising company on the brink of bankruptcy—the classic "turnaround" situation. Sprague has been called everything from a savior to a scavenger, but no one, not even Sprague, would deny he's an opportunist.

In a matter of days, in what Henry Kloss now calls "an atmosphere of panic," Advent was offered a deal by which Sprague would invest $575,000 for 375,000 shares of stock ($1.53 per share at a time when Advent stock was at $10—although there weren't any buyers at that price) *if* he was made chairman of the board. Sprague also wanted the voting rights of some of Kloss's stock, which would bring his share of voting control to 44 percent. It was a hard bargain—but then, it was a company that was losing money on every set it made. Sprague had the upper hand.

"One should have been working on some other way to raise capital before it came down to this, of course," admits Kloss ruefully, "but it was too late. Here was the bank making liquidation noises, and Peter, who was going to leave the next day for London, was willing to make enough of a commitment to calm them down, and we felt sure that if we said no, the bank would have said, 'Forget the whole thing, you people are just impossible' and foreclosed. It was completely risk-averse, unwilling to look at the *product* and say, 'Yes, you have a viable product here.' Anyone could have seen how well the audio part of the business was doing, at least. Certainly it could have given us a few more weeks to make another deal. But it said, and Peter said, if we didn't close the deal the company would go under. We were compelled to go through with it."

With Sprague on board, the bank agreed to a deferred-payment schedule on the loan. Then Sprague took control of sales and manufacturing, and insisted on a new president, a man Kloss did not want hired. He was hired anyway. Then Kloss was forbidden to personally authorize any expenditures. Although all his requests were promptly approved, he felt slighted. Eventually, he says, he had no input on product development either.

Within two years, Advent's sales reached $40 million, but many of the innovative people lured by Kloss had left. The continually expected competition from the majors had not yet come. And Henry Kloss was gone, about to become Advent's chief competitor.

With $1.5 million of his own money, the indefatigable Kloss formed Kloss Video and set out to improve the tube that formed the heart of the projection television system. But since he was nervous about going into manufacturing again, he decided that, like Ed Villchur, he would license manufacturing rights to his new tube to other companies, all of which would immediately see the commercial possibilities of his product and the glowing future of wide-screen television.

Some people never learn.

"One saw right away that the major companies weren't interested," he says, shaking his head. "When I went to Zenith with my new tube, they said they couldn't get involved in a technology that was so new. It wasn't so new. *I* had done it. But it was a matter of once they admitted that the product was do-able they would have to act. Rather than doing that and exposing themselves, they preferred to do nothing." And Zenith continued losing market share to the Japanese.

"Large American companies also seem to have this aversion to ideas from the outside," says Kloss. "They have these huge research-and-development departments, and if they don't come up with better products than some guy from outside, then what's the rationale for their existence? It becomes a hard thing for people in a large company to accept the fact that they didn't come up with a given idea. It's a real blow to their pride, and worse, a threat, so they turn it down.

"And then there's the problem of companies' relying on dealers for feedback about new products. Dealers are very short-term-oriented. The product they would like to see is the product they could have sold *yesterday*—a sale they didn't make because some other product had a slight edge and looked a little better to a consumer. So large companies often design their products accordingly—by adding on new, minor features to a product *everyone* is making in order to give the dealer that small edge he needs to make the sale. And then what one gets is an endless variety of the same old product which may make money, but not nearly as much as a really new product would."

As it turned out, Kloss couldn't find anyone in the United States to buy the rights to manufacture his new tube. But he did in Japan. And so today Nippon Electric (NEC) is making the Kloss tube. Advent, meanwhile, has gone bankrupt despite "professional management" and its cost/benefit emigration to inexpensive New Hampshire. Henry Kloss has taken over the remains of the company and moved it back to Cambridge. He is now turning out what is generally considered to be the highest-quality projection television on the market—in Advent's abandoned factory. Extra capital has come from friends ($800,000) and a public stock offering ($12 million). But that still isn't very much money in the TV-manufacturing business. Shunned by the professional money people and the large American television makers, Kloss continues to be haunted by the specter of high-volume foreign competition, which would be able to sell at lower prices.

The cautiousness of American business may once again have paved the way for Japanese business. Henry Kloss, for one, would not be surprised.

CHAPTER SEVEN ## The Eagle Scout Syndrome

When the legend becomes fact, print the legend, declares a character at the end of the film *The Man Who Shot Liberty Valance*. And so we do, again and again; for the truth is just the truth—often discomforting, almost always maddeningly complex—but a myth is something we can live by, teach our children about, and salute on holidays.

One of the more telling myths about who wins and who loses on the corporate battlefield is the myth of the entrepreneur. It's as much a staple of "how-to" business manuals as of the Horatio Alger books. According to the myth, the successful entrepreneur has a high level of self-confidence and the determination to solve problems. He or she sets clear goals, is not afraid of failure, seeks and uses feedback wisely, competes against self-imposed standards, and tolerates uncertainty well. He or she is also a persistent, independent "builder" with strong ethics, strong character, and great courage—in other words, a shrewd Eagle Scout, much cherished by society. Entrepreneurship, then, is something truly wonderful to aspire to.

Conversely, an unsuccessful entrepreneur is easy to spot by his or her "unentrepreneurial" attributes: he or she is self-centered, unwilling to listen to others, and prone to taking too-big risks or

167

too-small risks (but never just right ones), and has unclear goals. A born loser.

As for those without any interest in entrepreneurship whatsoever—why, they sound almost un-American!

Didn't De Tocqueville write, "No Americans are devoid of a yearning desire to rise ... All are constantly seeking to acquire property, power and reputation"?

Didn't Emerson write, "If a man can make a better mousetrap than his neighbor, though he builds his house in the woods, the world will make a beaten path to his door"?

And didn't our friend Ed say, "The killer-bee-honey business will make my fortune"?

We don't know why De Tocqueville and Emerson wrote such foolishness, but we do know why Ed uttered his famous words. It was some years ago, after several friends mercilessly kidded him about the business he had just begun. Ed took their teasing very well; he knew the jibes were born in jealousy. After all, it was he who had been the first to take the entrepreneurial plunge, leaving his friends behind. They had to wonder if they were somehow deficient for having reached their thirties without making any concentrated effort to build their fortunes.

One of them even had a nightmare in which Ed, having become a multimillionaire, did not recognize his poor, wretched friend who, having toiled in obscurity, was swept away by a great depression and cast upon Skid Row. The dream was so vivid that four years later, the dreamer could still remember the color of Ed's socks: gold.

Though they joked aloud about Ed's probable failure, the friends began to harbor secret thoughts about his possible success. Ed seemed to have not only a clever idea, but also many of the classic entrepreneurial attributes considered indispensable to a new business venture. What if he actually made it? How could they let pass an opportunity to see how an entrepreneur, in the great American tradition, starts from the beginning with almost nothing and builds an empire (or if not an empire, at least a very nice business)? They couldn't. The information might even come in handy for a venture of their own. (A chapter in a book about business, perhaps.)

His friends had reason to believe in Ed. He was smart and talented, and his background was impressive. Shortly after graduating from Cornell University, he started from scratch his own successful weekly newspaper in Harrisburg, Pennsylvania. And because he's a man of principle as well as enterprise, he decided to run George McGovern's press office in upstate New York during McGovern's bid for the presidency in 1972.

But Ed is also a realist. When McGovern was demolished in November, Ed decided to forgo a career in politics and turned instead to writing. As a free lancer, he wrote for the staid *New York Times Magazine,* the prestigious *Harper's,* the liberal *New Republic,* the hip *Rolling Stone,* the slick *Boston* magazine, and the muckraking *Mother Jones.* He interviewed the long-exiled King of Albania in Madrid, actor Jack Nicholson in London, and a talking chimpanzee in Oklahoma.

But Ed's was not an easy life. In the eternal search for good copy, his editors forced him to spend a weekend with the disciples of Sun Myung Moon, join a circus, carry a spear on stage at the opera, and jump out of an airplane. For his efforts, Ed was working twelve months a year with little security, no medical insurance, no pension, and a cluttered and cramped room in his apartment for an office. He was very tired. He did not like to jump out of airplanes and would rather not remember his day with an extremely laconic Jack Nicholson (although he did become quite fond of the chimp). Ed began to wonder whether there might be a better, easier way to earn a living.

In the summer of 1977, he found himself in French Guiana, a dismal place with only three points of interest: France's "space center" (France, as you probably know, is not famous for its space program); the Devil's Island penal colony, long abandoned but still an attraction for morbid-minded tourists; and killer bees, an attraction for American reporters sent to French Guiana by morbid-minded editors.

A colony of killer bees had been brought to Brazil from Africa twenty years before in an experiment to see if the sturdier, more adaptive and aggressive African bees would be more productive than their gentler South American cousins. Since then, the African bees had become the dominant strain in South America.

This phenomenon would be of less than passing interest had not some swarms of African bees escaped from their domesticized colonies and, over the years, spread north in large wild swarms as far as French Guiana. These belligerent bees are capable of stinging animals and even people to death. It seems they prefer to attack in battalions, not platoons like normal honeybees. An angry swarm can be very dangerous.

To South Americans, killer bees were not killers at all, but bees that made their honey and once in a while got out of hand. To American editors, however, killer bees sold papers. *Killer bees are heading north! Killer bees to devour Texas!*

And so our intrepid friend Ed found himself in a beekeeper's suit a few miles from the French Guiana jungle, trying to provoke an attack by a swarm of killer bees with the aid of an American entomologist there to study the insects. Ed counted with horror the hundreds of bee stingers that almost, but not quite, penetrated the thick cloth of his protective suit.

Afterward, he joined the hospitable entomologist at his house for tea. While Ed was discussing insect lore with his host, he noticed a small bowl of honey by his elbow. The honey proved to be a trifle thinner and sweeter than the kind Ed normally used, so he asked where it came from. His host answered that it was honey from the killer bees.

"I felt like Isaac Newton when the apple dropped," Ed explained later. "Killer-bee honey! Now, there's a product for you!"

Thus, in the tropical heat of that godforsaken country, Ed had the first vision of his very own company: a simple business that could free him from his life of constant travel and exhausting assignments. Yes, he thought, THE KILLER-BEE HONEY-NOVELTY-GIFT-IDEA-FOR-CHRISTMAS-AND-MAYBE-EVEN-VALENTINE'S-DAY-AND-BIRTHDAYS!

His mind raced. There would be a small bottle of the stuff and an amusing booklet, of course, and an inflated price to maximize profits, yet at the same time increase its respectability as a clever novelty gift. He would sell it in big department stores and small boutiques, in the mountains and in the plains. The new hula hoop!

For several months after his return home, Ed dawdled. Finally, he called up a friend who was attending business school and invited him to lunch. Top secret. Great plan. Killer-bee honey.

"Right," said the friend. "Great gimmick. Great novelty item. Who's going to do the work?"

"A group of us," said Ed. "Interested?"

"Interested," said the friend. "I know a lot about business. I'm willing to do your thinking for you. For a price. It is known as consulting."

"I will do the thinking myself," answered Ed. "What I need is people to go get the honey, get it bottled, packaged, distributed and sold."

"I don't have time for that," said the friend, "and neither do you. You have three free-lance articles to write by the end of the month. Pass the salt."

Other friends proved equally reluctant to get involved. But Ed was not ready to abandon the venture. He worked alone, a few hours here, an afternoon there, and decided he would first buy the honey with his own money and worry about the rest later. He tried to contact honey firms in Rio de Janeiro—but as he explained later, "People in South America don't seem to answer letters. I even began writing 'I will send you money' at the end of each one."

He tried telephoning, but after a few ludicrous attempts found that his ignorance of Portuguese was an insurmountable barrier. He hired a translator, but the translator did not have an easy time of it either, since the honey firms were extremely reluctant to fill a small order from an unknown American.

Ed joined the Brazilian-American Friendship Society in order to demonstrate his international goodwill. He continued to call Rio. In a fit of optimism, he hired an artist to design a box for the honey, although as yet he had no idea exactly how big the bottle would be. He consulted a lawyer about setting up a corporation.

On January 6, 1978, without an ounce of honey to his name, he toted up his expenses:

Translator's fees	*$ 73.60*
Phone calls	*324.06*
Legal fees	*469.03*
Box design	*75.00*
Postage and Xeroxing	*77.06*
Membership dues	*20.00*
	$1,038.75

Ed's gasping, choking business was running out of fuel, but he decided against borrowing any money or spending a greater portion of his time on the project than he already was. Searching elsewhere for more labor and capital, he found an unemployed friend who agreed to do the legwork for a percentage of future profits and a few relatives who agreed to put up $1,000 each for a share of the business. But the friend soon despaired of ever seeing a dime, and the relatives grew cautious and changed their minds.

Ed was desperate. It was late spring, with little time left to gear up for the next Christmas season, when he planned to make his killing. At one point someone remembered that killer-bee honey was the dominant honey in Africa as well as South America, and Ed made a few inquiries. He discovered that South African honey merchants were easy to deal with, spoke English, and were keenly interested in taking money from all sorts of people. It was very tempting, but Ed couldn't see himself doing business with the minions of *apartheid*. Oh, why couldn't they be progressive Mozambiquan honey merchants instead? he lamented.

At his lowest ebb, Ed turned to his old friend Kip, who had considerably more business experience. Kip offered the following deal: henceforth, Kip would supply half the labor and more money for two-thirds of the business. Ed reluctantly agreed.

Kip promptly flew down to Brazil, bought a ton of killer-bee honey for $1,000, watched as it was loaded on a cargo ship, returned to New York to see it unloaded, and then arranged to have it trucked home in four 55-gallon drums.

Success seemed at hand; but in fact their business was still in first gear. The partners thought they had found a beekeeper to bottle the honey, but after hedging for several months he pulled out. "Apparently some American beekeepers are afraid of the idea of killer bees," Ed complained. "They think killer bees are going to give bees in general a bad name and their neighbors are going to come with torches at midnight and drive them out of their neighborhood."

So Ed and Kip were forced to take their honey back. Since the 55-gallon drums proved too heavy for the partners to move, and since they were in a cost-cutting mood, they borrowed a pump and pumped the honey out of the drums and into plastic buckets so they could transport it more easily. Naturally, it was harder than they had expected. They got honey in their hair, honey in their ears, and honey all over their clothes. They even had angry bees chasing their truck down the highway.

Ed and Kip eventually found beekeeper number two, who agreed to fill hundreds of 5.75-ounce bottles, at 5 cents a shot, from a fauceted vat in his basement. He was a stalwart liberal and had nothing against killer bees, even if they were foreigners.

Meanwhile, back at the entrepreneurial hive, costs continued to rise. The partners had to buy 6,300 bottles, caps, labels, pamphlets, and glossy four-color boxes. Ed wrote the clever pamphlet relating the killer-bee-honey story himself, but the artist who designed the pamphlet, as well as the label and the box, had to be paid, as did the printing company. And once again, the lawyer. There were also the man who filled the bottles and the people needed to haul the cases of filled bottles out of the bottler's basement onto a truck to a warehouse, where more labor was needed to stick on the labels and box them and load them onto another truck to make deliveries.

When Ed and Kip added up their costs, they were aghast. The total was $10,000. A small bottle of killer-bee honey cost more than a dollar to produce, even without figuring in the start-up costs. They planned to sell the bottles wholesale to department stores for $2.50 a bottle, but Bloomingdale's, their first stop, told them flatly it would give the partners only $1.75 for each bottle sold. Thus with a profit per bottle of somewhat less than 75 cents, Ed and Kip would have to sell all their honey to lose $5,000. Just to break even, they would have to fill and sell another 6,700 bottles. To make $1 million, they would have to sell another 1.3

million bottles. To sell 1.3 million bottles, they would need a huge distribution system (which they did not have) and Christmas (which essentially they had missed).

They moved on to Valentine's Day. They bought more honey, and Ed valiantly donned a beekeeper's suit for a promotional stint at a small but chic department store. "GIVE YOUR KILLER BEE HONEY SOME KILLER BEE HONEY," read the display sign as Ed walked about the store in his suit, offering customers small crackers with honey. But sales, though respectable, were hardly as brisk as the partners had hoped. Ed understandably became testy and called out at uninterested browsers who passed up the samples: "What's the matter? It's free, isn't it?"

The store manager watched patiently as Valentine's Day drew to a close. "I think we'll give it one or two Christmases and then we'll move on to something else," he said.

The partners had spent another $10,000. They had next Christmas to look forward to, but very little Christmas spirit. Nevertheless, they pressed on. They hit the novelty-item-fair circuit. They assembled a team of commissioned sales agents operating from coast to coast. They learned everything there was to know about the novelty business. But it was too late. No one cared about killer bees anymore.

Ed is now working on a book and several free-lance articles.

Clearly, everything had gone wrong from the start. Supply had been haphazard and demand had been overestimated. Capital and labor needs had been underestimated. There never was a real marketing strategy, and promotion was too little, too late. Ed also had allowed his progressive politics to scotch a smart business move. Moreover, relevant business experience had been minimal, and planning nonexistent.

But it was the lack of drive—the missing compulsion to succeed—that doomed Ed most of all. He was not, like John W. Galbreath, the multimillionaire real estate developer and winner of the 1960 Horatio Alger Award, willing to work twelve to fourteen hours a day, including weekends, and "live" his business. Ed wanted the easy life, not the hard life.

Perhaps starting a new business is *not* the birthright of all Americans. Perhaps keen intelligence, strong ethics, and character are not necessarily entrepreneurial attributes, but Jaycee pap. Yet Ed, who never would have presumed to go into psychology, say, or plumbing without serving an apprenticeship of some sort, without making a total commitment, still thought he could start his own business—in the notoriously unstable novelty trade, no less—and his friends thought he could too.

Some people succeed by starting from scratch, of course, but most don't. In a typical year, 400,000 new businesses are started; five years later more than two-thirds of those have gone under. The average life-span of a company is six years; according to the Department of Commerce, about one-third of all new businesses will fail even before their first birthday. The only people who are left smiling are the authors of how-to business books.

As for the successful entrepreneur, he or she is too busy worrying to smile. Or too busy getting depressed. Or paranoid. Or euphoric. For many successful entrepreneurs, there is no easy life—ever. In fact, according to *The Enterprising Man,* the seminal study of psychiatric characteristics of entrepreneurs, maladjustment seems to be the key to their success.

The authors of *The Enterprising Man* studied 150 entrepreneurs with businesses in Michigan; 40 of those were given the Thematic Apperception Test (TAT), which requires respondents to make up stories about a collection of pictures. Most of the responses were either directly autobiographical or symbolic of feelings. The psychologist who analyzed the TAT results found that for the most part the successful entrepreneur lacks the social values of "getting ahead" and rising in a social hierarchy; experiences chronic fatigue; becomes suspicious of people who enjoy their work; has a weak ego, a dominant superego, and an ever-threatening id; and has satisfactory relations with subordinates only when they are on a patriarchal or patronly basis.

There is a striking absence of stable and reliable adult figures in the family histories of most of these men. They consequently have problems with both male and female authority figures. The former are perceived as "shadowy, remote beings ... cold and unsupporting [but] powerful—sometimes frighteningly so." The latter tend to be perceived as either "motherly (good) or seductive (bad)."

And so they see themselves as people who must go it alone, who do not fit in. Before their eventual success, they often drift from job to job, "looked upon by friends and relatives as hopeless big talkers who allow their wives and children to go hungry while they are out chasing rainbows." (Women entrepreneurs have the same problem. When Mary Kay Ash of Mary Kay Cosmetics was just starting out, she had to borrow $12 from a friend to attend a sales convention; the friend, said Ash, made a point of telling her she would be better off using the money to buy her children shoes than wasting it on some pipe dream.)

What forces are at work in the formation of the entrepreneurial personality? *The Enterprising Man*'s psychologist writes:

> Because of the unresolved fears of the father, the entrepreneur is uncomfortable in a situation which requires him to serve under strong male authority figures. . . . He finds it difficult to function effectively and gratifyingly within an organization which is not his own but belongs to a male authority. Such a situation too closely corresponds to the traumatic childhood experience in the family.

Some individuals have it more traumatic than others. John D. Rockefeller suffered a father who was an itinerant vendor of quack medicine, a sometime fugitive from the law, and a poor provider at best. He is said to have boasted, "I cheat my boys every chance I get. I want to make 'em sharp."

John's mother whipped him often with a birch switch. Once, in the midst of a whipping, she learned of his innocence of the misbehavior, but proceeded with the punishment just the same, saying, "Never mind; we have started in on this whipping and it will do for the next time."

To borrow from that great entrepreneur of ideas, Sigmund Freud (himself a noted neurotic), the entrepreneur, by starting a business of his own, may be trying symbolically to get through his Oedipal impasse. But he won't get out of the primal woods so easily. Often, he will experience an unconscious need to punish himself by bringing on his own failure. And so the careers of many entrepreneurs begin to resemble a roller-coaster ride, with steep ups and downs—dramatic success followed by dramatic failure, dramatic failure followed by dramatic success.

Consider the legendary Milton Reynolds who, like our friend Ed, went into the novelty business, but unlike Ed, was obsessive enough to try, try, try again—and fail, fail, fail again—until he finally succeeded.

Born in Minnesota in 1892, the son of a farm-equipment salesman, Reynolds went into the automobile-repair business in Chicago before he was twenty; by twenty-six he was on the verge of making a fortune when he lost it all in the stock market. In 1925 he borrowed some more money and went into the prefabricated-house business in Florida, but shortly after things began to hum along nicely, he lost everything in a hurricane which swept away a cargo ship full of his entire stock of unassembled houses.

Returning to Chicago, Reynolds launched his third would-be money machine at the age of thirty-five: the manufacture and sale of stock-quotation boards to brokerage firms—a rather clever way to ride the crest of the Twenties' great stock wave. Until the Crash, that is. November, 1929, found him with nearly empty pockets again, there not being much demand for stocks anymore, let alone stock-quotation boards.

Yet he pressed on. Within a few days he found still another business: a printing shop turning out sign-printing machines for department-store display advertising. He bought it with borrowed money and renamed it Print-A-Sign, and then raised the machine's price from $595 to $2,475—on the theory that with certain unique products, "the more you can sell something for, the easier you can sell it."

Print-A-Sign earned Reynolds a good living, but it was not the jackpot he so avidly sought. In June, 1945, however, he journeyed to Argentina on a business trip and chanced upon a new popular novelty which was unavailable and essentially unknown in the United States. As soon as he saw it, Reynolds knew he had to have it, to manufacture it, sell and promote it, to make it his own and get to the top. He saw in it an item *everyone* would buy at least once, the perfect holiday gift—a low-cost, high-profit product that could sweep the country. His killer-bee honey, if you will. It was the ball-point pen.

This marvel of the new technological age was more than sixty years old at the time. A pen using a ball point instead of a nib had been patented by an inventor named John Loud as far back as 1888, and the rights had long since expired; the basic invention was in the public domain. Only the exclusive features of any particular model were patentable.

In 1935, two Czechoslovaks in Prague had begun manufacturing a patented ball-point called the Rolpen, which worked on the ink-feed principle, with a tiny piston to press ink against the ball, but the pen sold badly and was subsequently swept away by the Nazi deluge. (Paul Eisner, one of the pair, commented later that it had been a time when you couldn't sell a dollar for 20 cents; his partner died in a concentration camp.)

Four years later, a Hungarian medical student–hypnotist–journalist–sculptor–inventor named Laszlo Biro took out a patent in Paris for his version of the pen, which worked by capillary action. It was the Biro pen which Reynolds discovered in Buenos Aires, Biro having wisely moved to Argentina when the war broke out, where he began manufacturing and selling the pen on a small scale. But by the time Reynolds saw his first ball-point, the Eversharp Pen Company already had acquired the U.S. rights to the Biro pen and was busy improving it before embarking on a major marketing effort. Had Reynolds been our friend Ed or almost anyone else, such competition would have stopped his scheme cold. But Milton Reynolds would let nothing get in his way.

As soon as he returned to Chicago, Reynolds, with an engineer he knew, designed one ball-point pen after another, searching for a model that could circumvent the Eversharp-Biro patent. They worked day and night until they came up with a pen that fed ink to the ball by means of gravity, which is about as unpatentable as you can get. August and the war's end followed soon after, and the public was ripe for a postwar wonder.

One fateful rainy evening shortly after the engineer constructed the prototype, Reynolds, as he later told *The New Yorker,* was sitting in a bar doodling on a soggy newspaper when he suddenly realized that his pen was able to write on a wet surface—a feat beyond the means of a mere fountain pen. He was overcome with joy. Returning to his shop, he filled a pan with water, placed a piece of paper at the bottom, and then took pen in hand and drew an unblurred line. Thus was born the great Reynolds Pen slogan: "It writes underwater!" As Reynolds confided to a reporter later, "The object was to make people tell each other what a ridiculous thing it was to boast about. While they were telling each other that, they were telling each other about the pen." The publicity proved to be worth millions. Now he had both the product and the promotion, and soon they would be inextricable, as Reynolds frantically promoted himself as well as his pen.

Reynolds had only one sample pen to work with in the beginning, so he took it to Gimbels in New York himself and, with great showmanship, demonstrated it to the department store's executives. They loved it, and he came away with an order for 2,500. The store agreed to use Reynolds's slogans for an advertisement the morning before the first day of sales: the pen, the copy read, would write not only underwater, but at high altitudes too. It was guaranteed to write for two years without refilling; it was the $12.50 "fantastic, atomic era pen" which cost 80 cents to make.

On October 29, 1945, Gimbels began selling Reynolds pens, and the response stunned the entire retail business community. The store was forced to summon fifty policemen to help restrain the crowd of five thousand who waited impatiently to get inside. It was a near riot. The promotion had worked brilliantly.

In Chicago, Reynolds was nearly overwhelmed. Only after he had received the initial Gimbels order of 2,500 had he concerned himself with production and hastily engaged a manufacturer of machine parts to turn out the components of the pen and then hired a few workers to assemble them. But they were no match for ball-point fever. Macy's, Gimbels' arch rival, wanted to sell the pens. So did everyone else. In San Francisco, a store would open that would sell nothing *but* Reynolds pens. Hundreds more workers had to be hired, including several just to count the money.

In case anyone in the nation had been asleep for the month in which his pen made headlines, Reynolds also filed suit in federal court for $1 million (treble damages) against two major pen manfacturers, Eversharp and Eberhard-Faber, for anti-trust violations. Reynolds claimed—completely unfoundedly—that the two firms had tried to prevent distribution of the Reynolds pen until they could get rid of their own "obsolete" pens (of the fountain variety) and produce a ball-point of their own. Eversharp and Eberhard-Faber quickly filed a countersuit, but neither suit came to anything, except that Reynolds got the publicity he was looking for. Though they knew all too well what Reynolds was up to, the giants could only grit their teeth and wait until their first ball-points came off the production line. They were too large, too complex to suddenly retool and get the product out much faster. Quality might suffer. There was the company name to consider, the relations with employees, the extra money that would have to be spent. A sudden move seemed too risky.

Meanwhile, Reynolds's business picked up speed. Reynolds pens were notorious leakers; no matter. They skipped; all was forgiven. They stopped writing altogether; an unfortunate problem. Hundreds of thousands were returned to the factory and Reynolds publicly announced he would replace every one, even though his company was barely able to fill the original orders.

After just six months, Reynolds had run a $26,000 investment into a profit of $1,558,608 after taxes—a fantastic, atomic achievement as these things go.

But by Christmas, 1946, a hundred manufacturers were making ball-points and the price began to plummet. Though Reynolds had made his pile, his ego was still at stake. In March he set out to break Howard Hughes's around-the-world flying record of 91 hours 14 minutes. With much hoopla, he bought a mothballed Douglas attack bomber, hired a pilot and engineer who had both flown extensively during the war, and appointed himself navigator (which, sniffed *Time* magazine, was a euphemistic way of spelling "passenger"). The plane, renamed the *Reynolds Bombshell,* worked far better than the Reynolds pen, as the press delighted in pointing out. From LaGuardia airport in New York, east across Europe, Asia, and the Pacific, the plane made the flight in 78 hours 55 minutes. The stunt cost Reynolds $175,000, but everyone, including *Time,* agreed it paid off handsomely. Ten days after Reynolds climbed out of his plane to greet a cheering crowd, advertisements in all the New York papers proclaimed the real news: "JUST ARRIVED! THE REYNOLDS BOMBSHELL PEN!" Sales boomed.

But Reynolds could not buck the realities of the marketplace forever. Inevitably, competition stiffened even further and prices continued to drop. Reynolds's last model, the Flyer, sold for 39 cents retail and cost 8 cents to make—a profit margin Reynolds felt was hardly worth bothering about. He didn't want to be in the pen business; he wanted to be in the bombshell business. He wasn't interested in managing a mature company; only the promotions really interested him anymore. But even those weren't working well now: a last attempt to stir public interest by flying across the Himalayas to find the world's highest mountain (for some reason Reynolds thought it wasn't Mt. Everest) fell totally flat. So after only three years, it was time for a divorce. Reynolds sold his company and sank from public view. Today, ball-point pens are made by the $2-billion Gillette Corporation, the $500-million Bic Corporation, and hundreds of other, smaller manufacturers who have carved out a niche with an easy-to-make commodity. There are no Milton Reynoldses in the pen business anymore.

In a way, Reynolds was lucky his run was so short: he got out before he was thrown out.

One venture capitalist, who has dealt with hundreds of entrepreneurs, tells of his problems with the ones who try to stick around:

"Most of these guys are egocentric people," he says, shaking his head. "They really don't know what *can't* be done. They've frequently attacked problems with low probabilities of success because of their egos.

"The guys I deal with have left IBM or GE because they were unhappy with the rate of progress they were making there. They *know* that on their own they could make it faster, even though all of the experience tells you that you only make it into bankruptcy faster when you're on your own. So these are the kind of people that we're dealing with. Their egos get them started, but they get to the point a few years later when their new company, if it's survived, can't afford them. They begin to get in the way of the company's orderly growth. Frequently we have to get that guy to step aside and bring in somebody with much more professional training, someone who's taken a company from, say, five to one hundred million. But the president, the entrepreneur, really doesn't want that. Oh, he probably senses other people's frustrations with his inability to get things to happen the way he wants, but he doesn't perceive himself as the problem. It's always all kinds of other things that are causing it.

"A while back, we were able to sell a guy who's running a small computer company on the idea that he needs a chief operating officer underneath him to work with his key managers. He quickly agreed to hire someone while he became chairman of the board and chief executive. So we hired a search firm to go out and find the right guy, but it's been eight months now and we haven't found anybody to do the job. When we parade people who are capable of doing the job in front of the president, it's clear that he wants someone who's at a considerably lower level in skills and responsibilities than what we have in mind. And yet he keeps insisting that he's willing to accept a chief operating officer.

"Look," says the venture capitalist, "in some cases entrepreneurs can stay on in some role and be productive. But in many cases they can't. A lot depends on their own emotions. The guy who does everything himself—buys better, sells better, negotiates the rent better, keeps the books better, does all these things better than anyone else, and consequently doesn't hire any good people and never lets go of anything—his company will reach its peak by virtue of his own span of control and personal skills, and then never go any further. That guy won't stay on and be productive.

"And since you can't just say, 'You've got to go away and

we've got to hire someone else,' you try to get someone underneath him with the management skills the company needs, even
though you know that after a year or two the entrepreneur won't
be able to stand the conflict and his own sad realization that the
company is doing better. Maybe he'll stay on as a major stockholder or a member of the board for a while, but eventually he's
gone...."

So even the successful entrepreneur's days can be numbered.
Sometimes, after a few years, the organization he created may
feel it no longer needs him. His presence may even jeopardize its
survival, for a chronic gambler is almost always a lousy manager.
He often can't leave the high-stakes table unless, humiliatingly,
he's forced to do so by his board of directors, or he has risked
everything and lost.

The entrepreneur myth may lead us to believe that American
business loves an entrepreneur, but in truth, many entrepreneurs
are best loved in the abstract.

CHAPTER EIGHT # The Anti-Business Business

In the late 1960s and early 1970s, a new type of business caught the public eye: the blue-skies–share-the-wealth-and-own-a-Porsche–anti-business business. Instead of those old, rigidly designed, "ravenous" companies of the past, these were supposed to be less formal, less standardized, less greedy, more human, and thus more attractive to all those stoned but fundamentally decent young people who had been repelled by traditional business careers.

The vast majority of these "anti-business" businesses, however, turned out to be different in style only. Employees could wear to work what they wished and call their bosses by their first names, but they were employees nonetheless: they still received a paycheck for services rendered, while their employers still determined the paycheck and the services. Though some firms had profit sharing, most did not. It was blue-skies–own-a-Porsche for the hip capitalists, who were both hip and affluent, but not for the employees, who were just hip—and usually badly paid. So when a truly *alternative*-seeming business was built, it was that much more worthy of note. Though cynics had scoffed, optimists had always maintained that an anti-business business was not a contradiction in terms.

The Real Paper, an irreverent weekly newspaper in Boston, was one of the more significant alternative business experiments of its time. It was the subject of innumerable articles in everything from the progressive weekly *The Nation,* which lauded its muckraking, to the ultraconservative magazine of the John Birch Society, which somewhat reluctantly called its reporting "superb." *The New York Times Magazine* devoted a story to the *Real Paper* phenomenon, and Hollywood produced a movie about it called *Between the Lines.* The paper even made *People* magazine. It won awards for its consumer reporting, influenced elections with its political coverage, and forced a high-level government official to resign. Its arts and entertainment writers were among the best in the country and were quickly scooped up by national magazines and television. Its alumni include a famous record producer, the university-press publisher of one of the world's great schools, numerous well-known writers and editors—and the authors of this book.

The significance of the paper, however, lay less in the individuals who began it than in its self-conscious attempt to bring the egalitarian politics of the 1960s and early 1970s into the workplace—to create a fair, equitable organization in which no one "exploited" anyone else; to prove that the anti-business business could survive—and even prosper—on the corporate battlefield.

The paper was founded in July of 1972, a few short months before Richard Nixon was elected to his second term and nearly two years before the collapse of South Vietnam. The children of the post–World War II baby boom had reached their mid-twenties. Demographically, they were becoming the nation's most important market.

The alternative press was in its prime in 1972, and the staff of one particular alternative weekly, the Cambridge *Phoenix,* was struggling not only against the conservative politics of the Silent Majority, but also against its own publisher, a Harvard M.B.A. with an inheritance, who had long been plagued by his militant staff's demands for more autonomy and unionization, and its contempt for his abilities. When he finally decided to retaliate, he sold out to his sole competitor, and his staff found itself on the street.

The *Phoenix* workers were so incensed by the sale, however, that they decided to strike out on their own and publish a new paper, *The Real Phoenix*. When they were legally enjoined from using the word *Phoenix,* they called it *The Real Paper*. It was a name hastily conceived by one staff member on his way to a televised press conference announcing the birth of the publication—and then regretted for many years after.

The first few issues were financed by cash in advance from several friendly advertisers who had patronized the *Phoenix,* and from the classified writers who, at $2 per "lonely white male," sought "lonely white females."

At first no one, including the staff, thought the paper could make it without outside investment. Prospective angels were courted, including an executive from *New York* magazine whose arrival on the Eastern Air Lines shuttle was met by a huge stack of *Real Papers* at the nearby newsstand. But impressed as he was, he deemed the workers "too independent."

And so they were. Although everyone said it was a pipe dream, within four weeks of the paper's birth a corporate structure had been set up in which each of the thirty-four founders received one hundred shares of stock. (The number of shares was, as in all companies, arbitrary; what mattered was that no one had more than anyone else.) Soon after, the positions of editor-in-chief, publisher, and advertising director were filled by staff election.

At *The Real Paper,* power was a function not of how much money you brought to the venture, but of the trust you inspired in your fellow employees. Your salary was based not only on your value to the paper but, at least in the beginning, on your individual need as well. It was to be a *just* company. Making money was necessary, to be sure, but it was secondary to "democratic management." Any managerial decision could be appealed to the publisher, then to the board of directors, and ultimately, to the stockholders, so that every stockholder would be protected from the whims of power and the enmity of an unfeeling superior.

To guarantee these protections, every regular staff member—

from the several-hours-a-week cartoonist to the publisher—was
an equal stockholder in the company, and only staff members
could be stockholders. If you left the company, you had to sell
your stock back. An employee who joined the paper after its
founding could become a stockholder after one year. Even part-
timers could become full stockholders after only eighteen
months of employment, and that meant equal voting rights for
them too.

The newspaper was not, however, meant to resemble closely
other common cooperatives: the volunteer efforts such as food
co-ops which are not intended to make any money at all; the re-
ligious organizations centered around one key individual to
whom all others renounce their wealth; the no-longer-profitable
operations (usually old factories) taken over by their workers
when the ownership decides to shut down for economic reasons,
with the capital often provided by the government in order to
protect jobs; or the collaboratives of highly paid professionals
such as lawyers or architects, in which profits and decisions are
shared only by those with equally high status.

The Real Paper had political goals, yet was not averse to profit.
It appeared likely to grow and prosper as a business. It was also
an organization, unlike law or architectural firms, in which
workers of unequal job status—from messenger to top executives—were treated equally in terms of ownership and voting
rights. It received no government aid. Though there were salary
distinctions, they were never very large. In 1972, the highest-paid
full-time employees were the editor and publisher, who each
made $175 a week. The lowest-paid full-time employees—staff
writers, the messenger, the receptionist—earned $110 a week.
Part-time salaries were prorated within this range. Everyone was
also included in the annual profit-sharing plan, which took both
salary level and length of service into account.

The Real Paper, then, was to be a profit-making institution
with political goals. It was touted by some as nothing less than a
bold new form of capitalism: "the bridge to socialism." It appeared to answer some of the age-old objections to traditional
capitalism—"unfair," "exploitive"—while providing the profit
incentive missing in socialism: a reconciliation of a "greed-

driven economy" and the Age of Aquarius, and as such the subject of a long and comprehensive case study at the Harvard Business School, now anthologized and taught throughout the country.

Yet amidst all this hoopla and high-mindedness there was one very large problem: *The Real Paper* was meant to be a "just" business; but no one on the staff was sure which—justice or business—ultimately took precedence.

Could such an unusual company actually be built and run smoothly? Or would it turn out to be a figment of thirty-four liberal imaginations?

In the beginning there was consensus. *The Real Paper* staff members, both editorial and business, worked shoulder to shoulder in a tiny basement room with no partitions, barely any office equipment, and windows that wouldn't open all the way. The heat was stifling, but everyone was feeling just fine: cheerful, excited, optimistic, ready to sacrifice. They worked long hours; ate breakfast, lunch, and dinner together; and looked very serious when the local television crews set up in the middle of the room for one of the routine interviews of the editor and publisher: "Plucky workers trying to make it on their own," "the *Phoenix* rises from its ashes" invariably ran the anchorman's copy later that night on the six-o'clock report.

They loved being plucky, throwing themselves into their work. Most were very bright, energetic, idealistic, college-educated, from middle-class backgrounds. Four were heirs to considerable sums. All were white, and two-thirds were male.

The leaders included: The Publisher—deliberate, unflappable, a bit Machiavellian, with a wry sense of humor; scion of a wealthy Midwest family, he renounced any help from home because he wanted to make it on his own. The Editor—a mercurial New Yorker, competitive, bursting with ideas, charming, infuriatingly unorganized; he knew everyone in town and wanted everyone to know him. The Associate Publisher—intense, magnetic, quick, explosive; he was the publisher's best friend and later his chief rival. The Advertising Director—supremely confident, slick, an elegant dresser; a devotee of "new consciousness" therapy, he was the "born-again salesman" of the 1970s. The Copy Editor—shy, private, reflective, extremely professional; she was trusted by everyone partly because she wasn't mercurial, supremely confident, or unflappable.

If it sounds like a soap opera, it was. Ironically, at the cooperative *Real Paper,* the individual was king, epitomizing one of the great ironies of the 1960s. For here was an experiment in sharing by a group of people whose impulses until now—from infancy through college protests—had been to a large extent indulged. This was the cosseted baby boom generation trying to buck its birthright of rampant individualism. Here were the free individuals produced by free enterprise, and what they wanted above all was to succeed as a group.

The first few months of *The Real Paper* were exciting, almost euphoric. Business was transacted professionally but informally, and many of the workers mixed socially as well. The receptionist felt free to chide the editor about a story she didn't like, and the company driver could argue with the publisher. Everyone was on a first-name basis.

With employee/stockholder equality, the work relationships among staff members were more often a product of evolution than anything else; it was all played very much by ear. Certain lines of authority were set at the very beginning, of course, but in practice they were open to informal "negotiation." If a manager wanted something done, he or she often would request, not demand; if workers felt that certain tasks were not part of their job, they would speak up. But a compromise was usually reached easily because everyone was eager to get the job done. In these early days, the welfare of the organization—"The Paper"—was paramount; no squabbling before the baby could walk.

Although all stockholders were created equal, however, some inevitably became more equal than others. The publisher had to be arbiter of business matters and the editor arbiter of editorial matters, so unless the stockholders felt compelled to step in and change policy, the day-to-day operations of the paper would be in the two managers' hands. But consensus was still sought, in those first few months, in almost everything the staff did. "I've never felt as close to the whole process of something I've worked on," said one reporter, Joe Klein (the author of *Woody Guthrie*), in an interview. "I've never been so interested in the business side, either. Everybody talks about how much like a family it is here."

The staff wanted it both ways. They wanted the security of a family without the "tyranny" of parents. Instead of a rigid, dehumanizing, stifling organization, the staff wanted a loose, creative, exciting one. They wanted total involvement, total fulfillment.

As long as the organization prospered, all was well. Though the paper was established with no capital and no means of distribution, within two months it was making a profit. Circulation was rising dramatically. Soon the staff agreed on a new, slightly more generous salary scale and a profit-sharing plan that would distribute at year's end any income not plowed back into the company (which turned out to be a considerable sum). And with an admirably conservative accounting system, the paper avoided the usual, often deadly optimism of new businesses and weathered easily the lean midwinter season. At the end of eight months its revenue had reached $462,000, with a net profit of $53,000, or 11 percent—an impressive record for any small business. Circulation was up to 30,000 paid and 20,000 free (delivered to local campuses). And the operation had moved to more spacious quarters.

Editorially, the paper had gained an enviable reputation. Several exposés had generated great public attention, and the editor of *The Boston Globe* was frequently quoted as a staunch admirer of the paper's enterprising reporters.

Years before the rest of the Boston media discovered the hidden epidemic of child abuse, Susan Quinn was writing about "Carol," a mother of four: " 'I don't like to feed babies,' Carol explains, 'because they're sloppy eaters, and so dependent.' With her first baby—a baby she didn't really want—Carol's dislike became so extreme 'I wouldn't do anything for him. I wouldn't feed him, wouldn't bathe him, wouldn't change him . . .' "

Rory O'Connor, lapsed Catholic, wrote a "Sinner's Guide to Confession: What you have to know to get the best deal on penance." St. Ambrose in Dorchester, a working-class neighborhood of Boston, received a rating of only 5: "Ten Our Fathers, ten Hail Mary's, and two days of fasting before the end of April? Bless me, Father! . . . That's the penance that I received from Father McGrath. He was an old-schooler and a prime practitioner of what is known in the show-and-tell biz as juridical morality. That is, a listing and full accounting of *all* sins in exchange for a judgment and penance based on the sheer quantity of sinning."

Harper Barnes reported from Twin Falls, Idaho:

> Most of us in the press-VIP enclosure have got it all figured out. In about forty-five minutes, after the high school band from Evel Knievel's hometown of Butte, Montana, has blasted through "Impossible Dream" and "The Star Spangled Banner," and Father Jeremiah Sullivan, Evel's fat, florid cousin, has droned through the benediction, Evel will push the button and thousands of naked, stoned, beer-crazed hippies are going to come crashing through the anchor fence separating them from us, go storming through the press enclosure, sweeping all of us before them, trample down the other anchor fence near the rim of the canyon, and Tom Fitzpatrick of the Chicago *Sun-Times*, Joe Eszterhas of *Rolling Stone,* Bill Cardoso of *New Times,* Leo Janess of *Time* magazine, Lucian Truscott of the *Village Voice,* my wife, me, all of us, are going to plunge to our deaths on the rocky ledges 600 feet below. As we fall, we will pass Evel floating down slowly on his parachute. He will smile and give us the finger.

The paper's advertising policy also received much favorable comment. There would be no ads demeaning women or promoting tourism to totalitarian countries or pushing unhealthful cigarettes. The staff voted overwhelmingly to reject a $14,000-a-year Portuguese wine ad contract when the controller, a white South African émigré, decried Portuguese colonialism in Africa.

But most important, relations among staff members had never been closer. There was a great feeling of *involvement*—in the paper, in one another's lives.

It was a terrible problem.

Because the structure so depended on this interdependence of individuals, crisis was only as far away as the first interpersonal break. And it came in the spring of 1973 when the common enemy—failure—had been vanquished and all the staff members had to do was get along. Suddenly the associate publisher's wife moved in with his close friend and inseparable business colleague, the publisher. The organization reeled; the "family" was stunned. Why, the three of them had been so close and had spent so much of their free time together! The publisher and the associate publisher's close relationship was one of the reasons they had been voted into their respective positions. The two men were at the center of the organization. Why, they depended on each other, and everyone depended on them. The woman was friends with many staff members. Many were friends with her and with both the men. Everyone was a close friend of somebody who was now an instant enemy of somebody else. It was a god-awful mess.

There were long, anguished lunches among friends of the trio: what to do? how to bring them together? how to keep them apart so they wouldn't kill each other?

The two men did not speak. They communicated by memo if at all. The atmosphere became feverish. One day the office was paralyzed when the associate publisher stole/took back his ex-wife's dog/his dog from the publisher's house. There were rumors: the associate publisher would destroy the dog rather than see it in the clutches of his ex-wife and her new lover; the publisher would take six friends and storm the associate publisher's apartment to retrieve the pet; the two men would fight it out and the loser would leave town.

In traditionally structured organizations, the problem, disruptive as it was, would not have lasted long. The associate publisher would have been forced out by the publisher because of the latter's superior position. Or the associate publisher would have left of his own volition, convinced of the hopelessness of the situation. But this was an egalitarian institution, and as such, not set up to resolve conflicts swiftly.

The associate publisher would not leave. Neither would the

publisher. The publisher did not feel he could fire the associate publisher, even though the animosity between them was tearing the paper apart, because the organization had made the firing of a stockholder extremely difficult and traumatic. You do not fire a "brother" or "sister" or equal shareholder.

In the early days, when peace reigned, it had been assumed that no one would *have* to be fired. It was protection from arbitrary dismissal that the staffers felt they needed just in case any manager became power-hungry. A simple precaution. Why form an alternative business only to be faced with the same insecurity and powerlessness of other workers? So it had been agreed that any firing could be appealed to the board of directors and if they did not overrule it, to the stockholders, among whom a simple majority would rule. Then everybody had forgotten all about it. Until now. But the publisher was afraid of losing that stockholders' vote and made no move against the associate publisher.

The Real Paper wasn't the first organization in history to split over a romance, of course, nor was it the first to botch the ensuing crisis, but it did suffer more than most because the incident set into motion the internecine struggles that an egalitarian organization cannot withstand if it does not resolve them at once.

Slowly the organization began to split into three camps: the publisher loyalists (including the editor, the advertising director, and the controller); the associate-publisher loyalists (mostly disaffected members of the editorial staff); and the unaligned, the largest group (most of the clerks, secretaries, salespeople, advertising artists), who could support one side and then the other.

This three-group configuration created grave problems. The first group, mostly managers (including the authors of this book), held the "power of position," but because they could not necessarily command a majority in a stockholders' vote, felt inhibited from making broad decisions for fear of precipitating an even greater crisis and a vote of no confidence. They became resentful that this should be so, and their resentment was then felt by their subordinates, who were wary of management in general and any attempt to seize power from the stockholders in particular. Eventually the managers' resentment was seen by many as arrogance, contempt for the staff as a whole, and even contempt for the organization's alternative structure. And as it became harder and harder to get things done because of the fear of appearing too autocratic, the managers became more disaffected from the idea of participatory democracy.

The second group was the smallest but the most vocal. Sharing an increasingly low opinion of top management's competence and objectives, the second group began to snipe constantly at the other's decisions, as well as the performance and attitudes of the publisher. Although they could not force policy changes, the members of the second group could inhibit them, and as far as the first group was concerned, inhibit them they did. Intergroup meetings became long-drawn-out affairs with great personal hostility, limited communication, and little possibility for consensus. The organization which was designed to run by consensus had become very sick.

The delicate balance between group mentality and personal expression tilted in favor of raving individualism. Everyone was self-absorbed; everyone expressed whatever dissatisfaction, however minor, he or she felt at the moment. It was a nightmare of self-expression.

And though everyone was upset by the constant bickering, no one would consider leaving the company. To leave voluntarily would mean surrendering one's stock for its book value—whatever cash and salable assets, like furniture, the paper had on hand divided by the total number of shares. The book value of each stockholder's holdings was at best worth a few hundred dollars. But the paper was now worth hundreds of thousands on the open market. The profit-sharing plan alone promised to net each stockholder several thousand dollars a year. And if the paper was sold one day it could mean tens of thousands.

The staff members seemed trapped by their own success. The bickering intensified.

The crisis brought to the surface a thousand latent conflicts, the most significant of which concerned the editorial direction of the paper. The market was beginning to change, but the paper was not. As the war in Vietnam wound down, the paper's readers became less interested in politics and cultural satire, and more in what was termed "life-style." The readers' income was rising and their tastes changing, but the paper's advertising base had remained the same: stereo equipment, records, and concerts—the youth market.

How would the paper respond? By seeking a younger, basically apolitical readership in order to keep and expand the same ad base, as the advertising director wanted? By following the original readership into a more affluent world and adding some "sex" to the usual political fare to attract a wider base, as the publisher wanted? Or by clinging to the 1960s tone of the paper in an attempt to convert new readers with reporting and writing, as the editor insisted?

Such conflicts are present in all publications, but here the situation was extremely difficult because the political commitment of the staff had been responsible not only for the paper's existence, but also for its first success. To abandon such an editorial slant now was tantamount to abandoning the paper's original principles and its only successful formula to date.

Often the editors felt compelled to print articles that they found tedious but worthy, such as an interminable, and inconclusive, three-part series about the mysterious death of a black man in a police holding cell. They also felt compelled to run the story on the cover, sensitive to criticisms that they had neglected the black community. But the readership of the paper was virtually all-white, and the issue that featured the first part of the series set a record for lowest sales.

The market brought other pressures. The carefully constructed equitable salary scale was becoming a great irritant. The top executives were painfully aware that they were being paid much less than people with comparable jobs outside. (In fact, the salaries of some executives doubled or tripled when they left.) As they grew older the executives seemed less willing to substitute "intangible" rewards for hard cash. Some of them threatened to leave if they did not receive sizable raises.

But none of this was as destructive to staff morale as the intense pressure put on them by the very nature of their cooperative organization. Since no one could agree as to how the paper should respond to the changing market—and no one had the power to decide for the others—*everyone* became alienated.

Consider a typical editorial meeting. The editor would begin by reluctantly asking for comments about the previous week's issue. The "anti-editor" writers would immediately criticize several stories the editor was either particularly proud of or defensive about. He would argue or stare stonily ahead as the criticisms continued: Why did we do this story about life in a carnival? someone would ask. Why can't we do more hard political stories like the one X (an anti-editor writer) did three weeks ago? Another anti-editor writer then would take the opposite tack and criticize the paper as too political. It was never "just right."

Let's talk about the managing editor, someone who disliked him would say. He's butchering my copy, turning it all into *Time*-ese.

I'm making it barely literate, that's all, the managing editor would growl.

This should be a writer's paper, not an editor's paper, a writer would say.

But what if the writer can't write? the managing editor would respond.

Meanwhile, downstairs in the advertising department, the salespeople were grousing about the editor's inability to keep his writers in line. My God, did you read what they wrote about our top advertiser? That's going to cost us big bucks, damn it. And why is there so much politics in the paper anyway? How about some more life-style pieces? How about some sexy circulation builders for once?

Finally the editor felt he had to do something to retain control. He fired a columnist—a stockholder—who had begun as a chronicler of community events but evolved into a self-styled poet. Of free verse, no less, frequently about American Indians. The columnist, who had a devoted following, often refused to write prose or to write about the local community ("The world is my community," he said). To the managing editor he was a symbol of unprofessionalism and self-indulgence; to a core of readers he was an oracle; to the editor he was a pain-in-the-ass.

The reaction to the firing was immediate—a perfect illustration of how irreconcilably split the organization had become. Although few staffers thought the columnist's work was beneficial to the paper, and most people had complained about him to the editor, his firing still caused a furor. It was a power grab, some said; a ruthless act. It was about time, others said; time to start cleaning house and get *serious.*

It was just like a rotten, heartless business, said some.

It was just like a good, sensible business—finally, said others.

The columnist went to every board member for support in preparation for his appeal. But the board, chiefly managers, would not overrule the editor's decision (the editor being a fellow board member and the columnist being a person who wrote free verse and walked in the snow in sandals).

So the columnist called a stockholders' meeting and went to every staff member to ask for support. A simple majority could win him back his job. He looked every person in the eyes with a soulful, spiritual look and declared that not only was his job at stake but also the very principles upon which the paper was built.

The anti-editor faction, the anti-publisher faction (which was the pro-associate-publisher faction grown larger over time), and every other faction (there were quite a few now) saw the crisis as a perfect opportunity to humble *someone.* Everyone saw the paper as *his* or *her* paper, in danger of being taken over by *them.*

The meeting began at 6 P.M. The tension was thick. The writer had invited several acquaintances to deliver testimonials in his behalf and they did so, rather self-consciously, imploring the staff to remember the columnist's idealism, sincerity, and dedication to good works which were, in fact, indisputable. Then they beat a hasty retreat.

The editor took the floor next and outlined the reasons for his decision: the long struggle over what he felt was the declining quality of the column, its bizarre and inaccessible style, the missed deadlines. "We asked him to be less self-absorbed, to stop using the word 'I' in his column so much," the editor explained. "So now he uses 'eye'—E-Y-E—instead."

The editor had decided the night before that a calm, reasoning tone would be most effective, and spoke without inflection, keeping his eyes on a spot two feet above the top of a file cabinet directly across the room. It worked until several stockholders

rose to question him and he found his voice rising several deci-
bels a second.

Didn't you have it in for the columnist because of his anti-authoritarian stance? one asked.

No, of course not, said the editor.

Wasn't it because you wanted to move the paper away from
political coverage to more arts and entertainment?

Ridiculous.

Oh, yeah? Then what about the time you said to X that he
shouldn't—

Wait a minute, that's not—

He was doing the best he could! How can you fire a stockholder who is doing his best?

Because his best is—

If they can fire him, why not me? Why not you?

Are you crazy? All I'm doing is—

Hey, I may not like the column either, but that doesn't mean
that—

The pro-editor forces decided to jump in. The managing editor
called one reporter an idiot. See! said one of the critics. That's
what they think of us. The managing editor snorted contemp-
tuously. (He was not known for his self-control.)

Both sides glowered at each other, then burst into angry debate again. Finally the columnist rose from the floor, where he
had been sitting Indian-style and smoking a long peace pipe. He
began speaking of the importance of the paper and its workers to
his life. His eyes traveled around the room as he recounted the
early days of the newspaper, by then eighteen months distant,
when harmony had reigned and the commitment of its staff to
the downtrodden had seemed clear. What had happened, he
asked, in the interim? Why was he now being fired for writing his
conscience, communicating to the world the anguish he felt for
the American Indian or the South Vietnamese or the—

The editor broke in. That was not the point, he said. No one
wished to ignore those people. It was just a matter of writing
about them in the appropriate place—not a community column—and appropriate style—not free verse.

The columnist shook his head. The editor did not understand the pain he, the columnist, felt. The world was in pain.

A number of stockholders exchanged glances. Pain? What the hell was he talking about?

The columnist caught one of the glances in transit and tried to make the most of it. He walked over to a neutral stockholder, held her hands in his, and looked deep into her eyes. She blanched and looked away. "Do you know how much you and everyone else here means to me?" he asked her. She mumbled, "Well, I . . ." He smiled beatifically and dropped her hands.

Holding the peace pipe in front of him, he then proceeded to travel from stockholder to stockholder, offering the pipe and delivering a short, deeply felt greeting to each until everyone was ill at ease—except, of course, the columnist, who, carried away by the ritual, seemed ready to drift into a trance. Instead he abruptly sat back down in a corner and waited for the proceedings to continue.

A stockholder quickly moved to cut off debate—anything to get out of there—and his motion was seconded. The vote whether to vote or not passed by a small margin, and the controller began to hand out pieces of scrap paper for a secret ballot. As he walked around the room, the associate publisher's faction caucused in one corner, and the editor and publisher in another. Everyone else milled about, predicting a close vote.

Ten minutes later there was a stunned silence. The vote was two for the columnist (including himself, presumably) and everyone else for firing him. The message was clear: even on an issue of virtual consensus, the organization was consumed by mistrust. And so that very night, a few hours later, the first murmurings of "Let's sell the damn thing and be done with it" were heard in various neighborhood bars.

When the next financial statement was completed, sales were above $1 million, but net income after taxes was only $75,000, or 7.5 percent. Circulation was stagnant. The market had split into two groups: the younger readers who had just discovered the paper and the older readers. But the younger readers did not have the same tastes as the editorial staff and clamored for more college- and rock-'n'-roll-oriented stories. The older readers were becoming more "upscale," and interested in college- and rock-'n'-roll-oriented stories not at all. They wanted a slicker publication that better reflected their interests: home furnishings, gourmet restaurants, sophisticated gossip, fashionable clothes, entertainment. The image of the paper was all wrong for them. It was tabloid size, newsprint, not glossy stock. Its ads proclaimed new bargains in stereo amplifiers, not men's suits.

The Boston Globe then attacked on the right flank, adding to its Thursday issue a free entertainment supplement with listings for movies, theaters, restaurants, and concerts. On the left flank came competition from national magazines and dailies, all eager to do investigative reporting and liberal muckraking. Why read about Watergate in *The Real Paper* when you could read about it in *The Washington Post* and *The New York Times*?

The Real Paper advertisers soon began to ask the sales staff why the paper couldn't make up its mind who its audience was. The youth-market advertisers were dissatisfied with the paper's politics; the "upscale" advertisers were not interested in a paper with so much rock-music criticism and articles about radical lesbians and personal classifieds with explicit messages.

To reconstitute its objectives and restyle its approach, the paper's staff would have needed a new burst of energy comparable to the one that had launched them into the business. But instead, the organization was spending all its energy on itself.

The main topics of conversation at the office were: (1) the editor's sudden resignation (exhausted, sick of fighting, he would become a reporter; no one actually left the paper, you understand—not as long as the stock might be valuable); (2) the publisher's purchase, with his own money, of the paper's printer (conflict of interest, shouted his critics; a valiant effort to keep the ailing printing company alive and secure good terms for the paper, insisted his allies); (3) the selection of a new editor (a predictably messy, bitter and endless affair). But withal, a consensus finally began to emerge. There was a growing sentiment for selling out. Perhaps the only way to deal with their own Gordian knot was to foist it upon some foolish, rich rope fancier. Perhaps what was needed was hierarchy, clean lines of command, peace and quiet, after all. Get out with some money before the paper fell apart; file the divorce papers—irreconcilable differences.

In April, 1975, *The Real Paper* was sold, by two-thirds vote, to a group of liberal Republicans that included David Rockefeller, Jr., son of the Chase Manhattan Bank chairman, great grandson of John D. Rockefeller. They inherited a staff used to stymying initiatives from the top. They lost most of their best writers. They were faced with a market in dramatic transition.

In 1976 they produced a brochure for advertisers that was headlined, "THEY DON'T THROW ROCKS ANYMORE." On the cover was a photo of student demonstrators breaking windows in Harvard Square during the Harvard student strike in 1969. The next page had a photo of a couple in their mid-twenties, lounging on an expensive couch and playing backgammon as their cat looked on. At their feet, a copy of *The Real Paper* and a volume of Robert Frost's poetry. The headline on this page read: "BUT THEY'RE STILL DOING THINGS THEIR WAY."

For six years the new ownership tried to straddle the two markets, but for lack of vision, an unwillingness to invest more capital, or the heartlessness of a dwindling market, they failed to rejuvenate the paper. The new staff, conscious of their paper's cooperative heritage, formed a militant union, further complicating the problems of management.

In November, 1980, *The Wall Street Journal* wrote: "Boston's famous Real Paper lambastes the Establishment and runs personal ads. . . . But it also recommends the poached pears and strawberries Romanoff at the Ritz-Carlton Hotel."

Ironically, where the original staff of the paper had come to realize that it was impossible to straddle two such completely different markets (but could not decide how to change), the later staff and owners never grasped the futility of their efforts until the end.

On Friday, June 12, 1981, the paper closed its doors after nearly ten years of publication. It was heavily in debt and losing thousands of dollars more each month.

But our story really ends in 1975, when the paper ceased to be a significant business experiment. At that time, the one question all observers asked was "Why?" Why did we sell it? Why did the experiment fail?

There were a number of theories. One—the "Tower of Babel Theory"—suggested that it was the unremittingly anti-authoritarian character of the stockholders which had doomed the paper. Another theory suggested that the reason for failure was precisely the opposite: the authoritarian character of some of the key stockholders who had never been really comfortable with sharing power. A third theory—the "Helen of Troy" one—pointed to the triangle between the publisher, associate publisher, and associate publisher's wife: it had stunted the organization at an early age. Then there were those who felt that people are just not taught how to function cooperatively in this economy, and hence their inadequate ability to compete against traditional businesses. A *Harvard Crimson* reporter called this the "Collectivist-Ship-Awash-in-a-Capitalist-Sea Theory."

Finally there was the notion, based on organizational theory, that collectives will not work well (or at all) in a business environment because of their very nature. It's not that they're impossible; it's just that they are exposed to too many dangers normal businesses are not.

According to organizational theory, the paper was clearly meant to operate under an implicit "cooperative compact" with shared responsibilities and power. But certain positions afforded more power simply because of their larger scope—because managers had to be allowed to manage. So as a trade-off, managers would be restricted to managing day-to-day operations and any decisions that affected the safety of the paper as a whole or the job security of any individual stockholder would be dealt with by everyone.

Thus there were two kinds of power: the managers' "power of position" and the stockholders' power. But if everything went smoothly the managers would manage and the stockholders' power would stay dormant. How could the secretary, clerk, or writer who had no power of position share regularly in decision-making if the stockholders' power stayed dormant? Only seven stockholders could be on the board of directors, and at least three of those were invariably managers. So the managers would manage and the stockholders would be managed—just as in any traditional business. How could a clerk feel truly equal in a place like that?

The employees with little or no day-to-day power became resentful. The goals upon which the paper had been founded—that all employees be content and secure—were no longer the same as the goals of the managers: that the organization be profitably and efficiently run. To secure their contentment and security, many employees wanted more power. To secure prosperity and efficiency, the experienced managers wanted to keep the power they had.

But the managers also felt that relying too heavily on rules and procedures when dealing with subordinates might only accentuate the already obvious differences in power, so they tried instead to exercise power solely on the basis of their popularity and acknowledged expertise. Unfortunately, however, the managers' popularity, which had gotten them elected to their posts in the first place, had waned considerably since they had ceased to be "one of the gang," and their expertise, insofar as they had any, began to rankle instead of comfort when their subordinates felt cut off from higher positions where new skills could be learned and expertise increased. The problem was compounded because no one ever left the paper, and new positions depended on growth alone in a market that was now stagnant.

The managers, in turn, felt dragged down by the organizational structure. Did they have power or not? Were they responsible or not? The paper ran best in the beginning, when it was possible to couch orders in the language of persuasion because it was not necessary to do so. But once they felt they actually *had* to persuade, it became very difficult for them to disguise their resentment. "Why don't we do this?" worked only as long as "we" assumed that the answer would always be yes. When that assurance faded, it became "Why don't *you* do this?"

At this stage the staff members in subordinate positions turned to the only kind of power available to them: "negative power"— the power to disrupt. If these subordinates could not decide what kind of stories to put in the paper or which lawyer to hire or which staff member to put in which office, at least they could make it harder for the managers to make those decisions.

And what do you do with such "malcontents"? If you can't neutralize them because their number is too large and they won't leave, you might try to force them out. But in a cooperative organization that's nearly impossible. Firing people destroys the very principles of the organization. Cooperation demands persuasion, not naked force.

And if persuasion becomes impossible because there is too much mistrust?

You fall apart.

Organizational theory may be the best analytic tool we have for explaining *The Real Paper*, but it isn't the only one. An economic analysis is needed to finish the picture.

People worked at *The Real Paper* for a variety of reasons. Some just wanted security. Others wanted to run a successful business. Still others wanted a sense of excitement and action. Some just wanted to *share*; they liked the idea of it. But everyone agreed upon one thing: no one wanted to feel like just another cog in the machine; everyone wanted an organization that was truly responsive to the individual.

Businesses, however, must be truly responsive to their economic environment. They must adapt to changing markets. They must be flexible, willing to abandon old ways of doing business when new, more profitable ways present themselves. Cooperatives, because of their heavy reliance on consensus, are inherently less flexible.

Still, there are thousands of cooperatives flourishing in the United States today. They range from a major metropolitan daily newspaper to small local food co-ops. But those which have prospered have learned a lesson that *The Real Paper* staffers did not: You can have a collaborative, you can have a traditional business, you can have any business you like as long as you remember what businesses are for: to make money. Security, fulfillment, righteousness, excitement, they're all possible, but secondary when times get tough. The individual is secondary. The organization comes first. Everyone in a business is replaceable in a time of crisis.

The Real Paper just forgot it was a company. Or never realized the implications of being one in the first place. It believed a myth and ignored the truth: anything that threatens a company's smooth operation, anything that exposes it unnecessarily to dangers that will reduce its competitiveness on the corporate battlefield is to be avoided.

A truly successful anti-business business is as likely as an anti-politics politician. That is, not very.

CHAPTER NINE

The
Intelligence Community

If business is as complex, tough, and uncertain as it plainly is, one would expect to find a considerable demand for experts who, for a price, could advise investors and companies on the significance of events taking place on the corporate battlefield. These experts—investment analysts and stockbrokers in particular—could then look behind the bottom line and judge the true health and prospects of each corporate combatant. They would be expected to know which companies will win and which will lose in the battles ahead.

That, at least, is what the members of the investment community are supposed to know. That is what they say they know. And that is what many people believe they know—and they invest accordingly. But how prescient are the professionals? Can they really tell the winners from the losers *before* the fight? Or is there so much smoke and confusion on the corporate battlefield that even the most handsomely paid observers spend the majority of their time hopelessly lost?

Dean LeBaron subscribes to the smoke-and-confusion hypothesis. One of the fastest growing pools of investment capital in the United States is under his control, and yet he represents a genuine threat to investment orthodoxy. In 1972, his firm, Batterymarch, managed $34 million in investments. By 1982, it managed more than $6 billion.

LeBaron states his position clearly. If some of the experts' stock-investment strategies *are* better than others', people with the greatest expertise should be able to consistently discern what they are. Yet all evidence suggests that they cannot.

Nowhere are there higher-paid, more prestigious, or more numerous experts than in the stock market, so one would expect the stock market to be the investment arena in which the experts truly excel. For years, Dean LeBaron himself was one of these experts: the director of research at F. S. Moseley, a brokerage house on the New York Stock Exchange. He went on to become vice-president and manager of one of the country's largest mutual funds, Keystone Custodian Growth. He was a great success.

But Dean LeBaron has a button he keeps on his desk. It reads: "DON'T CONFUSE BRAINS WITH A BULL MARKET."

Though his smile is understated, LeBaron is as blunt as the message on his button. He has been one of the most successful —and revered—proponents of "Random Walk," a by now thoroughly documented description of the stock market which states that stock prices move *randomly*. Therefore, no one can systematically predict them. But what are 30,000 stockbrokers passing along the advice of thousands of financial analysts doing if not providing some edge, some insight into the future of certain investments?

Earning commissions, says LeBaron.

"The investment world is loaded with myths," he declares. "The myth that earnings forecasts can be made. The myth that you can make forecasts about the economy as a whole. They're totally unsupported by independent studies. And yet almost all the activity of institutional investors [the giant mutual, pension, and corporate funds] and retail investors [the rest of us] is oriented around this activity. There are 25,000 members of the financial analyst community all rushing around trying to forecast earnings, yet if you pick up any kind of dispassionate study, it says they can't do it. You know, analysts can't even identify the difference between randomly generated numbers and sets of real numbers—of earnings per share, sales growth, dividends, and all the other key data of the trade.

"Some time ago, in the *Financial Managers Journal,* they took a series of analysts and gave them two sets of numbers, representing the sales growth, earnings per share, dividend growth, and so on of different companies. They told them that one set of numbers was real, the other randomly generated by a computer, and asked them which was which. *The analysts couldn't do it.*"

If you think about it, this is an astounding fact. Is there any baseball fan who, when confronted with, say, Pete Rose's career statistics—his batting average, home runs, and R.B.I.s—and an imaginary player's statistics composed of *completely* random numbers, could not tell them apart? And yet even the most self-confident baseball experts would be loath to predict *next year's* statistics for a given player.

Not financial analysts. They're happy to predict, happy to ask other people—us—to bet on their predictions. Amazingly, we do bet. And to make matters worse, we pay a brokerage commission on every bet we make, thus subsidizing the analysts.

Even if you don't have a dime in the stock market, you bet. If you have a municipal or company pension plan, your pension fund's money is invested in the stock market. In fact, pension funds are the biggest stock market players in the world. As of 1980, pension money controlled about one-fourth of the stock in all U.S. companies.

If you have insurance of any kind, you also are "playing the market," since much of your money may be reinvested by the insurance company in stock.

All these pools of capital are "managed"—that is, invested—according to the prognostications of financial analysts. Yet on average, financial analysts' stock predictions over the long term have been no better than had they played the market randomly. Corroborating evidence is plentiful. The most graphic form is the dart-board portfolio.

In the 1960s, the great economist Paul Samuelson testified before the U.S. Senate that mutual funds perform no better than random portfolios. He then promptly papered a wall with a listing of all 1,200 companies listed on the New York Stock Exchange and selected his portfolio by throwing darts at the list. Over the next decade, his random portfolio outperformed the average mutual fund; it even outperformed those funds dedicated to reducing risk and maximizing long-term capital appreciation.

Several years later, the top brass of *Forbes* magazine pasted the *New York Times* stock pages to the wall, also made ten stock selections by throwing darts, and invested $1,000 in each. A decade later their portfolio had outperformed most of the world's money managers. Yet to this day, *Forbes* continues to publish various investment columns and advice.

In 1981, the New York *Daily News* pitted five prominent brokers against a dart-board portfolio; four of the five brokers trailed the market in performance. The dart board equaled the market return and finished second in the competition.

Clearly, there are some money managers who, for any given period, have beaten the odds and outperformed not only their fellows, but the market itself. Are these analysts, then, the subspecies on whose advice one can become rich?

No. Consider this: If each of the country's 25,000 analysts picks 14 stocks and each stock has a 50–50 chance of going up or down, the law of statistics says that one of them will pick 14 consecutive winners. (That is, there's a 1-in-2 chance of picking one winner, and a 1-in-4 chance of picking two, and so on, up to a 1-in-25,000 chance of picking all 14. Since there are 25,000 analysts, a 1-in-25,000 event is expected to occur once.)

Now, if *you* followed the analyst who picked 14 out of 14, you might think you had discovered a genius. You would invest your money, tell your friends. Soon *Institutional Investor* would do a feature. Then *Money* magazine. There would be but one hitch: the odds of your analyst's repeating the feat are . . . 1 in 25,000.

In 1967, Dean LeBaron, with an enviable reputation as a top analyst, was given full responsibility for picking the portfolio of one of the country's most glamorous mutual funds, the $500-million Keystone Custodian Growth Fund, which invested in the so-called "high flyers"—the risky, speculative companies of the go-go years.

"I was trying to figure out how to do it," explains LeBaron, "and I sat down and said to myself, 'This is really pretty silly. I don't know anything. Maybe my record so far is just a function of luck.' So I decided to prepare for the job by taking six weeks off to ask a variety of people how I had done up until now. From my Wall Street sources I got the usual stuff: how brilliant my investment ideas were.

"But my academic friends said something different. They said my success was all random chance. That was disturbing, because if it was true, I was in trouble. Fifty percent of the time I would succeed, but it could well be that what lay ahead was the *other* fifty percent of the time, in which I wouldn't look so good. I was very discouraged. I realized that my brilliant investment ideas were nothing more than buying one stock, selling another stock (when almost all stocks were going up), and in the process generating commissions. I realized that that was the principal value of what I had been doing for seven years."

The academics convinced LeBaron with a simple argument: If, as institutional investors, he and his competitors managed most of the money in the market, then they *were* the market. If most of them were very smart and very well informed, they would quickly spot any over- or undervalued stocks, and correct the price by buying or selling. Thus the market was accurate, or "efficient," and success was likely to be a function of chance.

LeBaron began to feel that if there wasn't a better—or different—way of managing pools of money, then he would do something else. He didn't want to play a random exercise with his career.

In 1969, LeBaron left Keystone and with several associates formed Batterymarch Financial Management. Their major pitch was that the competition—the managed pools of money, whether mutual funds, trust funds, or pension funds—performed less well than the stock market as a whole, as measured by the average of 500 stocks tabulated by Standard and Poor's, the S&P 500. (The Dow Jones industrials, a small, unrepresentative sample of thirty older, larger companies, has, in the past decades, *underperformed* the S&P 500.)

LeBaron and company were betting that this trend would continue. After several years of thought and experimentation, they devised an investment strategy with the sole purpose of *matching* the performance of the stock market as a whole. It was called an "index" fund, and was made up of 250 stocks which closely approximated the behavior of the 500 tracked by Standard & Poor's.

"Doesn't this mean you will have virtually no chance of doing better than the market?" queries a hypothetical skeptic in a Batterymarch sales brochure explaining the index fund.

"Yes," the brochure replies, "and virtually none of doing worse either."

"But what is the point of matching the S&P? Surely investors should aim for superior, not average, results," asks the "skeptical investor."

"Study after study has shown that S&P results *are* superior results, somewhat above the average return on professionally managed money," Batterymarch answers.

True to its promise, Batterymarch created a fund which aped the performance of the S&P almost perfectly. Meanwhile, the money managers, as predicted, underperformed the S&P in every single year since 1969, when fund performance was first aggregated. Thus LeBaron beat the competition by doing nothing. The key to his operational strategy was that doing nothing costs less.

While other managers were analyzing, selling, buying, worrying, and paying out a small but noticeable chunk of the money in commissions, Batterymarch created a computer program to pick the stocks, assembled the portfolio, and then, more or less, sat on it. That meant far fewer commissions. But even on the commissions he did pay, LeBaron beat the competition. Since his strategy in no way depended on secrecy, he simply posted all the trades he wanted to make on the Batterymarch computer, offering notably low commission prices, and tied the computer to a phone number disseminated among all the major brokerage houses. Thus when a broker needed a piece of cheap, but still profitable, business, he or she had only to call Batterymarch and accept one of its trades. The normal commission on trades of LeBaron's size is much larger than LeBaron typically is willing to pay. Yet he has never had a trade linger more than a day. And since market timing is unimportant to him, he doesn't care about more immediate results.

"What we have done," he says, "is to mechanically cut into much of what is considered to be professional investment activity—having it done by machine, leaving a nub of judgment but trying to take the labor out of this process and not spend time on things over which essentially we have no control. That does appear to work rather well."

Interestingly, he appears to have no imitators, despite the fact that his business is successful. It may be that psychic factors are very important here. LeBaron says his competitors often come to see his operation; after he shows them around, they invariably leave shaking their heads and go back to their market forecasts. Batterymarch, it seems, has a similar effect to that of pop art, in which anything can be art, depending on how you look at it, and anyone can be an artist. Once the ego is removed from the process, which is what Batterymarch has done, there's no need for the analyst-as-artist.

LeBaron points out also that the investment industry, like other industries in the past, has "obsolete plant." If a steel company, say, has an obsolete mill, the company finds it very hard to abandon it. Brokerage houses are filled with analysts whose job it is to visit companies and forecast earnings and talk about stocks. The firms are set up that way, and as long as there is sufficient client money available to support them, there is no incentive to cut back.

LeBaron is so convinced that analysts by and large do not know what they're doing that he manages the money of clients who don't want to index with a strategy of always playing *against* the analysts.

In the middle 1970s, LeBaron saw that the institutional analysts—those who worked for banks, pension funds, insurance companies, universities, and foundations—controlled such huge funds of capital ($1 billion was a small amount) that they could afford to invest only in companies of one size: huge. Otherwise, an investment by, say, a teachers' pension fund in a small company would mean for all practical purposes the purchase of that company. Buying companies outright is not the way to diversify a stock portfolio and minimize risk.

LeBaron saw that the big players in the market were thus inexorably drawn to overinvesting in big companies and underinvesting in smaller ones. He put a series of numbers through his computer and, with his associates, came up with a bland formula for placing a value on a company. It was nothing new, nothing special, and it wouldn't have made him any money, were it not for the fact that a great many smaller companies seemed to be selling at a significant discount from their "true" price. So LeBaron based a portfolio on such stocks. Many were traded on the American Stock Exchange, as opposed to the better-known New York Stock Exchange. The Amex companies were smaller; the institutional analysts and the money that followed them were stuck with the NYSE.

LeBaron made money, but only for a few years. As soon as his theory—called the "two-tier market theory"—was generally accepted, it no longer worked. Institutions started breaking off chunks of their money and investing it in Amex companies. LeBaron's edge was gone.

So what would he do as his encore for the 1980s?

"We've been valuing companies by replacement costs," says LeBaron proudly, referring to the current cost of replacing a company's buildings, machines, and inventory. "Valuing companies that way runs counter to everything the institutional investors are doing at the moment. It has caused us to buy things like steel stocks and rubber stocks—companies with lots of physical assets and no earnings—which are not considered terribly attractive by the institutions. It has given us a portfolio which satisfies our desire to be different. We tested that assumption by showing the portfolio to our friends at the institutions. And they said 'Ugh.' That really appealed to us. And when our clients started criticizing us for buying these stocks, it reinforced our notion. We felt we were being sufficiently contrary."

"Contrarianism" is the name given to against-the-grain investing. It is a theory with several prominent adherents besides LeBaron and Batterymarch, but it is easier to theorize about than to apply with other people's money. LeBaron has been unable, for example, to implement the ultimate contrary portfolio: bankrupt, or nearly bankrupt, companies. Batterymarch invests money for institutions, and no institutional investor likes to own a potentially bankrupt company, even though the future rate of return may be very attractive. This reluctance may be a mistake. It is very hard these days for a large company to go bankrupt. Chrysler has tried very hard, but it has yet to succeed. And even bankruptcy itself may not be so bad. Penn Central went bankrupt and yet emerged a very powerful real estate company.

Bankrupt or nearly bankrupt companies are labeled by institutional investors "imprudent holdings"; but often, says LeBaron, the financial returns are attractive simply because it's not popular to have such things in your portfolio when you have to go to committee meetings and someone says, "Why the hell do we own that dog?" It just doesn't seem worth it. But that's exactly why you do want them: because no one else does. They're underpriced.

Why doesn't Batterymarch have a portfolio like this yet? Because, explains LeBaron, "whenever I talk with clients about it, they all say, 'That's very interesting, but don't do it with my money.' "

LeBaron says that one of these days he may yet get to institute his bankruptcy fund. But even if he does, it's bound to work only as long as the rest of the herd ignores it. Which will not be forever. Then LeBaron will be faced with a new quest for a workable short-term strategy. And even then he won't be guaranteed success. In the random walk, the herd is bound to be right sometimes.

"LeBaron knows what he's talking about," says "Tim Carter," a former analyst who now runs investor relations for one of the country's glamour computer stocks. (The stock's price increased ninefold in his first three years of dealing with the investment community.)

"Why do the standard analysts have results no better than random? Because they're all peas out of the same pod," he says.

Carter, whose name has been changed at his request, characterizes most Wall Street analysts as Ivy League graduates who got their M.B.A.s from Harvard and who have never held a job in an industrial corporation. They have become so accustomed to listening to corporate spokespeople, and so accustomed to talking to fellow analysts about what the corporate spokespeople are saying, that they have developed almost no independent sources of information.

On the other hand, if they *have* developed them, they could be headed for trouble.

"It's preposterous," says Carter. "When I was an analyst, what was I selling to the clients of my brokerage house? My ability to project earnings, to figure out the profits a company will make in the next few months or years. How was I supposed to do it? By understanding the company in all its intricate detail; to do what a good investigative reporter does, and get the inside story.

"A problem," says Carter. "An insoluble problem. I was not *allowed* to have the inside story. If I tripped over it, if an important piece of company data was foisted on me, if a confidential memo was sent to my home by mistake—if I came across *any* significant information that the public didn't have about a company—I was prohibited by law from sharing it with my firm and its clients."

According to law, the possessor of "inside information" cannot buy or sell stocks on the basis of that information. Legally, information is deemed "inside" if it is *material*—that is, if it were known to the public, it would have a material impact on the price of the stock.

"It's simple," says Carter, "and it's a Catch-22, since you don't know if it will have an influence on the stock unless you make it public."

One of the most famous cases involving inside information is the Ray Dirks affair. Dirks blew the whistle on Equity Funding Insurance, a company that boosted its earnings by making up bogus insurance policies, selling them to reinsurance firms, and pocketing the premiums. When Dirks discovered the scam, he revealed it—to several major institutional clients. He didn't go public. The institutions started unloading Equity Funding stock before the roof caved in. So the SEC censured him.

The better an analyst's sources inside a company, the better he or she understands what is going on there—the better, in other words, one does one's job as an analyst—the more information one is restrained from revealing to the people one works for.

"It's just plain ridiculous," says Carter. "What was I being paid to do? When my firm's management wanted me to write a report on a company, wasn't it expecting something special, something no one else had? If not, why did it pay me?"

Dean LeBaron, for one, doesn't even believe that inside information would make a difference in an analyst's long-term performance.

What if someone he knew had connections with the current Administration in Washington and learned that tariffs on foreign steel were about to be removed: a crushing blow to the U.S. steel industry—an industry in which Batterymarch was investing? What would he do with the information?

"Nothing," he says. "I wouldn't believe it. I'd figure if anyone I knew knew it, it was probably opposite the editorial page of *The New York Times* as an idea or rumor two weeks ago."

LeBaron was then told of an investor-relations operative who had called a reporter with a story about a company he was representing. The company, the man said, was about to receive a tender offer. Sure enough, three days later the offer was announced and the stock went up 40 percent. If that information had been passed on to LeBaron, wouldn't he have taken advantage of it as the best investment opportunity of the moment? Isn't that what an analyst is supposed to do?

"I don't doubt that there are conditions and circumstances where, in a single case, that kind of information is actually true," said LeBaron. "But I do doubt that if you took ten such opportunities you had had, and averaged out the ten, that you would make money. There may be one or two that actually work, but I think that you would then lose that money, and more, with the other eight—say, where the deals fell through, or the information was just somebody's attempt to inflate the stock's price."

LeBaron says he knows people who have tried to exploit various information pipelines, people with excellent connections, but even they have not proved successful. There are enough wrinkles in business—anti-trust, the Federal Trade Commission, the SEC—not to mention inflated egos—to cause any deal to come apart and make the information worthless.

Every purchase or sale of stock can be seen as *someone's* belief in his or her own special information. How many times have you heard of someone with a hot stock tip? People with such tips will try to play them as soon as possible, *before* the stock price rises to reflect the supposedly new information. As a result of this sudden flurry, the price will rise, but since there's no time to quibble over commissions, one must pay top dollar for the transaction.

Institutional investors get more hot stock tips than anyone else. Dean LeBaron's strategy is to play against them. With the money he actively manages, he very patiently, and therefore at low cost, sells to those who think they know a stock is about to shoot up, and buys from those who think they know a stock is about to drop sharply. His consistent success suggests that all that inside information isn't very inside at all.

Tim Carter, now that he's an insider, also admits that the number of opportunities to traffic in truly inside (which means illegal) information is very small, and that the people who are typically going to profit from such information are *not* going to be analysts; they will be officials of the company. (If a material change in the well-being of a company occurs, its officials are required to inform the stock exchange, which may then halt trading in the company's stock.)

So if inside information is not going to find its way to the stock analysts, what does a company's head of investor relations sell to the financial community?

"A rationale for buying a company's stock," says Carter. "To convince analysts of the value of my company's stock, I have to give them that rationale, and so I create investment theses, investment *arguments,* each tailored to the individual analyst.

"They all have their own little style. For example, one analyst puts great faith in capital assets. He thinks the more bricks and mortar you have, the firmer the long-term commitment. More is better. But our company is exactly the opposite—high growth, low capital commitment. So I had to turn him around. I had to argue that it didn't make any sense to sink a lot of money into machine tools in an industry which is changing so fast that they'll be obsolete in a couple of years.

"Another analyst says capital productivity is the magic formula. He measures several items on the balance sheet and comes up with a formula. He wasn't much of a problem, since luckily for me, our numbers fit his formula perfectly.

"Remember, it's hard for these people to find any truth—and they know it," says Carter. "So there's the constant search for the Holy Grail—something to grab on to, something to sell to clients. If an analyst can't sell inside information, second best is to come up with a magic formula. It's then my job to get my company to fit each of the formulae."

Some analysts are easy to please. Last year, on a tour of a General Motors assembly plant, a stock analyst for one of the country's largest investment firms found himself alongside a journalist also taking the tour. The journalist was constantly breaking away from the pack to ask questions of workers on the line, and would return to the analyst and apprise him of their attitude toward Chrysler ("Let it die"); the attitude of the male workers toward the women who made up 20 percent of the plant's work force (resentment); their assessment of management's receptivity to workers' suggestions (almost nil); and their satisfaction with their jobs (totally nil). But the analyst was only mildly interested—even though he was considering, during this very period, a buy recommendation on GM stock for the billion-dollar portfolio managed by his firm. Moreover, he had professed great interest in the issue of auto-worker productivity, for GM had been boasting that its workers were "as good as any in the world." The analyst had said he considered this a critical aspect of GM's ability to turn itself around.

Later that evening, in the lounge of a nearby hotel, GM's local P.R. man assured the businesspeople that Chevrolet still produced the number one and two best-selling autos in the United States, and that GM had a commitment to using many more industrial robots. (He also explained why, in the 1970s, the diesel engine cost $1,200 more as an option when it cost no more than a normal engine to produce: "Because it was what people were willing to pay.")

But the main topic was the disappointing quality of U.S. cars. The businesspeople in the group—one after another—seemed consumed by the topic. They took it personally; their questions typically concerned their own cars, and the various problems that befell them.

The P.R. man responded with earnest quotes from the company brass about GM's commitment to improve. Hence the redesigning and retooling and robots.

"But we say that our workers are second to none—in Japan or anywhere else in the world," he pronounced. "The company absolutely depends on them."

The session ended. The group began to disperse. The journalist hailed the analyst for a parting word. Would a recommendation on GM be forthcoming?

"I think I'm going to recommend that we buy. It looks like a good operation to me," he said as the P.R. man began shaking hands.

If those are the analysts, then who are the stockbrokers, the well-dressed middlemen who pass on the analysis to the poor unsuspecting public?

Salesmen, says Tim Carter.

Stockbrokers tend to buy and sell for the short term. Thus when Carter used to write up his analyst reports, he knew that the broker who was going to read them was going to make a sales recommendation to each client in a phone call lasting no more than a minute—perhaps as short as thirty seconds. "Friend," the broker might say, "here's an idea for you. The stock you've had in your account has done reasonably well; I think it's probably time to get out of that. It's made its move. Here instead is a new idea our research department came up with, called Centronics." Then the broker would read from Carter's report over the phone. "Look at the earnings trend. Two dollars a share in '76, $2.60 in

'77, and our analyst thinks they're going to do as much as $3.40. That's a pretty good progression. The stock is now selling pretty cheap—at only eight and a half times our analyst's estimated 1978 earnings."

So Carter tried to keep his reports simple, to provide enough numbers to give the broker ammunition, to make a few simple points at the end, because, he says now, the 30,000 brokers out there have one thing in common: first, foremost, and always, they are salesmen.

Any stockbroker with an ounce of introspection knows that Carter is right.

Ron, thirty-four, is an erstwhile stockbroker who runs a $2-million business in a wealthy Northeast suburb. He raised the money, he says, from *"alte Yidlach"*—an affectionate Yiddish phrase that means "old Jews." His only two rules for finding investors? "Make sure they're old, and treat them better than their children do," he says. "Which usually ain't hard."

Ron's story of life as a stockbroker will not win him favor on Wall Street. But then, he doesn't much care. He's gone straight:

"I was a good salesman," he says, "but I was working with a company with no prospects, so I figured I'd get into the 'money business' and become a stockbroker. If I could sit in an office and move around lots of money, and just take a tiny, tiny bit of all the money going through, I ought to do well for myself.

"Having always worked for smaller companies, I decided to go with the industry leader—Merrill Lynch—which accounts for about fifteen percent of all the shares traded on the New York Stock Exchange. After all, I didn't want to have the additional sales handicap of calling up someone and having to say, 'I'm from Flaigelbaum and Herbmeister' so they could say, 'Who? What?'

"So I walked into one of the Merrill Lynch offices, wearing a nice suit, looking like an attractive personality, and said I wanted to sell. And they said, Training program. Four and a half months. Taking tests, sopping up the business at the office. Merrill Lynch is very committed to training. They just bought a campus in Princeton. Rote memorization. Formulas.

"As if I was going to become a financial analyst. As if any broker is. But you have to know about balance sheets and ratios to talk knowledgeably about companies.

"So I went to their school and took the SEC and New York Stock Exchange tests and got my broker's license. But when I came back I had to confront the reality of being a stockbroker. It may impress somebody who doesn't know it's just a sales job. It seems glamorous because you're wearing nice, expensive suits you can't afford. But all it boils down to is coming to the office early in the morning and getting on the phone and calling a lot of people. Period.

"Now, I'm very ambitious, very competitive, so I figured it would be very easy for me, with lots of sales experience, to beat the other guys in my class. But to do really well, I had to come up with some good 'prospect lists.' Let's say Merrill Lynch put a fifteen-thousand-dollar ad in *The New York Times* on Sunday with a coupon for people who want tax-deferred income or bonds. The names of those people—those prospects—who send the coupons go first to New York and then on to the 'geographical managers' around the country.

"The manager, however, is not likely to waste a high-quality lead like that on some kid who just started the week before. He gives the leads to the people who have generated the most money and made the most commissions. Brokerage firms are totally performance-oriented. If you can bring in the commissions, they'll keep feeding you names. That's why one good guy can make as much as four or five mediocrities. They respect performance. If a guy is turning in money, all of a sudden he gets a bigger office, a full-time secretary; all of a sudden he's got a parking space where one didn't exist before. He's getting cuff links, coffee mugs, trips to Mexico. They reward performance. But if you're starting out, there's nothing to reward.

"They do throw you a few bones, of course—a few leads to pursue. But I found that the ones I got myself were the best.

"I would try to get lists of entrepreneurs who had just made money and 'hadn't yet paid sufficient attention to the careful husbandry of their resources.' I found the morning was the best time to call these guys, because they weren't yet spaced out—they were more crisp, more receptive, more open-minded. I'm talking about eight-thirty to eleven-thirty A.M. You've got to work afternoons too, of course, but by the afternoon I started getting depressed hanging around the office.

"I would 'cold-call' them. I tried different opening lines on the phone to try to refine my technique. In the end I found that the straightforward approach was best. 'Hello. My name is Ron ———. I'm with Merrill Lynch and I'm calling to offer you my professional services.' Then I'd shut up, and see what kind of reaction I'd get.

"I got everything from 'This is an invasion of my privacy. *Bang!*'—maybe one in fifty—to 'Say, gee, I was thinking I have to call you guys. My Treasury bills are coming due; I got $38,000 here. What do you think of Prime Computer? You guys like Prime?'

"It would run the gamut. And finally I realized that the success you have as a broker is going to be a function of how many phone calls you make. It's a numbers business. We used to call it 'Dialing for Dollars.'

"If I got forty contacts a day—making actual telephone contact with the people on my list, whether it was a list of prominent lawyers, or the corporate names on the annual report of one of the area's Fortune 500 firms—I would get one client.

"Now, most brokers, like most salesmen, are very lazy. If they call up a guy and he says, 'I'm not sure. Put something about tax-free bonds in the mail for me,' some brokers would just forget about the guy. But I would send the stuff and put his name on a call-back list for a week later.

"If they ask for a tax-free-bond report, it means they have a tax problem, they have money, and they have a portfolio kicking around. 'Well, I already have a broker,' most would say when you call them back.

" 'I'm not surprised you do,' I'd reply.

" 'And he's a pretty good guy, and frankly, he takes care of me.'

"I'd say, 'I appreciate that loyalty; I respect that. And I'm glad my clients are loyal to me. But don't you think that you're entitled, at this point in your finances, to have a barometer by which to measure your other broker's performance? Merrill Lynch has the largest and most highly regarded research arm on Wall Street. If you'd like to tell me the four or five stocks in your portfolio you're concerned about, I will get you Merrill Lynch's opinion, their most recent institutional reports, and you can see how you feel about it. Maybe they'll tell you that everything you've got is great, your broker's a genius, and it's been nice knowing you. Or maybe they will have some alternatives. If your objective is safety with some growth, what about utilities in the Southwest, for example—blah, blah, blah.'

"I'd keep it simple, with three or four points. Three or four points about a stock is all anyone can absorb. You get too far ahead of them and you confuse the issue.

"So with the utilities, I'd tell him about regular dividends. I talked about a good regulatory environment in the Southwest, not like the Northeast, where it can be hostile. And I talked about a freedom from too much dependence on foreign oil—blah, blah, blah.

"I had two or three utilities I liked to push—one in Kansas, I remember. And for the most part, the things I bought people looking for safety worked out well. Except for Three Mile Island. [He laughs.] We had some of that.

"So I'd say to potential clients, 'Look, I'm new at this. I've only done it for a couple of years,' I would lie. 'I'm very energetic. I'm not afraid to work for my money. Let me, free of charge, put you in touch with the research department Merrill Lynch is spending X million dollars a year to maintain.'

"Then I'd send them a report. I'd call back, try to meet them and talk some more. I found that if I could meet 'em, I could get 'em. I'd wear nice suits, make a nice impression. And I'd find that their current broker hadn't seen them for six or nine months.

"I was bashful the first year. I didn't want to just start slinging. But I learned. Slowly, I started to go after what the broker calls his 'total dollar.' After a while, you're not happy just selling a few bonds and maybe a Bar Mitzvah present for their grandchildren. You move in on some serious business, estate planning. Now, what the hell do I know about estate planning? But Merrill

Lynch had guys who knew it all, and if ever I had a big prospect, I would bring along an expert.

"Finally, I decided to find my own gambling stock. I felt I was turning down business because I didn't feel comfortable putting them in something that was a crapshoot.

"But the commission on even $50,000 worth of bonds was only $150 to $250, depending on what you were moving. If you can buy a guy $3,000 worth of Boeing options on a Monday which come due that Friday, however, you make 150 bucks and then, four days later, when you get him out, *bang,* another 150 bucks. The guys who made money were the traders, the gamblers, the in-and-out guys, always happy to have their clients subsidize their education—options, long, short, butterfly spreads.

"Any broker who has a big house and an airplane or a yacht is working every Saturday morning, calling people at home. He's working three evenings a week. Without question, he's always working. Always pumping. Always going.

"Not that I didn't pump. I found a couple of things I liked, stocks that had a good story. First there was something about an oil find off Indonesia—I got it from a little two-inch article in *The New York Times.* It had a nice ring to it, a lot of glamour. The stock was Redding and Bates. Actually, the year I was with it, it went nowhere but south, but since then it has had some success, they tell me.

"My other pet stock was Boeing. I read an article in *The Economist* my first month on the job that said the world's commercial airlines would have to replace twelve hundred to fifteen hundred planes in the next ten years. Boeing had 68 percent of the world market share, and *The Economist* said there was little question that Boeing was going to retain it, in spite of Airbus.

"I started getting people into Boeing at 27 and it went to 73. So the people I made a couple of Gs for became regulars.

"Around this time I also learned one of Merrill Lynch's best lessons: how to ask a guy for a hundred thousand dollars. If you don't suggest a thousand shares, you won't get a thousand shares. If they gulp or gasp, they'll suggest a more modest figure.

"I wanted the big spenders, so I came up with a list of people who had given a ten-thousand-dollar contribution the year before to a Jewish charity. It was a printout of hundreds of names of local people.

"It was a good list, although I was surprised at how many of them were deceased—in just one year.

"But I tracked down the rest, followed up phone calls, and met a few of them. I got some nice business, opened up some very substantial accounts. If the guy bought $25,000 worth of bonds, I made a hundred on that. Then maybe he had a brother who owned a couple of shoe factories and had a problem with a pension plan. That was another commission. And maybe his wife is concerned because their daughter married this son-of-a-bitch Mel, and they don't want Mel to get the kid's money, so how could they set up a trust?

"I would call these people cold and offer them my professional services. Some of them were very nice, and I opened up some business. But some were sons-of-bitches. I almost preferred the sons-of-bitches, though, to the guys who wasted my time. A lot of them were old—sixty-eight, seventy-four, seventy-six—with a few million dollars, and all experts on everything now that they had a lot of time on their hands. But instead of confessing in the beginning that they had no serious interest in what I was selling or what I was saying, they'd string me along, ask me to send them stuff. They'd want a half-point better return than the market was offering for tax-free bonds. They'd ask for the impossible and I'd come close, maybe even once or twice come up with the impossible, and then they would back out.

"It's okay to say yes. It's okay to say no. But these guys said yes, no, yes, no—wasted my time and didn't give me any money.

"So over the years, being an avid newspaper reader, I would begin to read the obituary page, and it would say, 'Nat Smegelbaum, seventy-two years old, founded vast leatherworks in Maine,' and I'd laugh.

"I'd read the obituaries and I'd say, 'Well, Nat, you *shmuck,* you should have listened to me.'

"But that perverse pleasure only took me so far. Here I was, making good money, building a base, and I wasn't happy. I had to work too hard. I had to work constantly. Evenings, Saturdays; always prospecting, always looking for clients. Leaks are always springing up in the bucket. One client's daughter marries a broker; another client dies on you; many you simply fail.

"It's tedious, a drag—nonstop selling, pick-and-shovel work. The reality was totally unglamorous, and I had hoped for a glamorous career.

"So when an old, sloppily dressed friend began coming by and trying to interest me in this venture he had in mind, I was vulnerable. He cajoled, he wheedled, he molested, he harangued. He came to Merrill Lynch every day and people began to think he was my best client, since they figured anybody that dressed that poorly had to be a rich eccentric. I had no idea if the venture would work—I'm still not certain. But it had to beat what I was doing.

"The bottom line was that I couldn't see being a broker for the rest of my life, or even the rest of the month. I didn't want to spend all my energy talking people out of their savings accounts and into utilities. I just couldn't take it anymore, and I'll never regret the decision to leave, even if I go broke.

"On the other hand, I sure did learn how to sell. . . ."

Harvard finance professor Jay Light sums up the "intelligence community" this way: "Wall Street is a multibillion-dollar business dedicated to getting people to change their minds and ringing the cash register each time they do."

EPILOGUE The
Corporate
Dilemma

From the battlefield, scouts Napoleon had sent out, and orderlies from his marshals, kept galloping up to him with reports of the progress of the action, but all these reports were false, both because it was impossible, in the heat of the battle, to say what was happening at any given moment and because many of the scouts did not go to the actual place of conflict but reported what they had heard from others; and also because, in the time it took a scout to ride the mile or more to Napoleon, circumstances had changed and the news being brought back was already becoming false.
—LEO TOLSTOY, *War and Peace*

As we finish our tour of the corporate battlefield, let's consider the dilemma of America's managers. Like Napoleon at the Battle of Borodino, they are usually far from the front lines. More often than not, the "intelligence reports" they receive are unreliable, partly because the battle is forever changing, partly because the observers often look for the wrong things, and partly because corporate managers are no more enamored of bad news than the rest of us, and so hear—and are told—what they want to hear. Remember that when Procter & Gamble test-marketed its liquid spray cleaner, the reports from the front were glowing, and victory seemed assured. As a result, the company marched right into Wilson Harrell's Formula 409 ambush. For want of "intelligence," the battle was lost.

That doesn't mean, however, that managers with good information are necessarily safe. If they embark on a particular course of action despite the uncertainty of the corporate battlefield, they face another kind of danger. Their new strategy will quickly alter the battle, and their opponents will probably shift *their* strategies accordingly. Thus the situation all the combatants entered just a short while before will be irrevocably changed. Bowmar fell victim to "Brain death" in the hand-calculator business not because it made a foolish decision to enter a new market but because the subsequent rapid changes in the business caught it by surprise.

What lies behind the bottom line? Uncertainty, as many managers know all too well. The head of corporate communications at Polaroid, for instance, admits that the right answer to many of the questions he's asked is simply "I don't know." But, he complains, "that's not what the security analysts or the press want to hear. It sounds as if we're covering up, instead of just being honest."

Managers are supposed to be leaders; their uncertainty might sound like indecision—or worse. If chief executives acknowledge the ambiguities of their business, do they risk losing their air of authority? How many times can a strategy be credibly changed? How much insecurity can a company take? How much insecurity can its leaders take?

Thus most press announcements, most annual reports, and most corporate interviews are unequivocal, enthusiastic, and Pollyanna-ish. A nod to the vagaries of the market—"We have seen some unexpected erosion in the housing industry"—is followed by assurance and reassurance. The corporate facade must show no cracks, no matter how extensive the damage within.

So where can one turn for truth? To the "professional observers"? The investment analysts and stockbrokers do seem, at first glance, to be above the fray; but as we've seen, their own self-interest—their deadlines, their "sales quotas"—will probably cloud their vision even when the smoke of the corporate battlefield does not. These seers of stocks and bonds are prized for their authoritativeness, their ability to predict, to *know,* in a world where the truly wise businessperson admits that in a profound sense, one cannot know.

Still, uncertainty creates anxiety, and anxiety opens up all sorts of opportunities for soothsayers. The professional observers sell an ability to turn uncertainty into certainty, and are paid handsomely for their efforts. They feed the great hunger for security that the insecurity of the corporate battlefield has created, taking the best data they can find and presenting it as expertly and persuasively as possible. Lacking true knowledge, what else can they do but sell guesses—sometimes educated ones, but guesses just the same? As long as investors themselves feel uneasy about guessing, they will turn to the professionals for help, even when one guess is as good as another.

The professionals, meanwhile, will convince themselves that they are not merely thriving on insecurity, but instead are providing a service of significant value. As with corporate managers, their job will be easier if they can sustain some degree of self-delusion in the face of uncertainty.

Time and again, this inherent uncertainty of the corporate battlefield will shape business behavior and dominate corporate thinking. Consequently, the avoidance of risk, as we have pointed out in earlier chapters, is a major form of behavior behind the bottom line. Companies—and managers—try to cope with uncertainty by seeking to protect themselves with numbers. They construct hurdle rates, make statistical analyses, and spend millions on market research until the numbers become a kind of security in themselves. Any framework for analysis, however unsatisfactory in practice, will usually seem preferable to the alternative: the even more uncertain territory of sheer intuition and judgment.

If a company decides that its hurdle rate for investment is, say, 20 percent, it will be that much easier to make an investment decision. A company needs guidelines that can be followed, rules that can be understood. Decisions must be coordinated; they must make sense in the context of corporate objectives. Decision-making-by-the-numbers, then, evolves naturally. Even when it is skewed by differing assumptions, it holds the promise of providing *some* measure of certainty. At least, everyone can start with the same basic equation.

Quantification and all the other devices of so-called scientific management are used precisely because they're designed to minimize risk—both to the companies and to the individuals who use them. A business tries as much as possible to minimize the risk to itself, simply because the battlefield has proved to be a very dangerous place. What else is a corporation, after all, but a legal entity whose primary purpose is to minimize risk? Incorporation enabled the owners to pool their money and spread financial risk, and also to limit their liability in case disaster should strike. (The great theorist of capitalism Adam Smith actually thought this a coward's solution to the problems of economic risk, and strongly criticized the notion of the corporation in *The Wealth of Nations*.)

But this minimization of risk, however much we might disapprove of it on a large scale, is a perfectly natural reaction to the uncertainty of the corporate battlefield. Most of us, after all, will try to minimize risk when it comes to our own money. We diversify our financial holdings; we buy insurance; we keep some of our money in a bank because we think it's safe, although the bank pays us much less of a return than we might get elsewhere. Some of our investments, such as stocks and bonds, are diversified in mutual funds.

Corporate executives are, in this respect, no different. They diversify their companies to buffer them against a disaster in any given market. They also promote corporate growth, sometimes paying enormous premiums, in the hope that size will protect their companies—and themselves. "A company is like a ship at sea," says Ken Fisher, the former C.E.O. of the Prime Computer Company, "and big ships weather storms a lot better than small ships."

Naturally, most executives would rather be captains of big ships than small ones—or sinking ones. And they would rather avoid storms entirely. Why risk steaming into uncharted waters—and risk losing your job—when you can anchor in the harbor?

This propensity to caution, however, has invited some serious theoretical attacks on our economic system. One of capitalism's most eloquent defenders, Joseph Schumpeter, claimed in 1942 that the system's aversion to risk would eventually rob it of the vitality it needed to compete with socialism. Twenty-five years after Schumpeter, at the height of the go-go years, John Kenneth Galbraith announced that the dominance of big firms in America meant that our system was not much different from socialism, in that risk taking had been replaced by the bureaucratic planning of the "corporate technostructure."

But both men—as well as many business executives—may have underestimated the uncertainty of the corporate battlefield. Caution, as we have seen, has its own pitfalls. Competition can force even the largest companies to take risks. Often, a company must change or die. When its market changes, when its competitors switch strategies, when its consumers develop new tastes or needs, a company must adapt. The change may not come for decades, but when it does, as in the auto industry in the late 1970s, the results can be dramatic. After decades of world dominance, GM, Ford, and Chrysler are now being *forced* to take risks. And still it may be too late for at least one of them.

Not long ago, a top executive of a Fortune 500 company served as jury foreman in a criminal trial. One middle-aged, pin-striped fellow juror turned out to be a banker, and during the deliberations he periodically put his hand to his face and rubbed his eyes, slowly shaking his head. The executive finally asked if the trial was getting to him.

"No," the man replied, "it's the banking industry. When I started in this business, I thought it was the safest job around. All I had to know about was loans. Now I have to learn how to be a stockbroker, an insurance salesman, and Lord knows what else. I'm going to have to take *risks*."

And so he will, as the banks and financial-services companies collide because of deregulation, technological advances, and the vicissitudes of the marketplace.

The banker is beginning to learn a hard lesson: when the only way to maintain profitability—or even survive—is to innovate, companies—and their executives—had better innovate. In a changing industry, the best way to minimize risk is to change with it. You never know when the graph of our typical industry's life cycle will go from this:

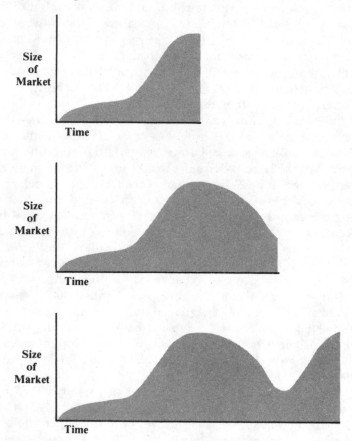

The lesson of the graphs: every boom market ebbs, but even a moribund industry can come alive again.

Behind all this, of course, lies the ubiquitous uncertainty of business. General trends are important, to be sure, but how does a company know *when* to change, or by how much? When is risk-taking the tempting of fate, a smart move, or a desperate, last-ditch defensive measure? How does an audio-equipment manufacturer, for instance, protect itself from the possibility that an innovative speaker will *not* sell, or that it will sell so well that it will transform the industry—and destroy the company's current line of profitable products?

Recently RCA launched a prime-time TV commercial that showed a family of four watching television in their living room. When Dad turns around, he explains that he, his wife, and the kids are watching not commercial television but RCA SelectaVision VideoDiscs of their favorite movies. "Just think of it," he says happily. "We can be watching all of this, while you're forced to watch us."

What is most fascinating about the ad is that it was broadcast on NBC, a subsidiary of RCA. In other words, RCA felt compelled to bet huge sums on the future of the VideoDisc even though the product's success might endanger one of its most profitable assets: NBC. It's a bet that no company would rationally take—unless, of course, it felt it had no choice. (As it turned out, RCA bet on the wrong technology and lost heavily.)

This is the crux of the toughest corporate dilemma of all: never to know when to risk but always to be compelled to guess. Sometimes business executives must dig in and minimize their risk, and sometimes they must charge ahead. Usually, of course, they will try to wait for another company to break new ground, which is why the Henry Klosses of the world are always forced to go it alone. But when it is finally demonstrated that a new business or product will make it, no one can afford to hang back. In remarkably short order, an industry that was peaceful, almost bucolic, can become a bloody battleground.

New conventional wisdom will then replace the old, and a crowd of corporate combatants, knowing full well the volatility of all markets, will rush into the fray lest they miss their chance to expand their territory and protect their flanks. That's why the commercial success of Milton Reynolds's ball-point pen was quickly followed by a rush of entrants into the marketplace, even though everyone knew that the laws of competition would doom a sizable percentage of the ventures.

But then, this is a system dedicated to results, not mercy. It is a constant battle for survival in which the average life of a company is six years and the average tenure of a chief executive is not quite seven. Both Karl Marx and Andrew Carnegie were right: in a market system, competition is inevitable and inexorable, and it takes a heavy toll. Once it is unleashed, neither cartels nor common sense can wholly restrain it. Uncertainty is the only certainty; what once worked will surely give way to something new, creating a boom, which in turn will lead to a shakeout. In a competitive system, someone is bound to lose. As financial guru Charlie Ellis puts it, "Gold rushes finish ugly." Or, as we learned from game theory, the logic of competition is to screw the other guy before he (inevitably) screws you.

The truth is clear to every smart businessperson: you can never rest easy. When Bruce Henderson of the Boston Consulting Group talks about competition, he does so in terms of economic natural selection: You must forever refine the concept of your business, the borders of your niche. You must forever pursue a mixed strategy: hawk today, dove tomorrow. No one strategy guarantees survival on the corporate battlefield.

Henderson's successor as the leading light of corporate strategy, Harvard Business School professor Michael Porter, expands the list of potential enemies even further to include not only competitors, but suppliers, customers, and possible substitute products.

It's enough to drive corporate generals to despair. In a continual reassessment of strategy and risk, they try to find the key to success on the corporate battlefield while always looking out for themselves. The right information can be critically important; so too can resources, experience, wisdom, and connections. But because there is so much uncertainty in corporate battle, luck can also be a powerful determinant of success. A brilliant strategy may prevail in one instance and a brilliant new product may spell victory in another, but behind the bottom line, there are many more crossed fingers than the traditional view of business would lead us to believe.

Index

Acoustic Research, 155–56
acoustic-suspension speakers, 154–58, 160–65
    invention of, 154
    marketing of, 155–56
    properties of, 154–55
Adams, Russell, 87
Advent Corporation, 105, 159–66
    audio equipment of, 160–62
    financial problems of, 163–65
    projection televisions and, 159, 162–63
advertising research and testing, 47
Airbus, 224
airlines, deregulation of, 61
Alger, Horatio, 167
Allegheny Ludlum, 33
All Savers Certificates, 74
alternative businesses, 184–205
    employees in, 184, 186–90, 193–94, 196–99, 202–4
    managerial structure in, 186, 189–90, 192, 202–5
    organizational theory and, 202–5
    political aspects of, 184, 187
    stockholders in, 186–87, 189–90, 193, 197–99, 202–3
    Vietnam era and, 184–85, 194–95
American Asbestos Textile Corporation (AMATEX), 106

American Brands, 90
American Research and Development Corporation, 142
American Steel and Wire Company, 80
American Steel Hoop Company, 80
American Stock Exchange, 213
American Tobacco, 90
American Tobacco Association, 90
Aminoil, 90
Anderson, Howard, 131–32
Andrews, Clark & Company, 77–79
Andrews, Samuel, 77–78
"anti-business" businesses, 184–205
anti-trust litigation, 24
Arizona Star, 106
Armco, 33
Armour, 138
asbestos mills, 106
Ash, Mary Kay, 176
Atomic Energy Commission, 35, 129
audio industry, 154–58, 160–65
    chromium dioxide tape and, 161–62
    Dolby noise reduction and, 161
    "explosion" in, 157–58
    see also high fidelity equipment
automobile industry, 218–19, 231

237

About the Authors

PAUL SOLMAN is Executive Producer for Business Affairs at the Public Broadcasting Service's Boston affiliate, WGBH-TV. He was the executive editor and co-originator of *Enterprise,* the Emmy Award–winning PBS documentary series about business; he was also founding editor of the award-winning Boston weekly *The Real Paper.* He spent a year at the Harvard Business School as a Nieman Fellow in Journalism. In 1979, he won an Emmy for his business reporting.

THOMAS FRIEDMAN is the senior editor of *Enterprise* and has produced and/or written many of its episodes. He has been news editor of WGBH-TV's acclaimed *Ten O'Clock News,* executive editor of *The Real Paper,* and a free-lance editor and writer. He won a 1981 Champion Media Award for Economic Understanding for the *Enterprise* episode "Bankrupt."